HISTORIES OF VIOLENCE

About the editors

Brad Evans is a reader in political violence at the School of Sociology, Politics and International Studies at the University of Bristol, UK. He is also the founder and director of the multi-media and interdisciplinary Histories of Violence project (www.historiesofviolence.com). His latest books include *Deleuze and Fascism* (with Julian Reid, 2013), *Liberal Terror* (2013), *Resilient Life: The Art of Living Dangerously* (with Julian Reid, 2014) and *Disposable Futures: The Seducation of Violence in the Age of the Spectacle* (with Henry Giroux, 2015). More at www.brad-evans.co.uk.

Terrell Carver is professor of political theory in the School of Sociology, Politics and International Studies at the University of Bristol, UK. He has published widely on Marx, Engels and Marxism and on sex, gender and sexuality. His most recent books include a two-volume study of Marx and Engels' 'German ideology' manuscripts (with Daniel Blank, 2014) and the *Cambridge Companion to The Communist Manifesto* (edited with James Farr, 2015). He is co-editor of the journal *Contemporary Political Theory* and co general editor of three book series: *Globalization* (with Manfred B. Steger), *Routledge Innovators in Political Theory* (with Samuel A. Chambers) and *Marx, Engels and Marxisms* (with Marcello Musto).

HISTORIES OF VIOLENCE

POST-WAR CRITICAL THOUGHT

edited by Brad Evans and Terrell Carver

Zed Books
London

Histories of Violence: Post-war Critical Thought was first
published in 2017 by Zed Books Ltd, The Foundry, 17 Oval Way,
London SE11 5RR, UK.

www.zedbooks.net

Typeset in Plantin and Kievit by Swales & Willis Ltd, Exeter, Devon
Index by Ed Emery
Cover design by Andrew Brash

A catalogue record for this book is available from the British Library.

ISBN 978-1-78360-239-1 hb
ISBN 978-1-78360-238-4 pb
ISBN 978-1-78360-240-7 pdf
ISBN 978-1-78360-241-4 epub
ISBN 978-1-78360-242-1 mobi

MIX
Paper from
responsible sources
FSC® C013604

Printed and bound by CPI Group (UK) Ltd, Croydon, CR0 4YY

CONTENTS

ABOUT THE CONTRIBUTORS

Jelke Boesten is reader in gender and development at the International Development Institute, King's College London, UK. Her latest book, *Sexual Violence during War and Peace: Gender, Power and Post-conflict Justice in Peru* (2014), received the Flora Tristan Best Book Award of the Latin America Studies Association – Peru section. In 2010 she published *Intersecting Inequalities: Women and Social Policy in Peru*. She has published widely on gender justice in Peru in international journals and books, as well as on gender, HIV/AIDS and activism in East Africa.

Ian Buchanan is professor of cultural studies at the University of Wollongong, Australia. He has published on a wide variety of subjects across a range of disciplines, including literary studies, cultural studies, communications studies and philosophy. He is the editor of the *Oxford Dictionary of Critical Theory* and the founding editor of the international journal *Deleuze Studies*. He is also the editor of four book series: *Deleuze Connections*, *Critical Connections*, *Plateaus* and *Deleuze Encounters*.

Lewis R. Gordon is professor of philosophy and Africana studies, with affiliations in Asian and Asian American studies, Caribbean and Latino/a studies and Judaic studies, at the University of Connecticut, Storrs, USA. He is also European Union visiting chair in philosophy at Université Toulouse Jean Jaurès, France, and Nelson Mandela visiting professor of politics and international studies at Rhodes University, South Africa. His most recent book is *What Fanon Said: A Philosophical Introduction to His Life and Thought* (2015). More at http://lewisrgordon.com.

Kimberly Hutchings is professor of politics and international relations at Queen Mary University of London, UK, and has previously worked at the universities of Wolverhampton and Edinburgh and at the London School of Economics. She is the author of *Kant, Critique and Politics* (1996), *International Political Theory: Re-thinking Ethics in a Global Era*

(1998), *Hegel and Feminist Philosophy* (2003), *Time and World Politics: Thinking the Present* (2008) and *Global Ethics* (2010). Her interests include international ethics and political theory, feminist theory and philosophy, and the thought of Kant and Hegel. She is engaged in long-term collaborative work (with Elizabeth Frazer) on conceptualisations of politics and violence in Western and anti-colonial political thought. From 2011 to 2015 she was the lead editor of the *Review of International Studies*.

Mark Lacy is senior lecturer in the Department of Politics, Philosophy and Religious Studies at Lancaster University, UK. His publications include *The Geopolitics of American Insecurity* (co-edited with François Debrix, 2008) and *Security, Technology and Global Politics: Thinking with Virilio* (2014).

Gregg Lambert is dean's professor of the humanities at Syracuse University, USA, and principal investigator of the Central New York Humanities Corridor, an Andrew W. Mellon-funded research network between Cornell University, the University of Rochester, Syracuse University and the Liberal Arts Colleges of the New York Six Consortium. From 2008 to 2014 he was founding director of the Syracuse University Humanities Center. His publications include *Report to the Academy (re: The New Conflict of the Faculties)* (2001), *The Non-philosophy of Gilles Deleuze* (2002), *The Return of the Baroque in Modern Culture* (2005), *On the New Baroque* (2008), *Who's Afraid of Deleuze and Guattari?* (2008) and *In Search of a New Image of Thought: Gilles Deleuze and Philosophical Expressionism* (2012). More at www.gregglambert.com.

James Martel teaches political theory in the Department of Political Science at San Francisco State University, USA. He is the author, most recently, of *The One and Only Law: Walter Benjamin and the Second Commandment* (2014). He focuses on political theology, radical left politics, anarchism and critical race theory. His new book, *The Misinterpellated Subject*, will be published in 2017. He is currently working on a manuscript entitled *The Misinterpellated Subject*.

Marcelo Svirsky works at the School for Humanities and Social Inquiry at the University of Wollongong, Australia. He researches questions of social transformation and subjectivity, decolonisation, settler–colonial societies and political activism. He has published several articles in the journals *Cultural Politics*, *Subjectivity*, *Intercultural Education*, *Deleuze Studies*, *Holy Land and Palestine Studies*, and *Settler Colonial Studies* among others, and various books and edited collections: *Deleuze and Political Activism* (2010), *Arab–Jewish Activism in Israel–Palestine* (2012), *Agamben and Colonialism* (with Simone Bignall, 2012) and *After Israel: Towards Cultural Transformation* (2014, Zed Books). He recently edited a special issue of the Australian journal *Settler Colonial Studies* under the title 'Collaborative Struggles in Australia and Israel–Palestine'.

Paul A. Taylor is senior lecturer in communications theory at the University of Leeds, UK, and editor of the *International Journal of Žižek Studies*. His research interests focus on critical theories of mass media culture (in particular, the works of Theodor Adorno, Siegfried Kracauer and Jean Baudrillard), psychoanalytically influenced media and film theory (including Friederich Kittler and Slavoj Žižek), and philosophically informed perspectives on the media (particularly in relation to the work of Martin Heidegger). In addition to *Žižek and the Media* (2010), he is the author of several books, including *Critical Theories of Mass Media: Then and Now* (2008).

Keith Tester is adjunct professor in the *Thesis Eleven* Centre for Cultural Sociology at LaTrobe University, Australia, and senior fellow at the Centrum Myśli Jana Pawła II, Poland. He is the author of *The Social Thought of Zygmunt Bauman* (2004) and has worked on a number of books with Bauman, including *Conversations with Zygmunt Bauman* (2001) and *What Use Is Sociology?* (with Michael Hviid Jacobsen, 2014).

1 | THE SUBJECT OF VIOLENCE

Brad Evans and Terrell Carver

Modern societies are saturated with images and representations of violence. From twenty-four-hour news coverage to the extreme torture of Hollywood blockbusters, shock art and theatrical performance and increasingly brutal interactive gaming formats, the realities and resemblances of violence have arguably never been so embedded in our cultural, economic and social fabric. Some might even argue that it has become so normalised that violence saturation is reaching the point of the banal as its entertainment value supersedes any considered political and ethical questioning. Maybe not without coincidence, this comes at a time when political thinkers and policy practitioners are facing considerable challenges as they try to respond to a broad spectrum of insecurities and vulnerabilities. Not only does this raise some searching questions concerning the ways in which we are to understand and conceptualise the problem of violence but it also demands new thinking on how we might teach about violence with a proper ethical care for the subject. In short, echoing the challenge identified by Walter Benjamin, our task remains to develop a critique of violence that is adequate to our times.

The purpose of this book is to take up this challenge by emphasising the importance of thinking about violence in a critically astute and sustained way. While many of us might agree that a world without violence is preferable, that still doesn't answer the question as to why so many groups and individuals engage in devastating acts of brutality and slaughter upon one another, almost on a daily basis. Violence, then, is both a problem and a political imperative. It demands our attention in such a way that the supplementary question 'what is to be done?' immediately appears before us. It also asks how we might deal with contemporary spectacles of violence to which many of us are forced witness, without simply becoming voyeuristic to the suffering.

So what can we say of violence? Violence is undoubtedly a complex phenomenon that continues to defy neat description. It comes in many forms, ranging from very intimate and shocking attacks upon individuals to the planned and calculated slaughter of tens of thousands from remote aerial distances. Our concern in this book is decidedly with *political* forms of violence. Yet what actually constitutes a political act of violence is no clear-cut affair. While many authors continue to write about the politics of violence – for instance, by drawing upon state theory, questions of ideology or issues pertaining to terrorist acts and revolutionary struggle – such reductive typologies often reflect only part of the complex fabric of violence in the contemporary period. Indeed, as Nancy Scheper-Hughes and Philippe Bourgois explain, 'What constitutes violence is always mediated by an expressed or implicit dichotomy between legitimate/illegitimate, permissible and sanctioned acts.'[1] Depending upon the moral angle of vision, all forms of violence in fact might be afforded political ascriptions.

Understood this way, this book starts from the premise that it is not satisfactory to simply limit our enquiry by asking the already moralising and normatively loaded question 'What is political violence?' Such a leading question invariably results in a preconceived response that merely affirms existing ideas and paradigms of the world. Inspired by many of the selected authors in this book, we prefer instead to ask the question 'How does violence function politically?' This allows us to interrogate the violence of the battlefield while not forgetting the everyday violence that is often hidden in plain sight. Such a strategy exposes what we might term 'the tyrannies of reason' and its concordant banalities of suffering, and it insists that we find new conceptual tools adequate for interrogating the present. So, instead of searching for some 'foundational truths' or 'root causes' of violence – as if some singular explanation were possible for all times and places – this volume broadly rotates around the following questions, which in turn raise a number of shared and widely debated themes: *How does violence function politically? Can we neatly separate legitimate and illegitimate forms of violence? Are there differences between violence, power and force? Is nonviolence an attainable political goal? Can violence ever be justified? Does violence necessarily require physical harm? Should we describe structural inequalities as forms of violence? Are there meaningful*

1 Nancy Scheper-Hughes and Philippe Bourgois, *Violence in War and Peace: An Anthology* (Oxford: Blackwell, 2003), p. 2.

distinctions to be drawn between violence, force and war? Is violence a particularly human problem? Why is the desecration of the environment or death from preventable disease now written in violent terms? And how might we better listen to those on the margins of existence who are forced today to live in conditions of unending emergency and vulnerability?

Despite the recent emergence of a number of important anthologies and books on this subject (see further reading below), the study of violence still remains an open field for critical enquiry. In his recently published book *Violence*, Richard J. Bernstein spells out the intellectual and pedagogical challenges facing us today when confronting the problem. As he writes, 'We live in an age when we are overwhelmed with talk, writing and especially images of violence.'[2] And yet, as Bernstein explains, despite 24/7 news reporting and ongoing proliferation in depictions of violence in many formats, there is a real poverty of attempts to deal with the problem at a political and philosophical level: 'Even a momentous event like 9/11 does not provoke much *thinking* about violence. Our age may well be called "The Age of Violence" because representations of real or imagined violence (sometimes blurred and fused together) are inescapable. But this surfeit of images and talk of violence dulls and even inhibits thinking.'[3]

Responding to Bernstein's concerns, this volume brings together a number of selected theorists who we believe have pushed the intellectual boundaries on violence in the post-war period. And, in doing so, they continue to offer alternative insights on the very nature of the political itself. Why study violence, after all, unless more peaceful relations among people are to be imagined? It is no coincidence to find that each of the thinkers selected is decidedly trans-disciplinary in their methods. Beyond offering meaningful connections between politics, theology, culture, economics and philosophy, they are also notably influenced and inspired by writers, artists and poets who attend to the injustices of history through more lyrical and aesthetic means. Such forms, it is argued here, are not divorced from reality. In fact, they add another layer of critical insight that exposes the violence of positivism, arising from a reductionism

2 Richard J. Bernstein, *Violence: Thinking without Bannisters* (Cambridge: Polity, 2013), p. viii.
3 Bernstein, *Violence*, p. ix.

that is said to characterise social science. Once politics becomes pure survival, the artisan often becomes the first casualty (literally), for it is the poets of history who imagine different worlds.

In terms of our selection criteria for this volume, we consciously opted to bring together those post-war theorists who are often associated and categorised within the Continental political and philosophical tradition. Our collection is by no means exhaustive. Within this canon we might have included, for instance, Theodor Adorno, Georges Bataille, René Girard, Wilhelm Reich, Susan Sontag, Pierre Bourdieu, Jacques Lacan, Elaine Scarry, Jean Baudrillard, François Laurelle, Antonio Negri, Simon Critchley, Adriana Cavarero, Jacques Rancière, Peter Sloterdijk, Alain Badiou, Étienne Balibar, Gil Anidjar and Henry Giroux, to name but a few. Our selection criteria was challenging, as there was good reason to include all of those mentioned. Nevertheless, we wanted to begin by introducing readers to those critical thinkers whom we felt would allow for a necessary introduction to some of the key conceptual debates shaping many of our contemporary concerns, which in turn points to their widely acknowledged position within the Continental tradition. That does not mean to say that we believe these authors should be prioritised over the others in broader discussions. On the contrary, we hope that this volume will encourage students to broaden their critical horizons and to further engage with the important and insightful authors identified above.

There is, however, a more pressing issue that certainly needs to be acknowledged in any study of contemporary violence. With the exception of Frantz Fanon, the Continental focus ensures that what is presented here is ultimately a product of very particular Western canons of thought. Hence, while Fanon's omission would have been unacceptable due to his profound influence over many of the theorists addressed here, critics could rightly point to the importance of many post-war thinkers beyond the anglophone tradition, not least Malcolm X, Mahatma Gandhi, Steve Biko, Edward Said, Gayatri Spivak, Angela Davis, Subcomandante Marcos, Cornel West, Achille Mbembe and even more provocative figures such as Sayyid Qutb. Thinking beyond the Western canon, however, deserves a dedicated volume in its own right, just as we might consider developing more focused anthologies on classical thinkers from Aristotle to St Paul to Machiavelli, and on to the modernists, ranging from Immanuel Kant,

Friedrich Nietzsche and Karl Marx through to Rosa Luxemburg, Antonio Gramsci, Primo Levi, Carl Schmitt and Martin Heidegger.

Violence belongs to the realm of thought as well as to the realm of physical action. Ideas give rise to violence just as it provides reasoning and explanations. Violence as such (as even the selection process here shows) is a very fraught intellectual affair. Even its most vocal advocates, however, prefer not to have the term applied to their belief systems, opting instead for terms such as 'force', 'warfare' or even 'interventions'. Critiquing violence can therefore be perilous and intellectually damaging. Most of the authors who feature in this book have certainly placed themselves in the firing line and faced a barrage of personal attacks. That, however, shows their true strength of character, for, if politics is all about asking the right types of questions, the most perilous of questions to ask concerns new angles of vision on the problem of human destruction.

With this in mind, there are a number of principles we can identify from the authors featured here and in the Continental tradition that are pedagogically useful for studying violence in the contemporary period:

- The study of violence is not about searching for foundational causes or neat explanations. It is more concerned with how violence functions politically.
- Violence is all about the violation of bodies and the destruction of human lives. For that reason, violence should never be studied in an objective and unimpassioned way. It points to a politics of the visceral that cannot be divorced from our ethical and political concerns.
- Violence is all about inscribing political markers. It points to the authentication and disqualification of certain lives and ways of living that quite literally mark out the inferior, the disposable, the expendable and the damned.
- Violence is a performance. What makes violence political is forced witnessing by audiences. Understanding more fully the spectacle of its occurrence is central to our pedagogical concerns in the contemporary moment.
- Violence cannot be explained solely through regime theories or ideologies. Just as we might point to the violence that takes place in the name of universal principles, so there is a micro-physics of

violence that points to more subtle forms of everyday violation no less pronounced in their political markings.

- Violence cannot simply be explained in terms of the negation of life or a posited death drive. It has proved, time and time again, to be integral to civilisational claims to truth, harnessing the discursive power of human progress, security and emancipation.
- Violence is not carried out only by irrational monsters. Sadly, most violence is not exceptional or deviant – it is rationalised, calculated and perfectly in keeping with political and social norms and legal frameworks.
- Violence will remain poorly understood if it is accounted for in terms of how and what it kills, the scale of its destructiveness or any other element of its powers of annihilation. We must not lose sight of the fact that violence concerns the violation of human lives. But this can also include an attack on a person's dignity, their sense of selfhood and their belief systems.

James Martel begins this book by introducing Walter Benjamin (Chapter 2). This is both an important and an intellectually daunting task. Benjamin's work on the problem of violence is among the most difficult and contentious for political theorists. His 'Critique of Violence', in particular, remains a source of great inspiration and yet consternation for scholars as they try to unpack its complex and philosophically rich narrative and to tease out many of its wider implications. It is perhaps fair to say that this particular article, written in 1921, offered the first serious attempt to think about the problem of violence in ways that specifically address questions of political theology. Benjamin's understanding of Jewish mysticism and religious lore notably inspired these connections. His work also proposes a more subtle dialectical interplay between the violence of law-and-order-making (mythical violence) as against the violence of the revolutionary impulses of lawbreakers (divine violence), with an evident nod to literary figures such as Franz Kafka.

In Chapter 3, Kimberly Hutchings provides a critical introduction to the work of Hannah Arendt, a towering figure of twentieth-century political thinking. Indeed, not only can we see in Arendt's work early traces of the modern concept of bio-politics, which demands a foregrounding of 'the human' as central to our understandings of power and violence, but Arendt also forces us to confront difficult and challenging questions regarding a population's capacity for violence. As Arendt famously explained, mass violence is not simply reducible to the dictates of a handful of extreme psychopaths; rather, it is about creating conditions such that order and obedience to rulers thrive in ways that produce thoughtlessness on behalf of perpetrators. This lack of critical agency in the face of modern forms of oppression and tyranny she termed the 'banality of evil'. Like Benjamin, Arendt insisted on the need for a theological turn in explaining the violence of the times. Her resounding question remains, why do normal people commit such evil acts?

Lewis R. Gordon provides a critical introduction to the work of Frantz Fanon in Chapter 4. Of all the theorists featured here, it is fair to say that Fanon has had the most impact and continued resonance. It is with Fanon perhaps more than with any other writer that the idea of an objective and neutral study of the problem of violence breaks apart. Fanon attends to the wider historical developments of regimes of colonial violence and moves on to the ways that it operates viscerally at the level of individual lives, quite literally marking out in an all-too-naturalising way the rulers from the subjugated. He connects systems of rule with the psychic life of power in order to ask uncomfortable questions of us all. As someone trained as a psychologist in the colonial stronghold of Algeria who then became a wartime soldier *cum* revolutionary fighter, Fanon witnessed the raw realities of colonial oppression and its modalities of violence at first hand. He also understood the dialectical logic of colonialism such that revolutionary violence often repeats the violent cycle of history. Thus Fanon's question 'who actually constitutes the wretched of the earth?' remains as important as ever.

Brad Evans provides a critical introduction to the work of Michel Foucault in Chapter 5. While already having considerable influence across the social sciences and humanities in terms of thinking about question of the body, subjectivity and the power of language and discourse, the relevance of Foucault's work to the question of violence has undergone a notable revival. This owes a great deal to the translations of his lectures at the Collège de France, which have encouraged scholars to rethink his work on bio-politics and the question of subjugation. Central here is the attempt to understand violence at the level of life itself, not simply by drawing on the failure of modernity or on some Freud-inspired death drive but rather by asking why so much killing takes place so that life can thrive. This paves the way to understanding how violence often appears necessary, especially when it is loaded with all-too-human justifications and exculpations.

Gregg Lambert provides a critical introduction to the work of Jacques Derrida in Chapter 6. Undoubtedly a provocative and polarising figure, Derrida nevertheless remains one of the most important thinkers of the past century. He offers a number of explicit contributions to thinking about the problem of violence, from his philosophically rich explorations of the force of law on to more reactive engagements to particular events, from the Holocaust to 9/11. It is also important for us to recognise here how his deconstructive methods open up new understandings of violence that go beyond mere bodily violence. As Derrida recounts, there is violence to language as much as there is violence to thought. The fact that it remains difficult to establish a Derridean position on this or any issue is not incidental. These *aporia* evidence his successful attempts to overcome the violence inherent in any fixed positioning, which – in the process of reducing politics to facile identifications – often results in self-serving pronouncements of moral victories and intellectual triumphs. At best these posturings decontextualise a situation, and at worst they preclude serious questioning into the relations of and between victims and perpetrators. These identities will always be shaping our politics 'to come'.

Ian Buchanan provides a critical introduction to the work of Gilles Deleuze in Chapter 7. Foucault's claim that the twentieth century will be known as 'Deleuzian' seems less mischievous today than years ago, given the widespread reception of Deleuze across disciplines. Notably inspired by Nietzsche, among many others, Deleuze understood war to be a defining organisational principle for societies. Borrowing from an array of sources including anthropology, military strategy, the human sciences, literature, aesthetics and history, he exposes us to a plethora of competing Deleuzian dualisms that constitute the very of order of battle: *nomos/polis*, smooth/striated, deterritorialisation/ reterritorialisation, lines of flight/lines of articulation, active/reactive, movement/strata, rhizome/arborescent, minor/major, singularity/ totality, heterogeneity/homogeneity, molecular/molar and so on. In doing so, not only does he attend to the organisation of violence in its various historical formations but he also forces us to think beyond ideology as we begin to come to terms with the desire for violence and with our own shameful compromises with power.

Jelke Boesten provides a critical introduction to the work of Judith Butler in Chapter 8. Without question one of the most important and insightful theorists in the world today, Butler has developed a formidable corpus of work on the problem of violence, ranging from the targeting of bodies to the power of mourning and the constitution of grieveable lives and then to understanding violence itself as a performance that is often mediated and filtered through authenticating/disqualifying frames for public reception. Evidently inspired by many of the authors featured in this volume, Butler's intervention is profoundly ethical and tasked with a clear ambition to bring into question the violence that often remains hidden but paradoxically confronts us in plain sight. In doing so, not only does she force us to face the violence of the norm and its logics for rule but she also opens up new thinking on the question of vulnerability and what this might mean for political transformation.

Keith Tester provides a critical introduction to the work of Zygmunt Bauman in Chapter 9. Bauman speaks to the present, having personally seen, intimately known and barely survived the worst excesses of twentieth-century totalitarianism. His warnings for contemporary generations should be heeded, precisely because he understands all too well the ability of mass violence to regenerate in novel forms that nevertheless reveal historical traces. From his work on the Holocaust, which reveals its all-too-modern drivers in terms of 'order-making' and 'progress', he moves on to the violence that we confront in our 'liquid' modern times. This is violence that unsettles previous demarcations between friends and enemies, inside and outside, and times of war and times of peace. Bauman brings under his critical microscope the production of disposable lives that defines all modern projects regardless of their ideological emblems. Bauman's message is thus stark and urgent: in a world where ideas of technological progress continue to shape ideas of human progress, the ability to cast aside entire populations is arguably easier than ever.

Mark Lacy provides a critical introduction to the work of Paul Virilio in Chapter 10. A renowned urbanist and cultural theorist, Virilio has been at the forefront of rethinking the new geographies of violence. Moving beyond reductionist and static frames for understanding the spatial dimensions of violence, Virilio offers a number of new conceptual tools for making sense of the border-traversing nature of violence, along with the bunkerisation of life as an 'official' response. Central here is the concept of speed and what this means for the violent way that human relations are being shaped, especially in the embattled urban landscapes of the modern global city. Eschewing conventional academic boundaries, Virilio has responded to the violence of the times by specifically addressing its speed and intensity. He does this across many intellectual domains, thereby examining how all aspects of life in the modern world are formed through histories of violence.

Marcelo Svirsky provides a critical introduction to the work of Giorgio Agamben in Chapter 11. One of the most cited and debated contemporary theorists on the problem of violence, Agamben encapsulates the Continental approach, which concerns itself with violence at the level of human subjectivity. He thus extends our thinking on the bio-political by taking into account its theological heritage. Developing in novel and critical ways the contributions provided by Benjamin, Arendt and Foucault, among others, Agamben raises fundamental questions concerning what happens when politics is reduced to questions of pure survival and life to pure biological facts of being. Central to Agamben's project is a triangulation between politics, law and theology that provides new insights into many diverse fields of study, not least the politics of the life sciences, the political practice of aesthetics and the potential for revolutionary struggle.

Paul A. Taylor provides a critical introduction to the work of Slavoj Žižek in Chapter 12. Once described as the 'Elvis of cultural theory', Žižek – a Lacanian-inspired philosopher – provokes admiration and criticism in equal measure. He might be described as the *enfant terrible* of the modern academic scene, with his penchant for provocation as a distinct art form and critical *exposé*. Beyond his evanescent stardom and media-savvy populism, however, there is a sophisticated critical architecture to his work that appears across numerous volumes and articles. Žižek uses provocation strategically in order to ask difficult – or as he might say 'sideways' – questions relating to the problem of violence, often highlighting our unrecognised investments in its continuation. Nothing and nobody is spared his critical scrutiny and satirical ripostes. From postmodernists, anarchists and liberals to humanitarian workers and even Nelson Mandela, Žižek demands an account of violence that does not retreat from revealing what he declares to be its unidentified manifestations. He is now central to many strategic encounters on crucial questions in numerous disciplines where political thinking meets digital modernity.

Finally, Terrell Carver provides a critical introduction to the work of Cynthia Enloe in Chapter 13. A pioneering theorist working at the forefront of feminist politics within an international setting, Enloe has, through her work, transformed a number of disciplinary fields by pointing to the simple absence of women in theoretical and empirical concerns. Central to some of Enloe's contributions has been a concern to disrupt familiar ideas regarding the homeland and abroad, thereby challenging conventional understandings of violence as they appear through neat paradigms of war and criminality. Enloe's move is both rhetorical and deeply personal. Indeed, by bringing into question the location of violence as it actually impinges upon the bodies of victims, she inverts the reified and top-down explanations of violence in the everyday, focusing instead on the insidious effects of the violence of the everyday. Hence, what might appear trivial or marginal to hierarchical forms of political enquiry actually points to the capillary ends of power and violence, which is often more revealing than a focus on a military dictator or authoritarian personality.

Setting out to provide an accessible introduction to these key theorists, this book provides a useful way in to the vexed problem of violence as an empirical reality and intellectual concern. Our aim is to open further debate on violence's complexities and all-too-political ascriptions. This is not a book that aims to offer definitive conclusions to the problem of violence. Nor do we promise to resolve the problem through some universal claim or positioning. If the problem of violence is multiple, it is also mutable and its logics and modalities subject to change across space and time. Our task then is to understand these contingencies in order to draw out points of commonality and important novelties and departures. Having said this, we do not buy into the idea that violence is as natural as it is inevitable. Such a challenge must, however, begin as an intellectual project that moves us beyond the comfort of rehearsed orthodoxies, whose dismissive and vocal concerns with so-called esoteric categories such as the performative, the aesthetic and the everyday often proves to be the mask of mastery for compromises with more legitimate or tolerable forms of violence.

In this spirit, we hope that the book works as a provocation to thought. If it can provide alternative insights into the problem of violence, encourage its readership to consider the contested histories of violence and the novel and subtle forms it takes as part of the everyday, and provoke new discussion and further research, then its purpose will have been fulfilled. As Bertolt Brecht might have said, 'So there you sit. And how much blood was shed. That you might sit there.'

Further reading

Since there is a comprehensive list of further reading provided by the contributors for each of the authors selected at the end of every chapter, there is no reason to reproduce those recommendations here. What we have listed is a highly recommended anthology, which is an indispensable accompaniment to any study of violence, along with some of the more important and accessible contemporary texts on violence with which we would strongly encourage students to engage.

Anthology

Scheper-Hughes Nancy, and Philippe Bourgois, *Violence in War and Peace: An Anthology* (Oxford: Blackwell, 2003).

Books

Bernstein, Richard J., *Violence: Thinking without Bannisters* (Cambridge: Polity, 2013).

Cavarero, Adriana, *Horrorism* (New York: Columbia University Press, 2008).

Collins, Randall, *Violence: A Micro-sociological Theory* (Princeton: Princeton University Press, 2008).

Debrix, François, *Tabloid Terror: War, Culture and Geopolitics* (New York: Routledge, 2007).

Evans, Brad and Henry Giroux, *Disposable Futures: The Seduction of Violence in Age of Spectacle* (San Francisco: CityLights, 2015).

Franco, Jean, *Cruel Modernity* (Durham, NC: Duke University Press, 2013).

Forti, Simona, *New Demons: Rethinking Evil & Power in the World Today* (Stanford: Stanford University Press, 2014).

Galeano, Eduardo, *The Open Veins of Latin America: Five Centuries of the Pillage of a Continent* (New York: Monthly Review Press, 1973).

Giroux, Henry A., *The Violence of Organized Forgetting* (San Francisco: City Lights Publishing, 2014).

Goldberg, David Theo, *The Threat of Race: Reflections on Racial Neoliberalism* (Malden: Wiley-Blackwell, 2008).

Hanssen, Beatrice, *Critique of Violence: Between Post-structuralism and Critical Theory* (London: Routledge, 2000).

Pinker, Steven, *The Better Angels of Our Nature: Why Violence Has Declined* (London: Viking Press, 2011).

Sen, Amartya, *Identity & Violence: The Illusion of Destiny* (New York: Norton, 2006)

Zimbardo, Philip, *The Lucifer Effect: Understanding How Good People Turn Evil* (New York: Random House, 2008).

2 | WALTER BENJAMIN

James Martel

Biographical details

Walter Benjamin (1892–1940) was a German–Jewish theorist and philosopher. He spent his life as a scholar and writer, analysing and critiquing various phenomena and currents of his time. In terms of his politics, Benjamin tended to call himself a communist, although a strong argument can be made that he was actually an anarchist (as I will argue further). His principal opponents were capitalism, and, especially towards the end of his life, fascism (which for Benjamin was just the culmination of capitalist doctrine). For Benjamin these phenomena were rife with violence – not just actual physical violence but a deeper violence committed by the state, by commodity fetishism and even by the subjects of such forms of oppression who responded with a violence of their own. In his work, Benjamin devoted himself to battling this phenomenon. His political interests were matched by an abiding interest in theology and, especially, political theology. In part through his friendship with Kabbalah scholar Gershom Scholem, Benjamin was interested in Jewish mysticism and lore. His political theory and his attitudes towards violence reflect these theological themes. In his view, the origins of all forms of violence come from the Fall of Adam, from humanity's attempt to replace the truth of God with false forms of representation. All of Benjamin's leftist politics – his interest in Marxism and commodity fetishism, his interest in revolutions and why they have failed – stems from his basic political theological positions.

Benjamin did not come about these ideas all at once. He began his intellectual life as a scholar who was distinctly more moderate, more interested in issues such as culture and pedagogy than revolution and resistance. In his early days, Benjamin was interested in Gustav Wyneken's idealistic ideologies about youth culture and also in cultural Zionism (in both cases, he held himself perhaps a bit aloof, already striking very idiosyncratic positions).[1] By 1914 he had already broken with Wyneken. Later on, from the mid-1920s, he was much more interested in Marxism, influenced by his friendship with Theodor Adorno and also Bertolt Brecht (the latter whom he encountered in the 1920s) as well as by his relationship with Asja Lacis, who had been Brecht's assistant and who was a committed Bolshevik (and for whom he divorced his wife Dora).[2]

Benjamin pursued a career in academia. In 1919 he completed his dissertation on German Romanticism, but his subsequent *Habilitationsschrift*, a 'second dissertation' required to become a professor, was rejected, and he had to give up his career at that point. Afterwards, Benjamin made his living by writing reviews, translations, journalism and criticism. Despite his inability to become an academic, Benjamin was well regarded in the community of scholars and writers of his time in Germany. Works such as *Goethe's Elective Affinities* (1924–1925) made him an early name. And, quite paradoxically, his 'failed' *Habilitationsschrift* was later published as the now very famous *Origin of German Tragic Drama*, one of Benjamin's best-known writings. Other important works are his 'On Language as Such and on the Language of Man' (1916), 'Critique of Violence' (1921), 'One-Way Street' (1928), 'The Work of Art in the Age of Mechanical Reproduction' (1936) and 'On the Concept of History' (1940).

Some of Benjamin's works remained unpublished and in fragments during his lifetime. *The Arcades Project* was one such text. It constituted his major inquiry into the formation of capitalism and the effects of commodity fetishism in nineteenth-century Paris. His study focused especially on the life and writings of Charles Baudelaire, a figure he considered to be highly compromised and to have bought into the fetishism of his day even as his poems are deeply resistant of and subversive to that phenomenon.

In 1933, Benjamin was forced to flee Germany due to the rise of the Nazi regime. He moved about Europe, eventually settling in Paris. At the outbreak of war with Germany in 1939, Benjamin was

---

1 Bernd Witte, *Walter Benjamin: An Intellectual Biography* (Detroit: Wayne State University Press, 1991), p. 26.
2 Howard Eiland and Michael W. Jennings, *Walter Benjamin: A Critical Life* (Cambridge, MA: Harvard University Press, 2014), p. 203.

briefly interned by the French (because he was a German citizen).[3] In 1940, with German troops advancing, Benjamin fled for the Spanish border. Armed with a US visa, he tried to gain access to Spain, but the border was closed when he got there, and he took his own life in the Spanish border town of Port Bou on 27 September 1940.[4] A manuscript that he was carrying at the time disappeared and has not been seen since.

In death, Benjamin was far more successful than he had been in life. His work was championed and introduced to a wider audience by Hannah Arendt and Theodor Adorno. Theodor and Gretel Adorno published two volumes of Benjamin's work in German in 1955.[5] Two books, *Illuminations* and *Reflections*, both put out by Schocken Books in 1969 and 1986 respectively, introduced Benjamin to an English-speaking audience (Hannah Arendt wrote the introduction to his work in *Illuminations*). Benjamin's collected works in German were published by Suhrkamp Verlag in seven volumes as *Gesammelte Schriften*, beginning in 1974. A later, Harvard edition of many of Benjamin's works in English, edited by Marcus Bullock, Michael W. Jennings, Howard Eiland and Gary Smith, was also published, beginning with volume one in 1996 (there are now four volumes). Thanks to these collections, Benjamin's influence in literary criticism, art criticism, social and political theory, political theology, and philosophy is very extensive and his posthumous reputation is enormous. Many contemporary thinkers, such as Jacques Derrida, Giorgio Agamben and Slavoj Žižek, have extensively considered Benjamin's work, further popularising his theory and reputation.[6]

Theorising violence

One of Benjamin's most important contributions to the field of social and political theory involves the question of violence. Critical to

3 Eiland and Jennings, *Walter Benjamin*, p. 647.
4 Eiland and Jennings, *Walter Benjamin*, pp. 675–676.
5 Eiland and Jennings, *Walter Benjamin*, p. 677.
6 On the question of violence and Benjamin's work, see, e.g., Giorgio Agamben, *States of Exception* (Chicago: University of Chicago Press, 2005); Jacques Derrida, 'Force of Law: The 'Mystical Foundation of Authority', in *Acts of Religion* (New York: Routledge, 2001), pp. 228–298; Slavoj Žižek, *Violence: Six Sideways Reflections* (New York: Picador, 2008). See also Simon Critchley, *The Faith of the Faithless: Experiments in Political Theology* (New York: Verso, 2012).

understanding his view of violence, as already noted, is Benjamin's political theology. Also as noted, for Benjamin, the origins of human violence go back to the fall of Adam (and Eve as well, although Benjamin does not discuss her very much). In his essay 'On Language as Such and on the Language of Man', Benjamin describes this origin. He tells us that, in paradise, Adam had a direct and unmediated relationship to the objects in the garden; God gave Adam the task of assigning a spoken name to the objects of the garden. In this way, Adam did not engage in representation at all. Instead, he acknowledged what was present to him; his language was a direct path to what he spoke of. With the Fall, this relationship changed. As Benjamin puts it:

> the knowledge to which the snake seduces, that of good and evil, is nameless. It is vain in the deepest sense ... Knowledge of good and evil abandons name; it is a knowledge from outside, the uncreated imitation of the creative word.[7]

For Benjamin, forever after the Fall, human beings have been forced to engage in the 'uncreated imitation of the creative word' – that is, a failed reproduction of Adam's original language. Human beings henceforth have no recourse but to representation, but this means that we are eternally separated from the things of the world. Violence is our response to this separation. Or, more accurately, violence is our response when we refuse to acknowledge the separation. When we deny this basic aspect of the human condition, for Benjamin, we are rendered fetishists one and all, and the unreality that we produce (manifest especially through the practice of commodity fetishism in our own, capitalist times) is collectively referred to as the 'phantasmagoria'.

Reflecting this basic cosmology, the most important thing to consider in terms of Benjamin's understanding of violence is the distinction that he draws between 'mythic' and 'divine' violence (the latter, which is *göttliche Gewalt* in German, is perhaps better translated as 'God's violence'), which he explains in his famous essay 'Critique

---

7 Walter Benjamin, 'On Language as Such and the Language of Man', in *Walter Benjamin: Selected Writings*, vol. 1, *1913–1926*, ed. Marcus Bullock and Michael W. Jennings (Cambridge, MA: Harvard University Press, 1996), p. 72.

of Violence.' Mythic violence is Benjamin's term for the widespread practice of projecting authority – whether of the political, legal or economic variety – onto screens such as God, nature, reason or other such devices. These externalisations serve to anchor and bolster a set of politics and other practices that constitute the phantasmagoria. This miasma of misrepresentation and idolatry determines what passes for reality in our world. As already noted, for Benjamin, every one of us is compromised by and a purveyor of such phantasms. This engagement with phantasm and fetishism is the true source of violence for Benjamin. It is for this reason, he tells us, that various leftist revolutions and uprisings of the past have not succeeded. Failing to recognise the endemic violence projected into the world, these revolutions have responded with a corresponding violence, a response that is equally prone to phantasm, so that, in the end, one false regime replaces another.

It is very important to note that, for Benjamin, the term *Gewalt*, which is usually translated into English as 'violence', does not mean violence per se. Instead, it means something more like force or power. The more ordinary sense of violence, such as stabbing or killing, can be considered part of mythic violence, but it is the larger forms of violence that Benjamin truly opposes. More accurately, he sees ordinary violence as reflecting this larger kind of violence; the arbitrary imposition of law and rules (erroneously attributed to higher and transcendental principles) means that, in effect, the law is enforced haphazardly and according to the whim and interests of those in power.

The most obvious material manifestation of this, for Benjamin, lies in the actions of the police. Thus, for example, in 'Critique of Violence', Benjamin writes:

> The assertion that the ends of police violence are always identical or even connected to those of general law is entirely untrue. Rather, the 'law' of the police really marks the point at which the state, whether from impotence or because of the immanent connections within any legal system, can no longer guarantee through the legal system the empirical ends that it desires to attain at any price. Therefore, the police intervene 'for security reasons' in countless cases where no clear legal situation exists … Unlike law, which acknowledges in the 'decision' determined

by place and time a metaphysical category that gives it a claim
to critical evaluation, a consideration of the police institution
encounters nothing essential at all. Its power is formless, like
it's nowhere tangible, all pervasive ghostly presence in the life of
civilized states.[8]

Here, the arbitrariness of the police reflects a deeper arbitrariness;
whereas we ordinarily look to the state to protect us from violence,
for Benjamin the state is the source of it. The police fill in the gap
between the appearance of legitimacy and the fact that all the bases for
this legitimacy are, as already noted, false and unreal. For Benjamin,
to have the police come to protect the citizenry is to have the veritable
fox come to guard the henhouse. In response, the community itself is
rendered prone to violence (again, taking this in the ordinary sense)
whether out of a duty of self-protection or because such actions are
modelled after the higher arbitrariness and violence of the law.

This also helps to explain the violence of the state. For Benjamin,
the state is marked by a condition of permanent anxiety about its
status as legitimate, precisely because of the way it falsely attributes
its authority to sources that it has no true access to. Thus he writes:

> If violence, violence crowned by fate, is the origin of law, then
> it may be readily supposed that where the highest violence, that
> over life and death, occurs in the legal system, the origins of law
> jut manifestly and fearsomely into existence. [The purpose of
> capital punishment] is not to punish the infringement of law but
> to establish new law.[9]

The law's origins must 'jut manifestly and fearsomely into existence'
in order to prove (or at least assert) its right to exist. The law
sanctions killing as the prime marker of its power. The state needs
a sign (usually of blood) to mark and produce its legitimacy. Even
when the state refrains from capital punishment (as many states in
our own time do), the fact that it retains the power to kill or not to

8 Walter Benjamin, 'Critique of Violence', in *Walter Benjamin: Selected Writings*,
vol. 1, *1913–1926* , ed. Marcus Bullock and Michael W. Jennings (Cambridge,
MA: Harvard University Press, 1996), p. 243.
9 Benjamin, 'Critique of Violence', p. 242.

kill is a key marker of state authority, masking or papering over an *aporia* of authority in the process.

Benjamin uses the story of Niobe to illustrate his concept of mythic violence. Niobe had twelve children and bragged that she had many more than Leto, the mother of Apollo and Artemis. In punishment, Apollo and Artemis slew Niobe's children. Niobe herself was turned into an eternally weeping rock that marked the boundary between the world of the gods and the world of human beings. In this new state, Benjamin declares Niobe to be 'more guilty than before through the death of the children'.[10] The point of this illustration is to show once again how mythic violence, insofar as it has no true basis (and is hence 'mythic'), must resort to great shows of power, to the shedding of blood, to the marked borderpost that Niobe herself has become. This violence is both the true source of power of the state and the sign of its permanent weakness, its vulnerability to challenge (a vulnerability that makes it even more violent in response).

For Benjamin, the answer to mythic violence is divine violence (the already noted *göttliche Gewalt*). As Benjamin writes:

> This very task of destruction poses again, ultimately, the question of a pure immediate violence that might be able to call a halt to mythic violence. Just as in all spheres God opposes myth, mythic violence is confronted by the divine ... If mythic violence is lawmaking, divine violence is law-destroying; if the former sets boundaries, the latter boundlessly destroys them; if mythic violence brings at once guilt and retribution, divine power only expiates; if the former threatens, the latter strikes; if the former is bloody, the latter is lethal without spilling blood.[11]

Here we see that divine violence needs no sign to ensure its existence. It is God's direct power and so is rooted in ontology and reality, as opposed to myth and phantasm. It is therefore 'violent' in an entirely different sense, not as a false imposition but simply as a power that serves as a counterforce to the myths that otherwise determine human life.

10 Benjamin, 'Critique of Violence', p. 242.
11 Benjamin, 'Critique of Violence', p. 250.

Benjamin's discussion of Niobe is followed by a discussion of Korah in order to illustrate the concept of divine violence. Korah was an idolater, a Levite priest who led a rebellion against Moses' authority to speak for God. In response, God swept Korah and his followers into the earth, leaving no sign at all of their previous existence. This example tells us that divine violence brings no new truths into the world (because, if it did, they would quickly become subsumed into phantasm and idolatry). It serves only to remove and unmake the falsities of mythic violence.

For Benjamin, human beings live situated in the space between mythic and divine violence. Although we ourselves are the source of mythic violence, we remain beneficiaries of God's messianic actions to unmake the inevitability and hold such myths have upon us. We are not therefore doomed to be idolaters for Benjamin. In fact, as will be explained shortly, for Benjamin, not only is it possible for human beings to live without recourse to violence but we already do so all the time (albeit in ways that are not usually recognised as such).

Another important concept that relates to the question of violence in Benjamin's work is the notion of 'pure means'. Pure means are the way towards nonviolence for Benjamin. He uses this language in 'Critique of Violence', where he writes:

> To induce men to reconcile their interests peacefully without involving the legal system, there is, in the end, apart from all virtues, one effective motive that often enough puts into the most reluctant hands pure instead of violent means: it is the fear of mutual disadvantage that threatens to arise from violent confrontation, whatever the outcome might be. Such motives are clearly visible in countless cases of conflict of interest between private persons.[12]

Here Benjamin is describing how we frequently do engage in nonviolent behaviour even under conditions of mythic violence. It is perhaps due to the ubiquity of mythic violence itself (as the quote above suggests) that we seek alternative means of reaching decisions and agreements. In 'countless cases of conflict of interest between private persons' resolutions are frequently made without recourse

12 Benjamin, 'Critique of Violence', p. 245.

to the legal system (Benjamin also adds later that they are done without contracts).[13] These nonviolent resolutions are moments of 'pure means' because they do not involve any (inherently false) ends. Although all human beings are motivated by and orientated towards such ends (a result of our location in the midst of phantasm), it is nonetheless possible to break off from those ends and turn instead to 'pure means' – that is, means that are no longer connected to phantasms of truth and authority. As such, these means help us to partake of the openings created by divine violence, which are everywhere and always unmaking phantasm. For Benjamin, the entire material world is in a constant state of rebellion against the phantasms that human beings project onto them. By turning to 'pure means', we align ourselves with this rebellion, and as a result a nonviolent approach becomes possible (or indeed, as we already saw, something that we already practice widely).

Key aspects of Benjamin's contribution to thinking on violence Having laid out some of the basic concepts and terms Benjamin uses in relation to violence, we can now turn to the way these concepts actually work in his system – how they lead, in his view, to certain political possibilities that are not fated to return to phantasm and idolatry. One of the key mechanisms that Benjamin speaks of as partaking in nonviolence is the revolutionary general strike. Benjamin uses Sorel's distinction (from 'Reflections on Violence') between the political strike and the general strike. In Sorel's view, the political strike (what we normally call a strike, involving picketing, organising and so forth) is not itself a radical move. The political strike remains violent insofar as it is essentially a form of extortion. The workers, in this case, try to force capitalists to share profits with them. They do not fundamentally challenge the hierarchies of capitalist forms of production. Instead they simply try to readjust the way resources are distributed in that system. In the general strike, on the other hand, there is no bargaining or even threatening of the state (or the corporations that the state backs up). Thus he writes:

> Whereas the first form of interruption of work [the political
> strike] is violent, since it causes only an external modification of

13 Benjamin, 'Critique of Violence', p. 247.

labor conditions, the second [the proletariat general strike], as
a pure means is nonviolent. For it takes place not in readiness
to resume work following external concessions and this or that
modification to working conditions but in the determination to
resume only a wholly transformed work, no longer enforced by
the state, an upheaval that this kind of strike not so much causes
as consummates.[14]

Here again we see Benjamin employing the term 'pure means' to
refer to a nonviolent action, a form of resistance to endemic forms of
state and capitalist violence. Here, too, the mythic ends of the state
and capitalism have been rejected. There is no deal to be made with
such forces. The general strike represents simply saying 'no' to the
whole enterprise of capitalism. It is for this reason nonviolent (and
its nonviolence, once again, is made possible by the space opened up
by divine violence).

Benjamin further tells us that 'for this reason, the first of these
undertakings [the political strike] is lawmaking but the second
anarchistic'.[15] This passage is one of those that offers evidence for
the earlier claim that Benjamin may be more of an anarchist than
a communist. Anarchism emerges here as that form of politics that
best accords to 'pure means' and also to nonviolence.

Does this mean, therefore, that no one who engages in a general
strike ever hits or hurts anyone else or that, to effect political change,
Benjamin gives up entirely on any form of physical aggression,
regardless of how terrifying and powerful the opponent? Benjamin's
response to this question is somewhat ambivalent. On the one hand,
he does offer a view, in an essay fragment that he wrote a year before
'Critique of Violence', that a completely passive form of resistance to
violence is possible. In that essay, entitled 'The Right to Use Force',
Benjamin writes:

> When communities of Galician Jews let themselves be cut
> down in their synagogues without any attempt to defend
> themselves, this has nothing to do with 'ethical anarchism'
> as a political program; instead the mere resolve 'not to resist

14 Benjamin, 'Critique of Violence', p. 246.
15 Benjamin, 'Critique of Violence', p. 246.

evil' emerges into the sacred light of day as a form of moral action.[16]

Benjamin tells us that we cannot consider this example to offer us a 'political plan'.[17] Such a plan, what he calls 'ethical anarchism' in that essay, is not necessarily the model that Benjamin espouses, but it does show that, even in the face of overwhelming power, human beings are not fated to choose violence themselves.

Yet, on the other hand, when we think about the example of the general strike, we can see that a far more active stance is possible without losing the sense of being nonviolent. It is probably more accurate to say that humans can be generally nonviolent, because we must remember that Benjamin's focus is not on preventing acts of physical violence so much as larger actions of states, societies and economies that make violence basic to the very fabric of the world. It is *this* violence that Benjamin principally opposes, and it seems possible that, for Benjamin, occasional acts of physical violence are not completely out of the question. At the same time, I also think that, for Benjamin, the criteria and responsibility for such acts of violence would be very, even dramatically different from those we usually associate with such acts of violence.

There is some textual evidence to support the idea that Benjamin countenances occasional acts of physical violence. In considering how even a divine commandment like 'Thou shalt not kill' is not true as such but a representation of a truth, Benjamin tells us that:

> neither divine judgment nor the grounds for this judgment can be known in advance. Those who base a condemnation of all violent killing of one person by another on the commandment are therefore mistaken. It exists not as a criterion of judgment, but as a guideline for the actions of persons or communities who have to wrestle with it in solitude and, in exceptional cases, to take on themselves the responsibility of ignoring it.[18]

16 Walter Benjamin, 'The Right to Use Force', in *Walter Benjamin: Selected Writings*, vol. 1, *1913–1926* , ed. Marcus Bullock and Michael W. Jennings (Cambridge, MA: Harvard University Press, 1996), p. 233.

17 Benjamin, 'Right to Use Force', p. 233.

18 Benjamin, 'Critique of Violence', p. 250.

This is a critical moment in 'Critique of Violence' because it is the closest that Benjamin comes to addressing our course of action as subjects (and authors) of violence. It suggests that we cannot take even an adage such as 'never kill' too literally. Benjamin is generally against such programmatic and across-the-board decrees insofar as they smack of the kinds of ends-orientated morality to which he is adamantly opposed. Thus neither violence nor nonviolence can be absolute dogmas in his view. Benjamin reminds us that the Jews 'expressly reject … the condemnation of killing in self-defense'.[19] Thus we have one example already of how one can resort to violence from time to time in a way that is not necessarily mythic.

But, if we do choose violence, it cannot come from a conviction that this is certainly the right thing to do. When we resist the larger violence that makes such acts of violence seem necessary to us, we are rejecting those ends and engaging, as we have already seen, in 'pure means'. Thus any sense that we are hurting or killing another because 'God has commanded me to do so', or because there are other metaphysical reasons to act, is inherently false. We do not have this refuge for our actions. When we act, in Benjamin's view, we are taking on full responsibility as ourselves or as members of a community. We 'wrestle' in solitude with the implications of the commandments but we reserve the right to refuse them, to ignore or even abandon them (the German term *abzusehen*, which is translated as 'ignore', literally means 'to look the other way', suggesting less an indifference to than a deliberate separation from the law).[20]

More generally, for Benjamin, nonviolence reflects a set of practices that are not continuous over time. Each time we confront a situation marked by violence, we must revisit this question anew. We cannot even rely on precedent, on our own previous actions as a way to determine what to do. We do not have a criterion for judgement but, as we saw, only a guideline. At times we may follow this commandment, but at other times we may modify or even reject it. In each decision the burden is entirely on us.

Couldn't one at least say that, for Benjamin, once violence was eliminated, we could practice a perfect and permanent nonviolence for

---

19 Benjamin, 'Critique of Violence', p. 250.
20 Walter Benjamin, 'Zur Kritik der Gewalt', in *Gesammelte Schriften*, vol. 2.1 (Frankfurt: Suhrkamp Verlag, 1980), p. 201. I am grateful to Marc de Wilde for pointing this out to me.

the end of time? The answer to that question must be no, because for Benjamin there will never be a moment when violence will completely leave the world. This is why understanding Benjamin's political theology is so important. For Benjamin, we are ontologically connected to violence; it reflects the most basic state of human existence, reflecting the Fall of Adam and the ongoing crime of commodity fetishism. This is not to say that we cannot seriously disrupt the workings of the phantasmagoria. To say that would similarly be to deny the upshot of Benjamin's cosmology. For our ability to resist violence is as much given by God as our status as idolaters reflects our distance from God. For Benjamin, we forget this double legacy at our peril; the day we decide that we have finally got rid of all forms of violence, all forms of myth and projection, is the day that these things come rushing back into existence. Hence the struggle between violence and nonviolence is a permanent one for Benjamin. Instead of looking for a form of revolution that ushers us into an entirely better world, we must instead look to a set of practices (and revolution is one of them) that maximises our ability to avoid being determined by violence. Put another way, we look for opportunities to maximise those nonviolent practices that we have been practising all along, in order to expand the occasions for decisions and relationships that are not in service to idolatrous ends but serve only our local and subjective positions.

Benjamin's relevance today For all of the reasons cited above, Walter Benjamin is as relevant today as he has ever been, perhaps even more so as the alternatives to capitalism seem to be vanquished one by one. In our present neoliberal age, it appears that fetishism and rampant capitalism are utterly unopposed. This is of course not literally true insofar as we have seen an enormous resurgence of popular activism against various forms of capitalist domination. Thus, for example, we have the widespread demonstrations in Greece and elsewhere against 'austerity', one of the key mechanisms by which neoliberal institutions seek to break down the welfare states throughout Europe and expose their citizens that much more to the full ravages of capitalist forms of production and domination. We have also seen resistance to capitalism more generally in the form of Occupy Wall Street in the United States and in the Gezi Park demonstrations in Istanbul, and indeed the entire and ongoing phenomenon that is called the Arab Spring.

Benjamin is critical for these movements because his theorising about why revolutions fail might help these and future movements to avoid repeating history. This is already happening in many instances. Even in Egypt, where the promise was perhaps greatest, where a sustained response to state violence was continued over the course of several years and where individuals became professional revolutionaries with a kind of self-created division of labour among themselves, we see the steady reimposition of state control in progress. In the case of Egypt, quite inexplicably, many (at least those at the more liberal end of the spectrum) of the revolutionaries sided with the army when it decided to turn against Mohamed Morsi, then president. I say this not to defend Morsi but only to suggest that aligning oneself with a state military apparatus serves to ensure that state violence will return (as it has, and with a vengeance).

A Benjaminian analysis of nonviolence, it will be recalled, does not guarantee or even demand that those who act nonviolently will never turn to physical means to defend themselves or refrain from attacking those who hold the means of violence. Rather, it focuses on the ways in which authority is created, how we make decisions and on what basis. We can see that many of the demonstrations across the world in recent years have had a strong Benjaminian element, a kind of decentralised, anarchic approach to revolution that above all refuses to engage in ends.

Occupy Wall Street, for the most part, steadfastly refused to come up with a programme of action. At the time this was considered to be a serious weakness. What were its demands? What did the occupiers want? Yet, once a radical movement enters into this kind of negotiating language, the jig is already up. Capitalism is superb at making accommodations with alternative forms of power and economic organisation. It is willing to share some of its profits if necessary when it becomes clear that doing otherwise might spell real trouble for it. Capitalism managed to wait out Soviet communism by this means. Social welfare states were created across Europe and even, to some degree, the United States (the New Deal and its later iterations) to avoid having communism become endemic across the globe (of course, the moment that threat disappeared, global capitalism began busily taking back that redistribution; this is the basis for 'austerity', among other recent developments).

In his discussion of the difference between the political and general strike, Benjamin reminds us that any compromise, any negotiation (any 'demand') is doomed to failure. Once we get into such a stance, we are returned to a relationship with (false) ends; we become re-ensnared within the operations of violence and, insofar as capitalism will always have both a greater affinity to this violence as well as the greater stock of money and weapons, capitalism will always win this fight (certainly it has won the lion's share of such fights to date).

From a Benjaminian perspective, the answer to such a dilemma, once again, is not to try to out-violence the state but to simply say no to it. Occupy Wall Street, never a monolith, had a mixture of responses to the 'demand for demands'. And this debate occurred under the drumbeat of attacks in media precisely for the failure to put forward any conditions to serve as the basis of negotiations with existing power structures.[21]

Many of the great movements of recent years – the Maple Spring in Quebec, the demonstrations in Greece, Spain, France, Brazil, Turkey and elsewhere – are orientated towards specific demands. The Maple Spring was mainly about student tuition. The demonstrations in Greece are against austerity. But to be against austerity (while a perfectly legitimate goal) is different from being against capitalism. It is to ask for the previous form of capitalism rather than demanding that capitalism remove itself entirely from the equation. From a Benjaminian perspective, as noble and wonderful as these movements have been, they are not radical or at least not radical enough. At best, such demonstrations and protests will result in a return to welfare state capitalism (although this seems highly unlikely), which, while clearly preferable to rampant neoliberalism, is not in and of itself a way to break with global capitalism and hence with violence.

Once again this is why Benjamin speaks of engaging in 'pure means'. When our means are 'impure', we remain to some extent either accepting of or acquiescent to capitalist demands; we remain

21 Not everyone is in agreement that it was a good thing that Occupy Wall Street failed to have any demands as a whole. For an interesting opposing view see a web essay by Marco Deseriis and Jodi Dean on this question: 'A Movement without Demands', *Possible Futures* (3 January 2012), www.possible-futures.org/2012/01/03/a-movement-without-demands. They make the interesting point that demands are not ends but rather are themselves means. This would necessitate, at the very least, a rethinking of how such demands are made and what relationship they would have with capitalist entities.

trapped in the cycle of violence and counter-violence. When we refuse such ends, not partially but entirely, then our mean becomes something else, something that we may never have anticipated or thought possible.

Confronting violence in the world

Elsewhere, in 'On the Concept of History', Benjamin spoke of a 'weak messianic power'.[22] This is a power to oppose fetishism and violence in all forms that is, Benjamin tells us, given to each generation. Such a force, once again, is a result of divine violence. While he uses the term 'weak', in fact this power can be very strong and very decisive. We have all seen how, in an instant, decades or centuries of political oppression can be lifted just like that. The capitalist regime, as ensconced as it is through centuries of domination, as much as it correlates with our larger ontological status as fallen beings, is not fated to succeed. For Benjamin the very concept of fate is a capitalist conceit, a sense of inevitability that causes despair in its enemies and allows the status quo to carry on. But beneath that bold assertion of fate lies, once again, capitalism's greatest anxiety. It is, once again, capitalism's greatest vulnerability that is not based on any real substance, that it must 'jut manifestly and fearsomely into existence' in order to exist at all. Here, too, its necessary turn to violence is both its most fearsome weapon and the sign that it is not, in fact, invulnerable, and that nonviolence and the breaking up of capitalist systems are possible.[23]

22 Walter Benjamin, 'On the Concept of History', in *Walter Benjamin: Selected Writings*, vol. 4, *1938–1940*, ed. Howard Eiland and Michael W. Jennings (Cambridge, MA: Harvard University Press, 2003), p. 390.
23 This is why Benjamin was able to answer Carl Schmitt so readily. To Schmitt's claim that 'sovereign is he who decides on the exception', Benjamin offers the example of the portrayal of kings in German Baroque plays. Carl Schmitt, *Political Theology: Four Chapters on the Concept of Sovereignty* (Chicago: University of Chicago Press, 2006), p. 5. Whereas the playwrights sought to portray images of these kings as decisive and powerful, Benjamin demonstrates that in fact they are shown to be incapable of making any decision at all. He writes: 'This enduring fascination of the downfall of the tyrant is rooted in the conflict between the impotence and depravity of his person, on the one hand, and, on the other, the extent to which the age was convinced of the sacrosanct power of his role.' Walter Benjamin, *Origin of German Tragic Drama* (New York: Verso, 1998), p. 72. For a discussion, see Giorgio Agamben, 'The Messiah and the Sovereign', in *Potentialities: Collected Essays in Philosophy* (Stanford: Stanford University Press, 1999).

This is not to say that capitalism or some other forms of mythic violence will vanish once and for all (as we've seen, it is very dangerous to think that way). In fact, a politics of pure means – an anarchist politics, in other words – must remain constantly engaged with a kind of endlessness, not just in the sense of rejecting false ends but also in the sense of not assuming that those ends will actually end. For Benjamin, it could be said that nonviolence is a practice, a way of life and a method of engaging with material reality. We have all already been practising it for all of our lives but we always have the opportunity to turn that practice into something bigger and more collective. The more widespread and sustained this practice, the more we can flip the relationship between violence and nonviolence wherein it is violence that is occasionally and intermittently practised and wherein nonviolence dominates and prevails, at least for a period of time.

Further reading

Benjamin, Andrew, *Working with Walter Benjamin* (Edinburgh: Edinburgh University Press, 2013).

Benjamin, Walter, 'Critique of Violence', in *Walter Benjamin: Selected Writings*, vol. 1, *1913–1926*, ed. Marcus Bullock and Michael W. Jennings (Cambridge, MA: Harvard University Press, 1996), pp. 236–252.

Benjamin, Walter, 'The Right to Use Force', in *Walter Benjamin: Selected Writings*, vol. 1, *1913–1926*, ed. Marcus Bullock and Michael W. Jennings (Cambridge, MA: Harvard University Press, 1996), pp. 231–234.

de Wilde, Marc, 'Meeting Opposites: The Political Theologies of Walter Benjamin and Carl Schmitt', *Philosophy and Rhetoric* 44(4) (2011), pp. 363–381.

Derrida, Jacques, 'Force of Law: The Mystical Foundation of Authority', in *Acts of Religion*, ed. and trans. Gil Anidjar (New York: Routledge, 2002), pp. 228–298.

Eiland, Howard and Michael W. Jennings, *Walter Benjamin: A Critical Life* (Cambridge, MA: Harvard University Press, 2014).

Hamacher, Werner, 'Afformative, Strike: "Benjamin's Critique of Violence"', in *Walter Benjamin's Philosophy: Destruction and Experience*, ed. Andrew Benjamin and Peter Osborne (New York: Routledge, 1993), pp. 228–298.

Hanssen, Beatrice, *Critique of Violence: Between Poststructuralism and Critical Theory* (New York: Taylor and Francis, 2000).

Weber, Samuel, *Benjamin's -abilities* (Cambridge, MA: Harvard University Press, 2010).

Witte, Bern, *Walter Benjamin: An Intellectual Biography* (Detroit MI: Wayne State University Press, 1991).

3 | HANNAH ARENDT

Kimberly Hutchings

Biographical details

Hannah Arendt (1906–1975) was born in Hanover, Germany, and brought up, mostly by her mother owing to her father's early death, in Königsberg (then in Germany, now Kaliningrad in Russia). Her family background was that of the secular, professional, progressive middle class, with a strong commitment to education. As she noted herself, the fact that she was Jewish figured little in conversation at home; it was something to be taken for granted as a fact, though one was reminded of it by anti-Semitic comments from others. Famously, Arendt's mother taught her always to defend herself by going home at once if a teacher addressed anti-Semitic comments towards her.

Arendt was a brilliant but also rebellious student. She was expelled from school for organising a boycott of unpopular classes, but, after spending some time in Berlin attending university lectures, she returned and completed her university entrance examination a year ahead of the rest of her class. She then went on to university and studied philosophy with Martin Heidegger (with whom she had a love affair) and Karl Jaspers. She engaged deeply with Husserlian and Heideggerian phenomenology, was part of a very vibrant intellectual community in Heidelberg and completed a doctorate on 'St Augustine's Concept of Love' in 1929. She also became increasingly politically engaged as Nazism gained ground in Germany. One of her closest friends was the Zionist Kurt Blumenfeld, and her first husband, Günther Stern, was a member of the Communist Party and a political journalist who fled to Paris after the Reichstag fire in 1933. Arendt was involved in trying to help political refugees in the wake of Hitler's gaining power, but, after being detained for questioning by the police, fled to join her husband in Paris and became a refugee herself. In Paris she worked for a variety of Zionist organisations. Unsurprisingly, she was disillusioned with philosophy and with the German intellectuals who had accommodated themselves to the

Nazi regime, including Heidegger, and started to think and write directly about political issues, most notably how to account for the phenomenon of European anti-Semitism. While in Paris, she was part of an expatriate intellectual and political community that included Walter Benjamin; she separated from Stern and met her second husband, also a radical political activist, Heinrich Blücher. Arendt and Blücher were interned in France in 1940 but managed to get away and eventually reach New York in 1941.

Once in the United States, Arendt found work as a journalist, commentator and editor, first in German-language outlets and increasingly in the medium of English. As the war came to an end, she became research director of the Conference on Jewish Relations. She revisited Europe in 1949, renewing her contacts with Heidegger and Jaspers. During this time she researched the historical conditions of totalitarianism and consolidated her thinking about its specific nature as a mode of rule, as well as developing a strong critique of Zionist aspirations to create a Jewish state in Palestine. Her book *The Origins of Totalitarianism* (first edition 1951; hereinafter *Origins*)[1] established her reputation as a major political thinker and public intellectual.

From the 1950s to the 1970s she was involved in many public discussions and controversies about US domestic and foreign policy, including the civil rights movement and the Vietnam War. She engaged critically with the emergent post-war discourse of international human rights and the issue of statelessness, and was inspired by the anti-Soviet uprisings in Hungary in 1956 and in Czechoslovakia in 1968. She was also always deeply engaged with the nature and fate of the Israeli state. Her most explicit engagement with the question of violence was prompted by student protest and other forms of resistant politics in the United States and Europe in the late 1960s. She held research and teaching posts at the University of California, Berkeley, the University of Chicago and the New School for Social Research in New York, and published a series of books and collections of essays as well as commentary and current affairs between the appearance of *Origins* and her death in 1975. Since her death, many of her earlier writings have been published or republished in translation, a huge

---

1 Hannah Arendt, *The Origins of Totalitarianism* (London: Andre Deutsch, 1986).

secondary literature on her work has emerged and her reputation as a profound political thinker, in particular in the US academy, has continued to grow. The most remarkable things about her work are its independence of voice, its capacity to unsettle the comfort zones of ideological right/left thinking and the impossibility of incorporating it under any particular 'ism'. It covers a wide range, from high theory and philosophy to the political theory of revolution to historical research to polemical and controversial journalism.

Theorising violence

Arendt became famous as the author of two books in particular: *Origins*, which examined the rise of totalitarianism in Europe and became an immediate classic, and *Eichmann in Jerusalem* (1963), which was her controversial report on the trial of the Nazi war criminal Adolf Eichmann. The latter work was controversial both because of its critique of the role of the leadership of the Jewish community in the Holocaust and because of its identification of Eichmann as fundamentally thoughtless rather than as radically or inherently evil. Her other major works include *The Human Condition* (1958) and *On Revolution* (1963), and a large number of essays, including one called 'On Violence' (1970), which was published in book form and also reproduced in the collection of essays *Crises of the Republic* (1972).[2] It is this essay that has made her work one of the standard reference points for the discussion of violence in relation to politics; however, violence is a crucial theme in almost all of her writings.

Arendt's work has become most well known in the anglophone world, but her theoretical and political concerns emerged out of her education in philosophy and her experience of the rise of the Nazi regime, of political persecution and exile and, more specifically, of the horrors of totalitarian rule. Her work was always driven by the urgency of the need to resist the complete closure of space for politics that she argued is characteristic of totalitarian societies. Her explicit arguments about violence are part of a larger argument about the

2 Hannah Arendt, *Eichmann in Jerusalem: A Report on the Banality of Evil* (New York: Penguin, 1994 [1963]); *The Human Condition* (Chicago: University of Chicago Press, 1958); *On Revolution* (Harmondsworth: Pelican Books, 1973); *Crises of the Republic* (Harmondsworth: Penguin, 1973); and 'On Violence,' in *Crises*, pp. 83–163.

nature of politics and of what it means to be human. I will therefore begin with a brief account of some of the themes of *Origins* and *The Human Condition*. The first of these texts gives Arendt's account of how an unprecedented and seemingly incomprehensible violence was able to take over the modern European state. The second presents her view as to the real meaning of politics and offers a positive republican ideal as a counter to the forces of a homogenising mass society.

Origins is an ambitious book. Arendt originally intended its analysis to be focused solely on the Nazi brand of racist totalitarianism but then extended the analysis to include the Soviet Union. The book is structured in three parts under the headings 'Anti-Semitism', 'Imperialism' and 'Totalitarianism'. It offers a complex and detailed historical and theoretical analysis that covers development in European states and societies in the period from the late nineteenth century to the mid-twentieth century. Its essential argument is that late nineteenth-century imperialism had what Arendt refers to in her essay 'On Violence' as a 'boomerang effect', in which ideologies of race and modes of rule developed in overseas empires rebounded on the metropole and created conditions in which totalitarianism and genocide in Europe were made possible.

Arendt's analysis in *Origins* has been criticised in a variety of ways. Historians have criticised it for not explaining fully how and why the boomerang effect occurred not in the most established imperial powers, France and Britain, but in countries that were latecomers to imperialism (Germany) or had a very different imperial history (Russia). Postcolonial critics have pointed to the very strong Eurocentrism of Arendt's account and to the problematic nature of her portrayal, in particular, of African peoples. Most readers have found the structure of the book, and the contrast between the detailed historical accounts in the first two sections and the much more analytic and general approach of the third section, somewhat unwieldy. For the purposes of this chapter, my aim is to bring out the themes in the book that help to make sense of Arendt's views about violence and its relation to politics.

A major theme of the book is the imbrication of late nineteenth-century European imperialism with scientific racism both at home and abroad. In the first part, on anti-Semitism, Arendt spends considerable time dissecting the Dreyfus Affair in France in the 1890s. In the second part, she traces how racist hierarchies legitimated imperial conquest and rule in the same period, and how the notion of a 'civilising mission' went hand in hand with the development of technologies of mass detention and massacre. The supposed inferiority of populations fed into the notion of the expendability of those populations. The intentional violence of colonialism had massive unintended consequences in terms of inter-imperial rivalry. The technologies of mass destruction and detention developed in imperialism against both native populations and imperial rivals (e.g., in the Boer War) came home to roost in the two world wars and the rise of totalitarian regimes in Europe. A significant theme in Arendt's discussion is how the consequences of violence are unpredictable and uncontrollable.

A second theme in the book relates to bureaucracy as a mode of rule specific to late nineteenth-century imperialism, in which rulers assumed their disconnection from the populations that they ruled and saw their job as one of government and administration. This form of rule not only lacked accountability to subject populations but was also dispersed and depersonalised. On Arendt's account, the complex and large-scale administration of imperial possessions separated process from outcome, thus enabling the shift of responsibility from rulers to rules so that myriad colonial officials were accountable to procedure and an organisational hierarchy rather than for the actual effects of their decisions. This meant that they did not have to think about what they were actually doing. It is this kind of thoughtless bureaucratic rule that Arendt argues characterises totalitarian society. Her infamous comment about the 'banality of evil' in relation to Eichmann is a point about his utter thoughtlessness: that in justifying the management of the 'final solution' he could only refer to following rules. Clearly, for Arendt, the disconnection between process and outcome in bureaucratic rule is one of the ways in which unimaginable, and ultimately incomprehensible, violence is able to be unleashed.

A third theme in the book, which carries through into all of Arendt's later work, is about the rise in the nineteenth century of organic understandings of historical and political processes, and how this is crucial to the development of fascist and communist ideologies that support totalitarian rule. Social Darwinism, Marxism and scientific racism are all, for her, grounded in a profound mistake, in that they position humans as subordinate to greater historical forces. Once this is believed, then anything may become permitted, either because it is on the side of history or because it is simply part of a necessary unfolding of history. A fourth, related theme is the rise of the 'social' as a distinct domain of government in nineteenth-century Europe. Arendt argues that the definition of humans in social terms is homogenising. Equality becomes defined as sameness, and humans are understood as producers and consumers, as objects of government but not as citizens. For her the domination of the 'social question' in European states, which began in the nineteenth century, reduced reformist and revolutionary politics to the pursuit of material improvements and allowed the significance of politics, as a distinct mode of activity that relied on a plurality of voices and perspectives, to shrink. The loss of the public sphere was linked to increased individualisation and isolation of people even in emergent liberal and social democratic states. Communist and Fascist states, which reduced the population to a completely manipulable mass, pushed the implication of the social turn to its extreme.

Although Arendt offers an explanation of how totalitarianism takes hold, she nevertheless drew a distinction between, on the one hand, developments of an imperialist mind-set or logic in which 'everything is permitted' in order to preserve rulers in power and, on the other hand, totalitarianism. For example, Kitchener's concentration camps in the Boer War, and even Stalinist show trials and labour camps, are identified as essentially products of an imperialist mind-set in which the point is to hold power. However, within Nazism, she argues, the logic was not simply one in which 'everything is permitted' but rather one in which 'everything is possible'. For her, the concentration camps were a massive horrific experiment in changing human nature – they had no instrumental rationale. In this sense the violence of the Nazi regime, although we may grasp some of its conditions of possibility, is beyond comprehension, and, as we will see later, beyond the scope of how we might normally understand violence in political life.

The Human Condition (hereinafter *HC*) is a very different kind of book from *Origins*, although there are continuities with themes from the earlier book. Whereas *Origins* is very much about the loss of politics in imperialism and totalitarianism, *HC*, drawing on Arendt's philosophical roots in phenomenology, sets out an argument for the meaning and value of politics. The argument is based on the identification of three modes of human activity derived from an interpretation of life in the city-state of classical Greece: labour, work and action. In summary, Arendt identifies labour with activities through which the possibility of the reproduction of the human species is ensured. This is the realm of necessity, of literal biological reproduction, of tending to material needs for sustenance and sleep. It is analogous to an organic process, in the sense that it is ongoing and never ending. Within the Greek city-state, it is identified with the private realm or household, the world of women and slaves. Arendt identifies work with making things. In contrast to labour, work creates a lasting world of artefacts and spaces. It creates the conditions for a shared world between human beings; in the Greek city-state it builds the city wall and the space of the *agora*; it also produces non-material things, such as poetry and history. It is an essentially public activity, but it is also thoroughly instrumental, always for the sake of something else. This 'something else' is action, the human activity that is distinctively political. For Arendt action is not instrumental; it is a mode of doing that in and of itself creates the 'in between' among citizens; it is public by definition. The classical Greek city-state exemplifies the sphere of action in the coming together of citizens in the *agora* to debate and vote. Action is about speech and new beginnings; it is inherently plural, in the sense that it relies on the revealing and disclosing of individual actors, assumed to be equal but also not the same, through words and deeds. Action, and therefore politics, is inherently unknowable in advance and unpredictable in its effects; it is risky and contingent.

Arendt argues that the preservation of the distinction of action from both labour and work is crucial to the possibility of politics. The problem with modern states, in contrast to classical Greece, is that the realms of labour and work have become identified with the realm of action:

> The triumph the modern world has achieved over necessity is due to the emancipation of labour, that is, to the fact that the animal *laborans* was permitted to occupy the public realm; and yet, as long as the animal *laborans* remains in possession of it, there can be no true public realm, but only private activities displayed in the open.[3]

3 Arendt, *Human Condition*, pp. 133–134.

While only fabrication with its instrumentality is capable of building a world, this same world becomes as worthless as the employed material, a mere means for further ends, if the standards which governed its coming into being are permitted to rule it after its establishment.[4]

Much of Arendt's work after the publication of *HC* addressed the question of how politics might be made possible within modernity. In *On Revolution* she examines the dynamics of the American and French revolutions in order to explore how politics as the capacity for new beginning might be enabled. Famously, she criticised the French revolution for diverting from its original inspiration in relation to the rights of humans as citizens to the demands of the mob for food, shifting focus from the realm of action to that of labour, and the consequent morphing of politics into tyranny. In contrast, she praises the American Constitution for keeping the space for politics open, although she is increasingly pessimistic about the fate of politics in any mass society in the latter part of the twentieth century. Many critics of Arendt have argued against her reliance on a typology derived from a reading of the Greek city-state and accused her of a kind of republican elitism and indifference to the political significance of poverty and economic inequality and social discrimination. One of her most notorious essays criticised the forcible integration of schools in the American South on the grounds of the need to restrict interference of the state in the 'private' or 'social' matter of education ('Reflections on Little Rock', 1959).[5] But for Arendt the drawing of hard lines between different aspects of the human condition was necessary to enable the recognition of politics as an autonomous sphere characterised by freedom and creativity. As becomes very clear in Arendt's essay 'On Violence', the reduction of action to work reduces politics to instrumental control, and the reduction of action to labour subsumes politics under inexorable and uncontrollable forces of history. With the former, you get authoritarianism; with the latter, totalitarianism.

'On Violence' 'On Violence' is a short but very rich text. It was originally published in the *Journal of International Affairs*, and it is

---

4 Arendt, *Human Condition*, p. 156.
5 Hannah Arendt, 'Reflections on Little Rock', *Dissent* 6(1) (1959), pp. 45–56.

impossible to make sense of it in abstraction from the political situation of the time or from Arendt's other theoretical and philosophical work. In terms of the historical context, the student unrest of the 1960s and the shift from the nonviolence of the civil rights movements to the explicit embrace of violence in resistance and revolutionary movements, as well as the ongoing situation of 'mutually assured destruction' in the Cold War, formed the backdrop to her analysis. In terms of her theoretical work, the analysis of totalitarianism and the labour, work and action categories from *HC* underlie the ways in which she makes sense of the meaning of violence and its relation to power. The crux of the essay revolves around the distinction between power and violence. Arendt insists that violence is inherently instrumental, which means that it is intentional and a means to an end, the end being to command obedience. Violence requires tools, and the logic of violence is linked to the kinds of technological development that culminate in mutually assured destruction.

> Violence – is distinguished by its instrumental character. Phenomenologically, it is close to strength, since the implements of violence, like all other tools, are designed and used for the purposes of multiplying natural strength until, in the last stage of their development they can substitute for it.[6]

Defined in this way, 'violence' sounds very like the Weberian definition of 'power' as the capacity of A to make B do what B would not do otherwise. For Arendt, however, in contrast to Max Weber, violence is defined as completely different from power. Power, in her view, is founded in the consent of a plurality of actors acting together and is the sole source of political legitimacy. In many ways power is treated by Arendt as equivalent to the categories of action and politics that she expounded in *HC*; it is contrasted not only with violence understood as an instrument but also with accounts that associate violence with natural or organic life forces. Arendt argues that predominant traditions in European political thought have been grounded in a mistaken identification of power with violence, assuming politics to be about rule ('the business of dominion') rather than about 'action' in the public sphere. Arendt notes that power

6 Arendt, 'On Violence', p. 115.

and violence are usually found together in political life, but she nevertheless argues that they are antithetical in principle. Violence may be a condition of power in certain contexts, in the sense that it may open the space for politics, for example in revolutionary uprisings or wars of independence. Violence may also destroy power in other contexts; for example, Arendt suggests the impossibility of nonviolent action in situations where the space for politics has been entirely closed down, arguing that movements such as Gandhi's nonviolence campaign against the British could not possibly have worked in Nazi Germany or Stalin's Soviet Union. Nevertheless, what violence is essentially about, compulsion, is fundamentally opposed to what power is essentially about, consent and free action. There are clearly parallels here between how Arendt sees the relation between the categories of 'work' and 'action' in *HC*.

> Power, far from being the means to an end, is actually the very condition enabling a group of people to think and act in terms of the means–end category.[7]

> Violence is by nature instrumental; like all means, it always stands in need of guidance and justification through the end it pursues.[8]

Looking a bit more deeply, we find Arendt identifying various kinds of mistakes in various aspects of the philosophical traditions that have been concerned with the relation between politics and violence and power and violence. One kind of mistake can be traced in what we might call statist and another in anti-statist political thought. Statist political theories, as in the work of Thomas Hobbes and of Weber, identify the state as the legitimate location of political authority. In this tradition of thinking, the state holds the monopoly of legitimate violence and is entitled to exercise it internally in the control of populations, and externally in war. Anti-statist political thought, as in the work of Karl Marx, of Georges Sorel and of Frantz Fanon, challenges the state's claim to legitimate power and identifies violence as a legitimate means in the cause of liberation. On the

7 Arendt, 'On Violence', p. 119.
8 Arendt, 'On Violence', p. 119.

statist side, as we have seen, Arendt argues that there is a mistaken identification of violence with power, in which violence is correctly conceptualised as a means to an end but power is misunderstood; on this view, violence is understood in Arendt's terms as an instrument for gaining specific ends, but power, rather than being seen as the capacity to act in concert, is defined instead as domination of A over B – and therefore as instrumental in the same sense as violence.

Anti-statist theories, on Arendt's account, are doubly mistaken. Here Arendt argues that both power and violence are misconceived by being subsumed under the logic of either natural or historical processes. Arendt identified this danger in the thought of theorists such as Sorel, who, she argued, had an organicist conception of violence as some kind of natural flow or energy that erupted in revolutionary movements. In 'On Violence', Arendt was particularly concerned to challenge the views she saw as prevalent in contemporary radical movements that drew on thinkers such as Sorel and Fanon, or on Jean-Paul Sartre's argument in his preface to Fanon's *The Wretched of the Earth*, in which violence was seen as liberating in itself.[9] That is to say, it was not just an instrument through which freedom might be obtained but an exercise or expression of freedom. The potential conflation of politics and violence in the case of this double mistake was particularly dangerous for Arendt as it subsumed human actions under broader organic and historical processes. This conflation of the realms of labour and action was for her, as we have seen, a key aspect of the rise of totalitarian rule.

> Nothing, in my opinion, could be theoretically more dangerous than the tradition of organic thought in political matters by which power and violence are interpreted in biological terms.[10]

This does not mean that Arendt disagrees with Fanon's view that violence may be necessary in order to fight against oppression. Arendt is not a pacifist. As mentioned above in relation to Gandhi, she argues that nonviolence becomes irrelevant in contexts in which power (in her sense) is absent. Repeatedly in her work she draws attention to

9 Jean-Paul Sartre, 'Preface', in Frantz Fanon, *The Wretched of the Earth* (London: Penguin, 1990), pp. 7–26.
10 Arendt, 'On Violence', p. 136.

revolutionary moments that are genuinely political. Her examples include the formation of the workers' and soldiers' soviets in 1917, the Hungarian uprising in 1956, the Danish evacuation of Jews while under Nazi occupation and the French resistance in World War Two, but also the Viet Cong in anti-colonial and anti-imperialist wars. She was also a firm advocate of the need for a Jewish army to fight in the Second World War. Arendt explains her acceptance of violence in certain circumstances with reference to a distinction between what is justifiable and what is legitimate. Justification, she argues, relates to the value of the outcomes of any particular action. Legitimacy, in contrast, relates to the nature of the grounds of action. In Arendt's view, violence can be justifiable, but it cannot be legitimate. Because Arendt sees the former as a prospective mode of validation, in which an act is justified in terms of the effects that it intends to bring about, she argues that violence can be justified if it rights a specific wrong that cannot be addressed in any other way. However, as a mode of action, violence can never be legitimate, because legitimacy derives from the nature of 'action' in the proper political sense, in which it is supported and enabled by power. Arendt is insistent that actors must not pretend that violence is anything other than violence, even when they have resorted to it for what they think are good reasons. Violence is not identifiable with building a better world, righting a wrong or achieving autonomy in the face of a colonial oppressor, even when it is the means by which these ends are served.

Moreover, Arendt argues that violence can only ever be justifiable as a short-term measure, and, even then, there is no guarantee that what will be brought about will match the intentions of the violent actor. Arendt is clear that violence breeds violence, and the most likely outcome of a violent action is a more violent world. As a long-term strategy, violence is ultimately self-defeating, since the compulsion of obedience, through threat of force, is extremely difficult to sustain. She points out that the first thing an invading force will do is to set up a 'quisling' government, to try to tap into power to help maintain it – in other words, regimes established by violence cannot be wholly maintained by violence for any length of time. Governments need some kind of legitimacy or consent to work at all over the longer term.

For Arendt the logic of both statist and anti-statist traditions of thought on violence is a logic of destruction and death. This linking of politics to death violates the meaning of politics and is a mistake made equally by Hobbes in his account of political authority as fundamentally the power over life and death; by what Arendt refers to as the 'suicide squads' of revolutionary martyrs; and, most obviously, by the nuclear stand-off that dominated the Cold War at the time she was writing. The policy of mutually assured destruction is the epitome of the equation of politics with rule and domination. Real politics, in contrast, is about creating and sustaining the space between plural actors through speech; it is about making commonality out of difference; about acting together and creating new beginnings, what Arendt elsewhere refers to as 'natality'. Even when it is justified, violence destroys space for action because it is silent in itself (it does not speak) and because it is silencing in its effects.

Arendt's discussion of violence in relation to power is highly distinctive. As with her analyses in *Origins* and *HC*, there have been a variety of criticisms of her views on violence and its relation to power. A common complaint is that Arendt's insistence on the hard boundaries between the categories of violence and power (and therefore politics) is too rigid, and difficult to sustain even in terms of her own analysis. For example, her suggestion that 'violence is the last resort of power', when referring to the treatment of criminals in the domestic state, raises the question of how the co-existence of power and violence is to be conceptualised and whether it can be done in such a way as to keep the categories as distinct as Arendt herself insists. In many ways, violence seems like a hybrid category in her account, somewhere between work and action. This problem appears at the macro-political level, where power uses violence and also – on Arendt's own account – depends on it, for example in relation to legitimate law enforcement or just war. It also appears at the micro-level of the individual subject, for whom violence may be the appropriate way to right a wrong. Clearly, Arendt's analysis is opposed to either psychoanalytic or Foucauldian accounts of the subject, and this can be seen to render her phenomenology of violence inadequate in certain respects – for example, in her account of the justifiability of violence. Within this account there is a tension between her awareness of how violence may corrupt the ends that it seeks to serve and the stark claim that violence may be the mechanism that rights a wrong, which implies that in some circumstances violence does not corrupt the end it serves. The problem here is partly Arendt's insistence on the instrumentality of violence, which is linked to her determination to resist naturalised accounts of violence. This means that the corrupting effects of violence are registered more in relation to its actual outcome or effect as against the intended outcome/effect than in terms of the ways it transforms the protagonists of violence (perpetrator and victim) in and of themselves, regardless of whether a specific wrong is righted.

Another key criticism of Arendt's treatment of the concept of violence is her restriction of the category to the intentional exertion of physical force against others. This means that it is difficult to make sense of either 'structural' or 'epistemic' violence in Arendtian terms. Structural violence refers to the ways in which economic and status inequalities and hierarchies structure people's life chances, determining poverty, hunger, suffering and death for many people, even though they are not being directly attacked. For Arendt, this phenomenon is not in itself either political or violent (since it is not being intentionally used to bring about a particular outcome), though she is clear that it is to be deplored. Critics have suggested that Arendt's lack of sympathy for the existential elements in Fanon's argument in *The Wretched of the Earth* is partly based on a misunderstanding of the nature of colonial violence, which, Fanon argues, is embedded in everything from the arrangement of, and differential access to, colonial space, to the ideological race thinking reproduced in the heads of the colonised themselves. Which brings us to the question of epistemic violence. There is clearly a sense in which Arendt does identify totalitarianism with a kind of epistemic violence, in terms of the ways in which it drives out the possibility of thought. But what she means by 'violence' cannot extend to this kind of process. Nor can it extend to the poststructuralist use of the term 'violence' to express the ultimate arbitrariness of the grounds of meaning or law. In contrast to her friend Walter Benjamin, Arendt was suspicious of the extension of the terminology of violence to express a moment of grounding, in either a negative or a positive sense. For her, violence is never either mythical or divine; it is always instrumental, intentional and defined in terms of its ends.

Confronting violence in the world

Arendt's work has continued to influence later generations of thinkers and also remains a site of controversy in terms of its internal coherence and its political implications. Those drawing on her work range from theorists of deliberative and agonistic democracy to profound critics of modernity, from both conservative and radical traditions. Her sharp distinction between violence and power was influential in Jürgen Habermas' development of his distinctions between strategic and communicative rationality and action.[11] Her analysis of totalitarianism is central to the critique of modernity in thinkers such as Zygmunt Bauman[12] and Giorgio Agamben.[13] In spite of her explicit dismissal of feminism as a political movement, many feminist thinkers have drawn on aspects of Arendt work to develop non-essentialist accounts of feminist politics, especially her conceptions of action and natality (Seyla Benhabib, Linda Zerilli).[14] International relations theorists have drawn on her analyses of human rights, statelessness and war (Patrick Hayden, Patricia Owens).[15]

There are two things in particular, I would argue, that draw such a disparate range of theorists back to Arendt's work again and again. The first is her analysis of modern forms of rule, emerging out of imperialism, as fundamentally historicist and bureaucratic. Historicism, whether in the form of the civilising mission, the future of the superior race or the ultimate victory of the proletariat, constructs an alibi for any current sacrifice in terms of a future good. Bureaucratic rule by no one in particular undermines the accountability and responsibility of decision-makers and constructs the population as a determinable creature, swayable by a complex set of carrots and sticks. Although modern states do not inevitably turn totalitarian, Arendt identifies this combination of historicism and bureaucracy as creating the conditions of possibility for the

---

11 Jürgen Habermas, *Theory of Communicative Action*, vols 1 and 2 (Boston: Beacon Press, 1984, 1987).

12 Zygmunt Bauman, *Modernity and the Holocaust* (Ithaca: Cornell University Press, 1989).

13 Giorgio Agamben, *Homo Sacer: Sovereign Power and Bare Life* (Stanford: Stanford University Press, 1998).

14 Seyla Benhabib, *Situating the Self: Gender, Community and Postmodernism in Contemporary Ethics* (New York: Routledge, 1992); Linda Zerilli, *Feminism and the Abyss of Freedom* (Chicago: Chicago University Press, 2005).

15 Patrick Hayden, *Political Evil in a Global Age: Hannah Arendt and International Theory* (London: Routledge, 2010); Patricia Owens, *Between War and Politics: International Relations and the Thought of Hannah Arendt* (Oxford: Oxford University Press, 2007).

emergence of a totalitarian mind-set. At best modernity, in terms of this combination of historicism with bureaucratic rule, enables unprecedented violence; at its worst, in totalitarianism, it exceeds the terms of violence as an instrumental category, because the injury, death and destruction wrought are not, any longer, for anything. Arendt's work offers a resource for contemporary thinkers striving to understand and critique the pathologies of modern states, and particularly the ways in which they render some lives disposable and without value, such as in twenty-first-century camps of refugees, migrants or the extraordinarily rendered, uncategorised, tortured prisoners of the 'war on terror'.

The second reason why Arendt's work remains hugely relevant for contemporary political thinkers is her vision of politics. She remains extremely unusual in the history of western political thought in offering an account of politics as not equivalent to rule or government. More generally, she refuses to reduce politics to any other category and identifies it as a fundamentally creative and common capacity. Politics is creative in the sense that it is an entirely human construct that is not controlled or determined even by its own authors. Revolutionaries, for her, are not forwarding the purposes of history but making something up, the consequences of which they can neither foresee nor control. This open and contingent understanding of politics offers an alternative way forward for thinking about resistance and democracy for those for whom liberal and communist ideologies of progress have been discredited. Unsurprisingly, Arendt's thought has become a resource for thinkers attempting to articulate participatory ideals of democracy and freedom outside liberal and Marxist vocabularies.

Of course, Arendt's thought also continues to be criticised as anachronistic, because of her reliance on the example of the Greek city-state; as governed by overly rigid categories; as dismissive of material and structural violence and inequality; and as inherently elitist, because only those for whom the work and labour is being done by others could have time for politics in her sense. Nevertheless, in spite of these critiques of her broader political thought, Arendt's account of violence in her essay 'On Violence' and in her other work is powerful and persuasive. She neither mystifies nor celebrates violence. She provides a set of tools for understanding the exponential increase in state and anti-state violence in the twentieth century, and her defence of uses of violence in politics is made in the full awareness of the dangers involved in any such use. As she says in 'On Violence', 'The practice of violence, like all action, changes the world, but the most probable change is to a more violent world.'[16]

Further reading

Arendt, Hannah, *Crises of the Republic* (Harmondsworth: Penguin, 1973 [1972]).

Arendt, Hannah, *Eichmann in Jerusalem: A Report on the Banality of Evil* (New York and London: Penguin, 1994 [1963]).

Arendt, Hannah, *On Revolution* (Harmondsworth: Pelican Books, 1973 [1963]).

Benhabib, Seyla (ed.), *Politics in Dark Times: Encounters with Hannah Arendt* (Cambridge: Cambridge University Press, 2010).

Frazer, Elizabeth and Kimberly Hutchings, 'On Politics and Violence: Arendt Contra Fanon', *Contemporary Political Theory* 7(1) (2008), pp. 90–108.

Villa, Dana R. (ed.), *The Cambridge Companion to Arendt* (Cambridge: Cambridge University Press, 2000).

Villa, Dana R., *Politics, Philosophy, Terror: Essays on the thought of Hannah Arendt* (Princeton: Princeton University Press, 1999).

Young-Bruehl, Elisabeth, *Hannah Arendt: For the Love of the World* (New Haven: Yale University Press, 1982).

16 Arendt, 'On Violence', p. 141.

4 | FRANTZ FANON

Lewis R. Gordon

Biographical details

Frantz Marguerite Victor 'Omar' Fanon (1925–1953) was born on the Caribbean island of Martinique. He was the fifth child in a family of eight, two of whom died in infancy. A volunteer for the Allied forces in the Second World War, during which he was a twice-decorated war hero, Fanon was subsequently able to secure support for his studies in psychiatry in Lyon, where he attended Maurice Merleau-Ponty's lectures in philosophy. It was there that he met and married Marie-Josèphe Dublé, a young woman of Corsican–Gypsy descent from a leftist family, with whom he had a son. He also had a daughter, Mireille Fanon-Mendès-France, who now directs the Frantz Fanon Foundation in Paris, from an earlier short relationship with a Jewish woman in Lyon. Fanon then achieved his licence to practise psychiatry, through training with the famed Catalan humanist psychiatrist François Tosquelles, which enabled him to serve as director of psychiatric wards in the French-speaking world. After brief employment in Norway, Fanon took a post at the Blida-Joinville hospital in Algiers in 1953.

Fanon's work as the head psychiatrist at Blida-Joinville is legendary. He implemented humanistic psychiatric techniques that involved recognising and affirming the humanity of his patients. Though not certain of the specifics, all of his biographers agree that his patients regarded his presence, methods and policies as emancipatory. The positive period, however, was short lived. He experienced radical shift at the advent of the Algerian war, which formally began in 1954 and ended in 1962. His response to the war was to train Front de Libération Nationale (FLN) members in techniques for resisting torture and methods of combat he learned from his years as a soldier. He eventually resigned from his post and became a full-time organiser, writer and physician for the FLN, and moved with his family to Tunisia.

The subsequent years consisted of Fanon serving as a representative for the FLN in 'black' Africa, where he set up agreements for the transportation of resources and soldiers. Such activities made him an outlaw in France and its colonies, the result of which was many attempts on his life. He became a Robin Hood figure in those years, eluding capture and assassination attempts, though he managed to participate in the 1959 Congress of Black Writers and Artists in Rome. He also wrote a critical text that year, *Year V of the Algerian Revolution* (available today as *A Dying Colonialism*), in which he both criticised the standard French interpretation of the Algerian war and offered his theory on the social impact of colonised people struggling for their liberation. By 1960 his health had deteriorated considerably, and upon seeking care had his suspicions confirmed that he had leukaemia.

Fanon first went to the then Soviet Union for treatment but was informed by the physicians there that the best care was in the United States, at the National Institutes of Health in Bethesda, Maryland. After planning some publishing projects and completing his last book, *Les damnés de la terre* (available in English as *The Wretched of the Earth*), he went to Bethesda under the name of Ibrahim Fanon. When he arrived in the United States, the Central Intelligence Agency detained him for ten days without treatment. He subsequently received a series of blood transfusions and eventually contracted pneumonia, which led to his death on 6 December 1961. His body was sent to Algeria, where he was by then a citizen, and, after a few days of ceremony and military recognition as an important revolutionary, he was buried in an FLN veterans' graveyard in Ain El-Karma.

Theorising violence

Fanon wrote on a variety of controversial topics ranging from racism to women wearing veils in Algeria. None has made him more notorious, however, than his thought on violence. The very idea of a black man unapologetically discussing the concept without the usual prescriptions and assurances against it scared so many white critics and what Malcolm X would call 'house Negroes' that it took some time for the actual content of his thought to receive even a modicum of understanding, much less careful reading. Much of his actual thought on the subject was distorted in the secondary literature and, in some cases, what critics thought he had said was actually the words of his white commentators, such as Jean-Paul Sartre and Hannah Arendt. Ironically, such secondary sources reinforced one of Fanon's criticisms in his first book, *Black Skin, White Masks*, against the tendency to seek thought in a white face instead of engaging what emanates from a black body. As he reflected in that inaugural work: 'I became disillusioned. That victory played cat and mouse; it mocked me ... When I was there, it [reason] was not; when it was there, I was no longer.'[1] The construction of reason as white entombs him, rendering his voice, even in texts where his words reach forth, muffled, if not entirely silent. To make matters worse, Fanon's biography, which includes his having joined the Algerian fighters in one of the twentieth century's bloodiest struggles for independence, was easy fodder for critics who already saw violence as the only role black men could play when fighting against colonialism, even though they were also deployed as its protecting forces, as in the regiments of black soldiers fighting in Algeria for 'mother France'. Exacerbating all this was Fanon's sharp tongue, which spared no opponent, even if that opponent was among the much-prized members of his own countrywomen and men. This latter tendency welcomed efforts to discredit him, especially among Antillean elites.

However, many of Fanon's critics miss a basic point. His relationship with violence began in the world in which he was conceived. A colonial subject from birth, he lived through the many manifestations of brutality and degradation unleashed against members of a subordinated humanity. Fanon grew up with a sense of pride in belonging to a nation supposedly carrying a torch of civilisation for humankind, which, presumably, included him. Accompanying such esteem was a sense of dignity premised on a belief in rights, or, more properly, the rights of 'men', which, again, presumably included him. Such bolstering of the spirit meant, then, the experience of violation where such expectations were not honoured. On the island of Martinique, where the demographics revealed a tiny number of whites who held most of the wealth, a

---

1 *Peau noire masques blancs* (Paris: Editions du Seuil, 1952), p. 96. I will refer to this text in English as *Black Skin, White Masks*. As I am not satisfied with most of the translations of Fanon's writings, all included here are my own except for the portion of his plays from his brother Joby Fanon's *Frantz Fanon, My Brother: Doctor, Playwright, Revolutionary*, trans. Daniel Nethery (Lanham: Lexington Books, 2014).

large number of blacks as the poor and disenfranchised cheap labour pool, and a fair number of 'mulattoes' and a tiny number of Asians as the mediating population between white and black, the primary interaction on matters of violence was without the wider logic of dehumanisation, because it was premised on basic rules of equality between black and black. Rhetorical equality is not able to sustain its legitimacy in the face of de facto inequality, however, and the contradictions do work their way through to many facets of social and indeed psychic life. The ongoing violence of colonial society works, in other words, on multiple levels of human, lived reality.

A confusion that often emerges in discussions of violence is the failure to distinguish it from force. An example from Fanon's childhood suffices to make the point. When he was around the age of ten, a friend visited, carrying his father's revolver. The boy hurt his finger when he fired the loaded pistol. Fanon dressed the wound, informed his mother that it was a toy backfiring and took his friend to the hospital. His friend was harmed, true, but 'violence' would not be the proper characterisation of what happened. Whereas force is simply the impact on one object of another, with at times the result of pain and suffering, violence requires a system of norms through which something *wrong* or undeserved or unjust happens. Running into a wall hurts, and at times even causes death, but it doesn't properly count as violence. Pushing someone into a wall is, however, a different matter. Violence, in other words, is part of the human world and its variety of norms. It would be remiss to describe what happens between predator and prey among non-human animals or at least those without reason (though not necessarily without rationality, since hunting and avoiding being hunted are very rational) as violence, although it would be correct to say it is brutal.

Fanon faced much brutality throughout his short life. Violence, however, is something he understood as endemic to the colonial situation. Additionally, once inaugurated, violence is not a phenomenon from which one can be easily disentangled. There is the dream of innocent dissociation from violence, but that, Fanon eventually argued, is naive. Ironically, he knew this through his humanism. Drawing on another period from his childhood, Fanon, then about fourteen years of age, was curious to witness an autopsy of a woman being conducted in a nearby church of his hometown of Fort-de-France. He sneaked up to an open window and watched the whole procedure, which disgusted him. This revulsion remained with him throughout his life. It was also what existentialists would call the inaugural moment of Fanon's reflective apprehension of himself. He realised his humanism through his incapacity, or perhaps refusal, to dissociate the person from the cadaver before him. This commitment haunted him in ironic ways. That he eventually became both a forensic and clinical psychiatrist reveals much about the man. In his day, forensic psychiatrists were often assigned the task of conducting autopsies. He eventually devoted his life to exposing knowledge held within flesh while continuously attempting to heal the soul.

Colonialism raises the constant threat of violence. This makes ignoring it in the name of pacifism and peace, as Fanon saw it, nothing short of complicity. Being nonviolent maintains violence; what is needed is intervention. The problem is also that, where the ongoing violence doesn't register as unjust, its adherents regard it at most to be a circumstance of force. Think, for example, of the expression 'police force'. The police are called such because their use of force is presumed to be legitimate. Where their legitimacy is eroded, their proper title would be 'state-sanctioned agents of violence'. This requires a further meditation on the relationship of force to power. To some extent, in agreement with Michel Foucault, all power is force.[2] Power is possession of the means – the relations or activities of force affecting other forces – to make things happen. Where limited to bodies, power is the physical reach of force, if but simply to move one object from one point to another. The social world, however, enables other resources such as language, desires and needs to produce a series of effects. Thus, beyond the body, an agent could potentially affect others on another part of the globe and even those in outer space. One could even be affecting another without being aware of it, as when one's desires, interests or obsessions focus on someone without one having any idea of what is transpiring.

Fanon was a radical democrat, which means he regarded all forms of government that limit the distribution of power to be pernicious and, as such, ultimately violent. Colonialism, he argued, was such an arrangement, and its use of force to limit colonised peoples'

---

2 See, e.g., Michel Foucault, *Power/Knowledge: Selected Interviews and Other Writings, 1972–1977*, ed. Colin Gordon and trans. Colin Gordon, Leo Marshall, John Mepham and Kate Soper (New York: Pantheon, 1980).

capacity to affect the world beyond the confines of their bodies and their immediate vicinity was an ongoing, lived reality of violence. We need to supplement this, however, with an important biographical reminder: Fanon, as his former student and one of his subsequent biographers, Alice Cherki, correctly argued, detested violence.[3] It is an observation shared also by his ambivalent early mentor Aimé Césaire.[4] Fanon's logic should be obvious: as illegitimate force, *justification* of violence is a contradiction in terms. Still, even such a straightforward rejection is rarely as simple as it appears, and, since a very brilliant and complicated young man endorsed such, it behoves us to learn more about him.

Revolutionary humanism Fanon is one of the most famous black revolutionary figures of the twentieth century. He is known as a revolutionary existential humanist whose writings are influential in such areas of thought as political theory, Africana thought, postcolonial thought and black existentialism, to name a few. His first book, *Black Skin, White Masks*, is a brilliant portrait of irony and struggle. He advanced what he called a 'sociogenic' theory of oppression. The colonised person of colour often tries to work within colonial and racist systems in good faith, but the system itself has no conception of a normal person of colour beyond models of separate normalities, where what is considered pathological white behaviour is supposedly the normal behaviour among coloured populations and vice versa. Thus it is abnormal for, say, a black to be as a white, and all the investments of viciousness are marked onto the bodies of blacks. Black psychology is therefore, from the perspective of white normative systems, abnormal psychology or psychopathology. How, then, can people be made well when there is no model of them ever being truly normal? The response, Fanon urged, is to fight against and effect a transformation of a society that fails to recognise the humanity of many of its members. In effect, he joined thinkers such as Anténor Firmin, Franz Boas and W. E. B. DuBois in pointing out that there are societies that make people into problems instead

---

3 Alice Cherki, *Frantz Fanon: A Portrait*, trans. Nadia Benabid (Ithaca: Cornell University Press, 2006), p. 72.
4 Aimé Césaire, 'La révolte de Frantz Fanon', in *Frantz Fanon: Par les textes de l'époque* (Paris: Les Petit Matins, 2012), p. 110.

of addressing the social causes of the challenges they face.[5] At the end of the book, Fanon applauded African Americans for fighting against their oppression, and he asked for himself and other people of colour in the francophone world to become people who *question* their condition.

There are many provocative theoretical insights in *Black Skin, White Masks* emerging from Fanon's analysis of socially generated meaning, the limits of semiological resistance, concepts of failure in the human sciences, colonial relativising of psychoanalysis, problems of closed dialectics, phobogenesis and more.[6] Particularly germane to the interests of this volume, however, is his critique of the dialectics of recognition and models of self–other relations. The colonised or racially subordinated subject who attempts to justify their existence through recognition from those who dominate them in effect makes the dominator the standard of legitimacy. As in effect not being the standard, such an effort is proverbially stillborn, because *the ability to be the standard* is what is at issue. There is thus the problem of failing by virtue of being who or what one is. This problem of recognition carries over into self–other relations. The logic of *self* and *other* requires a form of reciprocity in which the self is also an other and the other is also a self. This logic leads to a vicarious situation, the ability to see another's point of view or at least imagine oneself from such a perspective, which is one of the fundamental premises of ethical relations. The other, by this logic, is another human being. Colonialism and racism, Fanon argues, produce beings who are neither the self nor the other, trapped in what he calls the 'zone of nonbeing.' Such subjects imagine a world of others-whom-they-cannot-be except in relation to those horizontally located in the zone of nonbeing. Looking vertically, there are only asymmetrical relations from those others-whom-they-cannot-be-or-become.

---

5 For discussion of Boas, Firmin and Du Bois on this problem, see Lewis R. Gordon, 'Franz Boas in Africana Philosophy', in *Indigenous Visions: Rediscovering the World of Franz Boas*, ed. Isaiah Lorado Wilner and Ned Blackhawk (New Haven: Yale University Press, forthcoming).
6 For a detailed analysis, see Lewis R. Gordon, *What Fanon Said: A Philosophical Introduction to His Life and Thought* (New York: Fordham University Press, 2015), chs 2 and 3, though the entire book is relevant to what I am arguing throughout this chapter.

The crucial point here is that, in the zone of nonbeing, one does not move *down* to whiteness. It is a structured hierarchy that in effect makes whites (or similar colonial categories of people) relate to each other as human beings but to those in the zone of nonbeing in the form of being gods over them (from the perspective of those in the zone) and human beings above subhuman beings or animals (from the perspective of the dominating colonial group). The struggle against colonialism and racism, then, becomes not a struggle against being the other but instead one of establishing self–other relations without the trap of the dialectics of recognition. The problem, however, is that, in the pre-given sphere of ethical relations, this form of justice emerging from the zone of nonbeing is seen as a disruption of a presumed right order. It is seen as a violation, a form of illegitimate effect or wrongful force – in other words, violence – from the perspective of the governing regime of supposedly legitimate power relations.

A Dying Colonialism, Fanon's second book, defends the view that no people can be handed their freedom. It is something they must seize. Although the work's main purpose was counter-propaganda – that is, to argue against the French claim that the FLN was a group of thugs and terrorists – Fanon took advantage of the situation to outline his social theory of liberation. His main point is that fighting for national independence awakens new ways of living in the world. In the case of Algerian women, he argued that participating in the struggle created new understandings of the meaning of such practices as wearing the veil in Muslim communities. He was critical of the white French claim that colonising Algeria was the best way of liberating Algerian women. He countered by arguing that participating in the liberation of Algeria would raise the *internal* question of the liberation of Algerian women. Contemporary debates over the wearing of the veil in Europe reveal the prescience and continued relevance of Fanon's analysis. Fanon also made distinctions between colonial medicine and liberating medicine and between colonial use of technology and liberating use of technology. He pointed out how the Arab and Berber Algerians' views of medicine changed when they learned how to practice medical techniques on the battlefield, and how the need for information led to a new relationship with, for example, the radio. In the conclusion to this book, he pointed out that white French settlers who chose to fight on the side of liberation developed a different form of consciousness and were, consequently, new people or in the process of becoming such. His italicised concluding paragraph sums up his position:

Revolution, at its core, is truth, precisely because it changes man, renews and advances society. It is the oxygen that invents a new humanity. This, precisely, is the Algerian Revolution.[7]

The theme of struggle creating new people returns in Fanon's most famous work, *Les damnés de la terre* (1961), from which his thought on violence is most principally known. The English translations appear as *The Wretched of the Earth*, but, as 'wretched' is not identical to 'damned', which is what *damné* means, I prefer simply to refer to the book as *The Damned of the Earth*. Some critics may object because of the use of the expression in Eugène Edine Pottier's *L'internationale* (1871), but here we should be reminded of Fanon's critique of the blind application onto coloured subjects of concepts developed for white normative uses. Afro-Francophone intellectuals were also aware of Jacques Roumain's adaptation and transformation of *L'internationale* in his own poem, 'Sales nègres' ('Dirty *nègres*'), in his book of verse *Bois-d'ébène* ('Ebony Wood').[8] I have left the word *nègre* without translation since it means both Negro and nigger. Readers of *Black Skin, White Masks* would immediately recognise the connection here to the opening sentence of the fifth chapter, 'The Lived-Experience of the Black': 'Dirty *nègre!*' or simply 'Look, a *nègre!*' The *nègre* is not a being neatly tacked onto the proletariat or working class. It is a being beneath and as such is more properly an *underclass* category. Added to the poetics of all this is the deeper significance of the word 'damned'. Its etymology points in Latin to *damnum* (injury, hurt, harm), and further linguistic archaeology reveals the obvious connection to *adamah* (ground, clay, human), from which comes the name 'Adam'. The connection to the Genesis myth of Adam being made from dust or clay is evident, but the matter is complicated by *adamah* being what Adam would look like if rendered feminine in Hebrew. There is also the fact that the word Adam (or Adom as it appears in Hebrew) also literally means 'red', and, if one thinks of the ritualistic killing of animals, where the

7 Frantz Fanon, *L'An V de la révolution algerienne* (Paris: Maspero, 1959), p. 174.
8 Jacques Roumain, *Bois-d'ébène* (Port-au-Prince: Imp. H. Deschamps, 1945).

blood is drained into the soil, the connotations of blood and soil, spirit and soil, and life and soil become clear.

Rich with mythopoetic imagery, *The Damned of the Earth* is a book that speaks to the heart of the human quest for what is called our humanity. Called by the Black Panthers in the 1960s 'the handbook of the revolution', Fanon's book revolutionised and changed the lives of people from many walks of life. The chords he struck were many. Firstly, he was unapologetic about violence. The earlier arguments in *Black Skin, White Masks* and *Year V of the Algerian Revolution* were now more succinctly and forthrightly stated: imperialism and racism were ongoing practices of violence against people of colour. Since imperialists and colonialists saw themselves as having the 'right' to their empires and settlements, they then considered anything that threatened that relationship to be a violation of their rights. Thus colonised people must either accept their situation and be called nonviolent in doing so or attempt to change their situation and be called violent. Fanon's verdict? Decolonisation is a violent phenomenon, though that may not be the perspective of those manifesting their agency in such a struggle. To demand nonviolence results in maintaining colonialism – although that may not be the colonised's or even the colonisers' intent. This is not to say that Fanon rejected conventionally understood forms of violence, although he abhorred them. He argued that, since freedom must be fought for and because colonisers considered colonised people to be without a right to their freedom, to the point of even treating assertions of dignity as threats, then any assertion of their freedom would be considered violent. Thus the colonised must face violence as the underside of their pursuit of freedom.

Such a face-off poses ethical and political questions. Violence, after all, is by definition a special kind of harm, one that involves the degradation of human beings. In effect, the circumstance is premised on accepting one form of continued humiliation instead of imposing another on those who maintain the first. This places one set in the zone of nonbeing and another in a relation of being gods. As both limit the reach of human relations, Fanon in effect is arguing for those propped up as gods to be brought down to size, to a human level, which, unfortunately, is considered by the dominating group as beneath them. A controversial aspect of this observation is that it is not only structural but also psychological. Part of the damage colonialism imposes is a form of self-imprisonment in which many colonised subjects question their legitimacy and presume that of those who dominate them. The experience of realising that the latter are not gods has the cathartic effect of releasing the body from a soul that entraps it. The colonised subjects reach a point of not seeking legitimacy through or approval from those who colonise them. In other words, the assertion of their being violent, from the perspective of the colonising group, loses its currency. This shift releases the colonised subject from self-imposed chains and is thus cleansing or cathartic in the way Aristotle used the latter term to describe the effect of tragic drama in his *Poetics* (1449b21–28).[9]

Fanon was thus addressing the colonised, the being gripped by a system of colonial gods, *and* criticising discourses on revolutionary violence in processes of social change. To proponents of global revolutionary movements, the canonical figure against whom he was arguing came as something of a surprise – namely, Karl Marx's collaborator and benefactor Friedrich Engels, who, we should stress, supported armed struggle. Engels had portrayed the state as a violent institution (and hence intrinsically illegitimate) that is formed by violence. Thus the end of enslavement and alienation requires the elimination of the state (or states).[10] Fanon's critique is meta-theoretical, practical and existential. The meta-theoretical problem is whether an *a priori* works for dialectical argumentation. As Fanon proffers an open instead of a closed conception of dialectics, this

9 Literary drama is not accidental in Fanon's writings, as Keithley Philmore Woolward has shown in 'Towards a Performative Theory of Liberation: Theatre, Theatricality and "Play" in the Work of Frantz Fanon' (NYU dissertation in French, 2008). See also Alejandro J. De Oto's *Fanon: Política del sujeto poscolonial* (Mexico City: El Colegio de México, 2003), ch. 2; Clément Mbom, 'Frantz Fanon', in *Multicultural Writers since 1945: An A-to-Z Guide*, ed. Alba della Fazia Amoia and Bettina Liebowitz Knapp (Westport: Greenwood Press, 2004), pp. 211–215; Ato Sekyi-Otu, *Fanon's Dialectic of Experience* (Cambridge, MA: Harvard University Press, 1996), esp. pp. 4–5; Peter Worsley, 'Frantz Fanon and the "Lumpenproletariat"', *Socialist Register* 9 (1972), pp. 193–230. Finally, though not exhaustively, Joby Fanon's discussion of his brother's plays in *Frantz Fanon, My Brother* makes the case pretty clear.

10 Friedrich Engels, *The Origin of the Family, Private Property and the State*, ed. Tristram Hunt (New York: Penguin, 2010) and *Anti-Duhring: Herr Eugen Duhring's Revolution in Science* (New York: International Publishers, 1966), pt. 2, ch. 3. For Fanon's criticisms, see especially *Les damnés de la Terre* (Paris: François Maspero éditeur, 1961), pp. 95–98, 254.

means that the contingencies of the human world need to be taken into account, which leads to the existential point: human beings cannot build or live in foreclosed futures.

The colonial condition, as we have seen, is one of competing claims divided by a Manichean (Aristotelian) structure of contraries premised on apartheid or policed borders. The first or prior peoples see colonial regimes as rationalisations of organised theft of land and the resources it offers. The colonial settlers see themselves as simply going through legal transactions that give them the right to the land they own, and they often do so, as Carole Pateman has argued, through fictional appeals to *terra nullius* – that is, supposedly empty land.[11] The stage is thus set for a conflict of rights, as Hegel outlined in his discussion of *Antigone*; as in that classic play, both cannot win – someone must lose. Violence lurks in either direction: the colonial settlers' victory would be continued violence for the first or prior peoples; the latter's victory would be, to the colonial settlers, unjust or illegitimate achievements of force – that is, *violence*.[12] This is what Fanon means by saying that decolonisation is always a violent phenomenon: there is no outcome in which there isn't a side that suffers violence.

A critic may object that recognising both sides of the equation is fallacious. One side is actually right, and that conclusion depends on the *means* of social change, not the ends. Such an objection, Fanon would argue, focuses pretty much on the actions of the first or prior peoples and the criteria of assessment premised on what are suitable means from the point of view of the colonial settlers. What, however, would those means be other than those that don't challenge the legitimacy of the colonial settlers' presence and possessions? Recall that such a system does not see itself as unjust nor its rewards as

11 Carole Pateman, 'The Settler Contract', in Carole Pateman and Charles Mills, *Contract and Domination* (Cambridge: Polity, 2007), pp. 35–78.
12 I am using the expression 'first or prior peoples', as to do justice to the concepts of indigenous first people and prior people is beyond the scope of this chapter. For a detailed discussion, see (among other essays in the volume) Lewis R. Gordon, 'On the Temporality of Indigenous Identity', in *The Politics of Identity: Emerging Indigeneity*, ed. Michelle Harris, Martin Nakata and Bronwyn Carlson (Sydney: UTS ePress, 2013), pp. 60–78. For an excellent riff on Fanon's thought on these themes, see Glenn Sean Coulthard, *Red Skin, White Masks: Rejecting the Colonial Politics of Recognition* (Minneapolis: University of Minnesota Press, 2014).

unjustified, which means its overturn would be, from the perspective of its proponents, unjust, unwarranted – in a word, violent. This is the reason for Fanon's powerful, famous opening sentence: 'National liberation, national renaissance, returning the nation to the people, the Commonwealth – whatever the rubric or new formulas introduced, decolonization is always a violent phenomenon.'[13]

We should bear in mind that the first chapter, 'On Violence', rarely defends the claim that violence, in and of itself, is revolutionary. Fanon had no romantic views of violence. He was offering, almost clinically, a heavy dose of reality: decolonial violence is simply what is manifested in 'the replacement of one "species" of men by another "species" of men'.[14] Contraries, we should remember, are opposing sides of the same quantified scope: 'all' and 'none' pertain, as in Boolean logic, to entire domains of reference. The players are changed, but not necessarily the system. Only those who break this logic through the introduction of contradictions become what Fanon calls 'the truth'.

Take, for example, the concrete manifestation of the colonial state in relation to the colonised: the police. While the settlers regard the police as their protection, the colonised encounter them as their persecutors in a web of double standards bolstered by brutal force. The ensuing conflict means, then, that the status of outlaw falls upon all but the colonialists, and the treachery of state apparatuses comes to the fore through efforts to divide the illegals into those owned by the state and those not so owned. This observation has continued into recent times, as the terrorising behaviour of the Ferguson police in the area of St. Louis, Missouri, attests. Their practices are in fact part of norms as old as policing in the United States, despite attempts to treat them as anomalous. This means that taking seriously the lived reality of black and other colonised groups' relation to such avowed instruments of force requires thinking against the grain of ordinary models of legitimacy. Take, for example, the classic Marxist category of *Lumpenproletariat*. Marx and Engels, in *The Communist Manifesto*, regard the *Lumpenproletariat* as 'a dangerous class', immoral refuse to be avoided at all cost.[15] Fanon, however, argues for the necessity

13 Fanon, *Les damnés*, p. 65.
14 Fanon, *Les damnés*, p. 65.
15 See Karl Marx and Friedrich Engels, *Manifesto of the Communist Party*, in *The Marx-Engels Reader*, 2nd edn., ed. Robert C. Tucker (Princeton: Princeton University Press, 1978), p. 482.

of organising them into a cohesive, legitimate force in the struggle for national liberation. By focusing on their necessity, Fanon puts to the side the question of their moral character. He, in effect, renders that concern irrelevant. This critique brings us back to the self–other relation and the problem faced by those trapped in the zone of nonbeing. However ethical the colonial settlers and governors may present themselves to be, they must answer to the historical fact of Europe and its manifestations across the globe. Fanon lays their hypocrisy bare:

> Europe is literally the creation of the Third World. The riches that choke her are that which was stolen from underdeveloped peoples. The ports of Holland, the docks of Bordeaux and Liverpool specialized in the slave trade, and owe their renown from millions of deported slaves. So when we hear a European head of state declare, with hand on his heart, that he must help poor underdeveloped peoples, we do not tremble with gratitude. Rather, we say, 'It's just reparations owed to us.'[16]

Disavowing colonialism   Fanon takes us to the moment of avowed decolonisation. The way Europeans deal with each other, as in the case of what Germany was determined to owe as reparations following both the First World War and the Second World War, suggests this logic of debt unfortunately was suspended when it came to peoples of the global south, especially those in Africa. Accompanying this logic is the paradox of continuation in the face of disavowal. 'Colonies' became a bad mode of description. Colonialism became ashamed of itself, but its logic continued in mysterious ways, as Achille Mbembe later demonstrated with his concept of the 'postcolony'.[17] This idea is classically Fanonian. The 'post' in postcolony exemplifies the lost legitimacy of the colony, but colonies, as we all know, continue in other ways, and they often do so through those rallied to the cause of national liberation. For Fanon, this circumstance demanded theoretical resources beyond those offered by Marxism. It required mobilising rural populations such as the peasantry and those among

---

16 Fanon, *Les damnés*, 137.
17 Achille Mbembe, *On the Postcolony* (Berkeley: University of California Press, 2001).

the urban underclass. Peter Worsley, who attended some of Fanon's lectures in Ghana, agrees when he writes:

> It is high time that they [orthodox Marxists] stopped looking at the twentieth century through nineteenth-century eyes ... The new Third World cities cannot cope with the human flood, except where ruthless controls are operated to keep the inflow in line with the requirement for urban labour ... Every year, thousands of new recruits flock to the *favelas, barriadas, bidonvilles*, shanty-towns or whatever the local name is for the universal phenomenon of life in encampments made out of cardboard, flattened petrol-tins, and old packing-cases. Whatever term we use to describe this social category it is high time to abandon the highly insulting, inaccurate and analytically befogging Marxist term *Lumpenproletariat* which is so commonly used. 'Underclass' or 'subproletariat' would seem much more apt characterizations of these victims of 'urbanization without industrialization'.[18]

What orthodox Marxist critics miss is summarised in Fanon's famous dictum 'Each generation must, in relative opacity, discover its mission, fulfill it, or betray it.'[19] The historical facts suggest that the last in the series tends to hold. The generation that takes on the mission of decolonisation, while at first heroic, is not necessarily best suited for the next stage of national liberation. Here Fanon draws upon insights from E. Franklin Frazier's classic *Black Bourgeoisie* (1955), a work first published in French that was no doubt discussed at the Congress of Black Writer and Artists that Fanon attended at the Sorbonne in 1956 before heading to Tunisia as a full-time

---

18 Worsley, 'Fanon and "the Lumpenproletariat"', pp. 208–209. This surplus and cheapening of labour has led to the global return and increase of enslavement; see, e.g., Jane Anna Gordon, 'Degrees of Statelessness: Vulnerability and Political Capital', *Journal of Contemporary Thought* 32 (2010), pp. 17–39, and 'Theorizing Contemporary Practices of Slavery: A Portrait of the Old in the New', *Scrbd* (21 November 2013), www.scribd.com/doc/185968288/Theorizing-Contemporary-Practices-of-Slavery-Gordon; Joel Quirk and Darshan Vigneswaran (eds), *Slavery, Migration and Contemporary Bondage in Africa* (Trenton: Africa World Press, 2013).

19 Fanon, *Les damnés*, p. 253.

member of the FLN.[20] Frazier argued that, although there was a black middle class in the United States, it was one premised on the service economy and the mediating role of negotiating race relations. In other words, the 'capital' of the members of this class was purely political and cultural – forms of power to achieve symbolic things and limited ability to transform anything except their own individual wealth. Lacking material capital, they weren't able to build or transform the material conditions of black people in general and thus functioned more like the correlate of the so-called *Lumpenproletariat* to the working class – that is, as a form of '*Lumpenbourgeoisie*'. In similar kind, Fanon's verdict on the postcolonial bourgeoisie is biting: 'The national bourgeoisie discovers its historic mission: to serve as an intermediary.'[21] In this role, it holds the nation indebted to its moments of former glory.[22] The postcolonial leadership becomes parasitic.

A new dialectical struggle is formed between the postcolonial leadership and people, especially the younger generations, in the postcolony. The complicated question becomes what the younger generation should do as they, too, are at least affected by the process of decolonisation. Fanon's expertise as a psychiatrist comes to the fore here, as he raises some difficult questions with regard to the leadership and the population affected by the process of brutal transformation. Fanon here focuses on violence. I'm using the word violence here because Fanon is addressing the problem of ambivalent action, where the perpetrators aren't quite comfortable with their actions. The destabilisation of norms leads, as we have seen, to acts of brutality in an effort to equalise the value of life. Fanon, however, examines the traumatic guilt of an FLN soldier who killed a white French woman in an attempt to avenge the murder of his mother, and the seeming absence of remorse in two Arab boys who killed their close friend, a white French boy, in an environment with nearly no regard for the

---

20 E. Franklin Frazier, *Bourgeoisie noir* (Paris: Librairie Plon, 1955), available in English as *Black Bourgeoisie: The Book that Brought the Shock of Self-Revelation to Black America* (New York: Free Press, 1997).
21 Fanon, *Les damnés*, p. 193.
22 See also Amilcar Cabral, *Unity and Struggle: Speeches and Writings* (New York: Monthly Review Press, 1979); Olúf{eunderdotacute}mi Taíwó, 'Cabral', in *A Companion to the Philosophers*, ed. Robert L. Arrington (Malden: Blackwell, 1999), pp. 5–12.

value of Arab life. Why offer these case studies near the end of the book? These are hardly attractive portraits of colonised people.

These disturbing case studies support Fanon's not offering a romantic portrait of colonialism and the struggle against it. Colonialism, as we have seen, is a system of ongoing violence. As such, it produces monstrosity, and, even worse, its overcoming could also be monstrous. Consider the word 'monster'. It is derived from the Latin *monstrum*, which when placed in the infinitive is *monere*, which originally meant 'to show' (notice its presence in the word 'demonstrate'). In our book *Of Divine Warning: Reading Disaster in the Modern Age*, Jane Anna Gordon and I show that monsters are symptoms of greater forces at work.[23] They show us disasters and thereby often serve as signs of them. The word 'disaster', after all, is another way of saying 'fallen star' (from *dis astro*), and, as we all know, to fall from the heavens is not a good thing. Monsters' emergence, then, informs us of what must be addressed. They alert us to additional stages of transformation to come. Fanon argues that the system of values must also be changed, because, with its power relations of violence, it produces people whose relations are premised on such, on the contradiction of attempting non-relations (death, after all, involves being taken out of relations); his purpose in offering this grotesque portrait is to challenge the presuppositions of complete sciences of revolution.

The north–south model of economic and political development regards people of the global south – and, indeed, all people of colour – as in effect 'minor terms'. The violence of pushing some peoples into zones of nonbeing is not only material but also theoretical. The comparison here would be to make the conditions that such people face – brutality, degradation, racism – insignificant except when considered in relation to supposedly universal categories, such as class, or in relation to specific nation-states and their leaders. It is not insignificant that the subjects about whom Fanon wrote in those case studies were not national leaders or anonymous exemplars of economic relations. He is in actual fact offering a critique of revolutions that fail to address the suffering of ordinary people and the extent to which they inherit the traumas of social change, and, for better or worse, are

---

23 For more on this point, see Jane Anna Gordon and Lewis R. Gordon, *Of Divine Warning: Reading Disaster in the Modern Age* (Boulder: Paradigm, 2009), chs 2 and 4.

entrusted to be the agents of the future. Revolutions, he is reminding us, are not ushered in by perfect people. It is not only that each generation must find its mission but also that each stands on the very flawed shoulders of those who go first and stand as the troubled ones on which others must stand. Fanon thus brings an additional issue to the fore: change in and of itself is not necessarily revolutionary.

Fanon was analysing the historical circumstances of the largest group in the colonies under formalised post-slavery – specifically, peasants in countries governed by urban centres with large unemployment and thus many people relying on illicit economies for their survival. As the ruling elites are primarily mediators between the postcolony and former colonial centres, their role is moribund: in Fanon's words, they are useless.[24] How, then, do such governors make themselves legitimate? The earlier discussion of power suggests at least two possibilities: firstly, demonstrate their necessity to their constituents and secondly, if that fails, *force* allegiance despite rejection. The second should be called what it is: violence. The first, however, could be understood through exploring the affinities Fanon's thought had with that of the Italian Marxist activist intellectual Antonio Gramsci, particularly the latter's concept of hegemony. According to Gramsci, hegemony can be

'spontaneous' consent given by the great masses of the
population to the general direction imposed on social life by the
dominant fundamental group; this consent is 'historically' caused
by the prestige (and consequent confidence) which the dominant
group enjoys because of its position and function in the world of
production [and] ... state coercive power which 'legally' enforces
discipline on those groups who do not 'consent' either actively or
passively. This apparatus is, however, constituted for the whole
of society in anticipation of moments of crisis of command and
direction when spontaneous consent has failed.[25]

---

24 Fanon, *Les damnés*, p. 217.
25 Antonio Gramsci, *Selection from the Prison Notebooks*, ed. and trans. Quintin Hoare and Geoffrey Nowell Smith (New York: International Publishers, 1971), p. 12. For more discussion, see Jane Anna Gordon, *Creolizing Political Theory* (New York: Fordham University Press, 2014), pp. 136–137; Sekyi-Otu, *Fanon's Dialectic of Experience*, pp. 85–86.

Hegemony need not be in sync with the interests of a group. This concern comes to the fore in Gramsci's discussion of what he calls 'organic intellectuals', a concept that could easily be extended to leadership. What are the ultimate interests served by dominant groups or those to whom legitimacy is ascribed? There is here a collapse between identity and interests; thus, though the leadership may be members of a group, their ideas, policies and commitments may be organically linked to an opposing group or, radically extended, time.[26] Fanon's challenge to classical Marxism takes such observations into consideration: the national bourgeoisie and even the small proletariat in postcolonies of the global south may be organically linked to their former governors and, as ultimately counter-revolutionary, to the moment of decolonisation but not to the future. Other groups – such as the peasantry, the large, unemployed underclass and members of the illicit economies – may be more in tune with where the society is going, and intellectual work should take seriously the problems organically linked to their condition.

Failure to provide services demands rationalisations of mundane disorder. Xenophobia, ethnocentrism, racism and, as we could now add, homophobia become rallying efforts of purification to stave off the critical question of state interests. In effect, a 'cividicy' (a form of secularised theodicy of society) of the state and its leadership emerges, where the contradictions of the postcolony are blamed on those living within but are external to the society. If, however, the errors of cividicy are pointed out and result in a delivering state, one that is expected to be the exemplification of power in the interests of the people, a circumstance could emerge in which the distance from the leadership is such that its ability to maintain order becomes the coercive sovereign of *Leviathan*: one premised exclusively on fear and force.

Fanon, then, ultimately shows how necessary violence leads to new conditions of violence where power is in effect hoarded and retracted from sources of legitimacy beyond the machinations of hegemony. The dialectical movement here is to a new struggle, one against

---

26 Gramsci, *Selections from the Prison Notebooks*, pp. 5–15. For discussion of affinities between Fanon and Gramsci, see, e.g., Sekyi-Otu, *Fanon's Dialectic of Experience*, pp. 148–149; Hourya Bentouhami, 'De Gramsci à Fanon, un marxisme décentré', *Actuel Marx* 55 (2014), pp. 99–118.

those who stand in the way of subsequent generations organically linked to the problems of their time. As this is an appeal for the radical distribution of power as sovereign, of radical democracy, the Rousseauian question of the general will returns, but, as Jane Anna Gordon has shown, with innovation: instead of general will, Fanon raises the question of national consciousness.[27]

Nationalism, given the argument about hegemony above, carries the danger of hegemonic control over those not organically linked to the interests of the people. The question of the people's interest, however, is not an easy matter to articulate. For Fanon, the distinction between nationalism and nation is that the latter for Fanon is an open question while the former is premised on the presumption of a complete or closed nation. Legitimacy in the case of national culture doesn't emerge from proof of cultural heritage or racial authenticity but from actively building institutions and ideas that nurture and emancipate subsequent generations.[28]

Confronting violence in the world

Fanon's penultimate chapter brings forth the importance of philosophical anthropology for an understanding of how colonialism has a symbiotic relationship to violence. The colonial condition, he argues, forces colonised people to question their humanity. He explains this through making a distinction between domination and oppression. 'Under the German occupation', he writes, 'the French remained men; under the French occupation, the Germans remained men'.[29] Colonised peoples, however, suffer racial degradation and thus don't live in the world as human beings. He explains:

> Because it is a systematic negation of the other, a determined decision to refuse to the other all the attributes of humanity, colonialism forces the people it dominates to ask themselves constantly the question: 'In reality, who am I?'

Consider that this question is posed from the zone of nonbeing, which, we should remember, lurks beneath the self–other relation.

---

27 Gordon, *Creolizing Political Theory*.
28 Fanon, *Les damnés*, pp. 269, 282.
29 Fanon, *Les damnés*, p. 300.

The 'who' in the question is instantly transformed to 'what', creating the reformulation '*What* am I?' Add Pateman's discussion of *terra nullius* and the skewed logic of conquering peopleless land comes to the fore: the hell of suffering through the theft of land via the continued assertion of one's absence. To be present as flesh devoid of humanity is what Fanon appropriately calls 'zombification'.

My use of the metaphor of hell isn't accidental. Hell is the lived reality of an all-consuming environment of dehumanisation. As my earlier discussion pointed to damnation, it's appropriate here to explore what is perhaps the most enduring mythopoetic representation of the subject: Dante's *Inferno*. The poem is a long tale of a journey through layers of divine punishments, from being stuck in limbo to being at the centre of the greatest distance from holiness. At the cold, hateful centre of hell itself rests Satan consuming the worst of the lot, and this theme of consumption has its parallel in two close-by foes frozen from the neck down. One of them is so consumed by hatred that he stretches over and gnaws on the head of his enemy. Seeing the repulsive implications of being consumed by hatred, the protagonist lets go of his, and Virgil leads him out to where, under the dawn's sky, he is able 'to see – once more – the stars'.[30] Fanon, too, offers a portrait of the horrific implications of being consumed by hatred. His concluding message of *The Damned of the Earth* hardly makes the text an unqualified endorsement of violence. Its ending could be read in philosophical–anthropological terms as a paraphrase of Dante's concluding verse: 'For Europe, for ourselves, and for humanity', Fanon concludes, 'let us make a new start, develop a new thought, and try to establish a new man'.[31]

Many didn't read or see, or were not even willing to listen to, these many dimensions of Fanon's reflections on violence. Yet these observations and analyses continued beyond Fanon's time. Even a cursory look at history since 1961 reveals, in every equation, what is both poignantly and desperately asserted in early twenty-first-century efforts to declare that 'black lives matter'. Much of this would be to Fanon's chagrin. He was, after all, a paradoxical thinker. He thought so clearly, so presciently, in the hope that he was, in the end, wrong.

30 Dante Alighieri, *The Divine Comedy of Dante Alighieri*, vol. 1, *Inferno*, trans. Allen Mandelbaum (New York: Bantam Books, 1980), canto 33, l. 139.
31 Fanon, *Les damnés*, p. 376.

Further reading

Césaire, Aimé, *Frantz Fanon: Par les textes de l'époque* (Paris: Les Petit Matins, 2012).

Cherki, Alice, *Frantz Fanon: A Portrait* (Ithaca: Cornell University Press, 2006).

Fanon, Frantz, *Black Skins/White Masks* (New York: Grove Press, 2005).

Fanon, Frantz, *A Dying Colonialism* (New York: Monthly Review Press, 1965).

Fanon, Frantz, *Towards The African Revolution* (New York: Monthly Review Press, 1967).

Fanon, Frantz, *The Wretched of the Earth* (London: Penguin, 1967).

Fanon, Joby, *Frantz Fanon, My Brother: Doctor, Playwright, Revolutionary* (Lanham: Lexington Books, 2014).

Gordon, Lewis R., *What Fanon Said: A Philosophical Introduction to His Life and Thought* (New York: Fordham University Press, 2015).

Mbembe, Achille, *On the Postcolony* (Berkeley: University of California Press, 2001).

Sekyi-Otu, Ato, *Fanon's Dialectic of Experience* (Cambridge, MA: Harvard University Press, 1996).

5 | MICHEL FOUCAULT

Brad Evans

Biographical details

Michel Foucault (1926–1984) was born in Poitiers, France. His father, an eminent surgeon, hoped his son would follow him into the same profession, something that perhaps influenced his later bio-political enquires. Graduating from the Lycée Henri-IV, in Paris, Foucault had to his credit an impressive academic record and then gained entrance to the most prestigious French higher-education institution for humanities studies, the École normale supérieure. Here he gained a BA-equivalent degree in psychology in 1947 and a second one in philosophy in 1950. Passing the *agrégation* on his second attempt in 1951, he began work in a psychiatric hospital during the early part of the 1950s. From 1954 to 1958 he moved to Sweden to teach at the University of Uppsala. Following this he spent consecutive years teaching at the University of Warsaw and the University of Hamburg. In 1959 Foucault received his doctorate under the supervision of the famous French philosopher Georges Canguilhem.

In the 1960s Foucault was head of the philosophy department at the University of Clermont-Ferrand. During this time he met Daniel Defert, a philosophy student whose political activism made a profound influence on him, and the two entered into a relationship that lasted for the rest of Foucault's life. When Defert went to Tunisia, for instance, Foucault followed, teaching there from 1966 to 1968. They both returned to Paris when Foucault became the head of the philosophy department at the University of Paris-VII at Vincennes. Foucault tragically died in Paris in 1984 from an AIDS-related illness.

Foucault was a widely recognised and celebrated public intellectual during his lifetime. He was nevertheless troubled by his canonisation as a theorist. Such concerns cannot be divorced from his critical methods and his desire to emancipate thought itself from the entrapments of oppressive systems of rule. We find a remarkable example of this in an interview he gave for the French newspaper *Le Monde* under conditions of anonymity. The reasons for concealing his identity were straightforward. Foucault believed that when anybody encountered his work it would no longer be judged on its content alone. That is to say, the reader would already engage the writing with some pre-inscribed ideas of the author based on past works and previous arguments. Foucault was guarding against the fact that his work would not be taken on its own terms and would instead be situated within a wider and altogether more encapsulating frame. This frame would be akin to offering an authentic and predetermined 'Foucauldian perspective' – a theoretical mode of capture and foundationalism that was the complete antithesis to his entire critical endeavours. Anonymity thus provided a tactical solution to the formation of a 'universal Foucault', thereby allowing his work to speak on its own terms:

> I can't help but dream about a kind of criticism that would
> try not to judge but to bring an *œuvre*, a book, a sentence, an
> idea to life; it would light fires, watch the grass grow, listen
> to the wind, and catch the sea foam in the breeze and scatter
> it. It would multiply not judgments but signs of existence; it
> would summon them, drag them from their sleep. Perhaps it
> would invent them sometimes – all the better. All the better.
> Criticism that hands down sentences sends me to sleep; I'd like
> a criticism of scintillating leaps of the imagination. It would not
> be sovereign or dressed in red. It would bear the lightning of
> possible storms.[1]

This method clearly had its advantages. Firstly, it ensured that the critical cartographer (Foucault) was outliving the compulsion to commodify any personal identity, which ordinarily subordinated identity to the regulatory dictates of authenticating markets. It was, as Foucault explained, 'out of nostalgia for a time when, being quite unknown, what I said had some chance of being heard'.

---

1 Michel Foucault, 'The Masked Philosopher', in *Ethics, Subjectivity & Truth: The Essential Works of Michel Foucault 1954–1984*, ed. Paul Rabinow (New York: New Press, 1987), p. 323.

Anonymity was a 'way of addressing the potential reader' without them 'knowing who I am'. Secondly, beyond this, it enabled him, for a time at least, to carry out that most difficult of tasks, outliving the intellectual violence of one's own wilful capture. The problem Foucault acknowledged was that we encounter a sort of 'pseudopoliticisation that masks, beneath the need to wage an "ideological struggle" or to root out "dangerous thoughts", a deep seated anxiety that one will not be heard or read'. Anonymity thus enables the writer to 'dream of a new age of curiosity' that 'allows the individual to change at will'. More than experimenting with the possibility of critiquing some secure foundation of truth, what is being presented here is a new *ethical* disposition whose activity or movement could be forever orientated towards the possibility of genuine political change: 'The displacement and transformation of frameworks of thinking, and changing of received values and all the work that has been done to think otherwise, to do something else, to become other than what one is.' The 'very life of philosophy' is 'not a way of reflecting' but 'a way of interrogating ourselves'[2] akin to what a more recently published series of lectures would aptly term 'The Courage to Truth'.[3]

In terms of his major publications, Foucault's earlier works, such as *The Order of Things* (1966) and *Archeology of Knowledge* (1969), established his reputation as a leading critical thinker, notably in terms of the histories of systems of thought. However, it was the publication of *Discipline and Punish: The Birth of the Prison* (1975) that staked out his importance as a theorist on the questions of power and violence. In this text, Foucault explicitly rejected the enlightenment notion of juridical power and in doing so paved the way for a fundamental rethinking of the hidden order of politics. Indeed, if the disciplinary model would become central to Foucault's critique of the normalisation of power and hence its altogether more problematic abuses (especially its militarisation) in modern societies, it would be with the publication of volume one of *The History of Sexuality* (1976) that the foundational tenets of modern sovereignty would be transformed. In a remarkable chapter entitled 'The Right to

2 Foucault, 'Masked Philosopher'.
3 Michel Foucault, *The Courage to Truth: Lectures at the Collège de France 1983–1984* (New York: Palgrave Macmillan, 2011).

Death and Power Over Life', Foucault outlines the change from the sovereign right to 'make live and let die' to the modernist compulsion for 'letting live and making die'. It is also with this text that we are purposefully introduced to Foucault's concept of bio-politics, which will be the main theoretical focus of this chapter.

Theorising violence

While already having considerable influence across the social sciences and humanities in terms of thinking about the body, subjectivity and the power of language and discourse, the relevance of Foucault's work to the question of violence has undergone a notable revival more recently. Much of this is due to the influential works of Michael Hardt and Antonio Negri[4] and of Giorgio Agamben,[5] whose application of Foucauldian thought to the areas of security, global war and violence has highlighted his relevance to some of our most pressing political concerns. This has been matched by the translated publications of the series of lectures Foucault gave at the Collège de France from the mid to the late 1970s.[6] Illuminating his thinking on 'bio-power' and 'bio-politics', these texts have contributed to the numerous writings that have taken critical aim at what is now commonly termed the 'liberal way of war'. Invariably what has been taking place here is a necessary rewriting of Foucault's legacy. Not only have these works moved us beyond the normative 'question of truth' (which, to be frank, served the dialectical entrapments of Frankfurt theorists such as Jürgen Habermas more than it ever did Foucault) but they have also posed new questions concerning the nature of power in our modern societies. Foucault's resurrected spectre, however, has come with its challenges. As Foucault would explain, when one begins to pose the problem of power bio-politically, an entirely different

4 Michael Hardt and Antonio Negri, *Empire* (Cambridge, MA: Harvard University Press, 2000); Michael Hardt and Antonio Negri, *Multitude: War and Democracy in the Age of Empire* (London: Hamish Hamilton, 2004).

5 Giorgio Agamben, *Homo Sacer: Sovereign Power and Bare Life* (Stanford: Stanford University Press, 1995); Giorgio Agamben, *State of Exception*, trans. Kevin Attell (Chicago: University of Chicago Press, 2005).

6 Michel Foucault, *Society Must Be Defended: Lectures at the Collège de France 1975–1976* (New York: Picador, 2003); *Security, Territory and Population: Lectures at the Collège de France 1977–1978* (New York: Palgrave Macmillan, 2007); *The Birth of Bio-politics: Lectures at the Collège de France 1978–1979* (New York: Palgrave Macmillan, 2008).

'grid of intelligibility' is required that no longer provides us with the comfort of a rehearsed orthodoxy:

> Instead of deducing concrete phenomena from universals, or instead of starting with universals as an obligatory grid of intelligibility for certain concrete practices, I would like to start with these concrete practices and, as it were, pass these universals through the grid of these practices ... Historicism starts from the universal and, as it were, puts it through the grinder of history. My problem is exactly the opposite. I start from the theoretical and methodological decision that consists in saying: Let's suppose universals do not exist. And then I put the question to history and historians: How can you write history if you do not accept a priori the existence of things like the state, society, the sovereign, and subjects? ... Not, then, questioning universals by using history as a critical method, but starting from the decision then that universals do not exist, asking what kind of history we can do.[7]

Enthusiasm for Foucault's revival has been expectedly muted in certain quarters. Even some Foucauldian scholars – albeit of a distinctly liberal persuasion – have expressed their concern about the applicability of his lecture series to contemporary political analysis.[8] Leaving aside the claim that this body of work somehow represents Foucault's 'wasted years' – or, for that matter, that the concepts explored during this period were not really Foucauldian at heart (especially bio-politics) – the most serious charge concerns the lack of sufficient academic rigour in the lecture series. Beatrice Hanssen,[9] for instance, has correctly pointed out that, despite the attention given to race war during this time, the history of colonisation is scantily considered. It is also the case that, when Foucault did apply his bio-political method to colonialism, he only attended to

7 Foucault, *Birth of Bio-politics*, p. 3.
8 See in particular Paul Patton, Giorgio Agamben and Michel Foucault, 'Biopower and Biopolitics', in *Giorgio Agamben: Sovereignty and Life*, ed. Matthew Calarco and Steven DeCaroli (Stanford: Stanford University Press, 2007), pp. 203–218.
9 Beatrice Hanssen, *Critique of Violence: Between Post-structuralism and Critical Theory* (London: Routledge, 2000).

the colonial heartland, not the overseas dominions and borderlands, which have attracted a great deal of the contemporary focus. It is fair to say that Foucault's efforts leave us wanting more empirical and analytic depth. That is not, however, to deny their usefulness. As John Marks argues,

> the lectures are an expression of Foucault's attempt to analyse power in terms of its operation, functions, and effects, rather than in terms of sovereignty and juridical models. They are a continuation of his project to look at power from the perspective of its functions and strategies, as it operates 'under the radar' as it were, of the juridical system of sovereignty.[10]

Bio-political theorists, however, have proved to be far from a unified church. Hardt and Negri, for instance, have argued that contemporary bio-politics needed to be matched up with Gilles Deleuze's notion of 'control societies' in order to account for the new postindustrial cartography of productive relations. Then, taking this to be their point of theoretical departure, they invoked the notion of bio-political production (arguably another way of saying 'labour') to afford the concept the potential for liberation. The term bio-politics is therefore said to reveal both exploitative and resistive qualities, enabling us, diagrammatically speaking, to map out the entire social morphology of power relations in our modern systems. Truer to his academic style, on the other hand, Agamben has offered a more protracted genealogy in order to reveal how bio-politics is fully implicit in the production of those subjects that, open to the technologies of pure rule, are stripped of their political and moral values. Such desubjectivised souls connect and rework Carl Schmitt's 'state of exception' to refer us to 'bare life': 'the fundamental categorical pair of Western politics is not that of friend/enemy but that of bare life/ political existence, zoē/bios, exclusion/inclusion'.[11]

While these works have enjoyed notable academic success over the past few years, they have nevertheless tended to muddy the waters when

10 John Marks, 'Michel Foucault: Bio-politics and Biology', in *Foucault in an Age of Terror*, ed. Stephen Morton and Stephen Bygrave (London: Palgrave, 2008), p. 88.
11 Agamben, *Homo Sacer*, p. 8.

it comes to defining the bio-political. A return to Foucault's original provocation seems to be warranted. For Foucault, the bio-political specifically referred to the political strategisation/technologisation of life for its own productive betterment. Effectuating the active triangulation between 'security, territory and population', bio-politics forces a reprioritisation of those concerns ordinarily associated with human development and progress in a manner that complements traditional security paradigms. Importantly, for Foucault, since the bio-political takes issue with the open recruitment of life into political strategies for the internal defence of societies as a whole – doing what is necessary out of life necessity – the concept is best broached by raising the following critical question: what happens at the level of power and violence when life itself becomes the principal object for political strategies?

In terms of our concerns, as Foucault maintained, when dealing with the political problem of life we are also dealing with life as a political category. That is to say, the 'invention of life' as a political problem corresponds to the invention of race and the ability to quantify and to hierachicise the human species. Bio-politics in short gives rise to the very notion of race war. As Foucault points out, since the principal task set for bio-political practitioners is to sort out and adjudicate between the species, modern societies reveal a distinct bio-political *aporia* (an irresolvable political dilemma) in the sense that the positive promotion of lives ('making life live'), by selecting those ways of life that are fittest by design, inevitably writes into that very script those lives that are retarded, backward, degenerate, wasteful and ultimately dangerous to the social order. Racism thus appears here to be a thoroughly modern phenomenon. Or, to put it another way, since life becomes the author of its own (un)making, the bio-political assay of life necessarily portrays a commitment to the supremacy of certain species types: 'a race that is portrayed as the one true race, the race that holds power and is entitled to define the norm, and against those who deviate from that norm, against those who pose a threat to the biological heritage'.[12] As Foucault insistently argued, what is at stake here is no mere sovereign or juridical affair. An epiphenomenal tension aside, the question of race occupies

12 Foucault, *Society Must Be Defended*, p. 61.

a 'permanent presence' within the political order.[13] Bio-politically speaking, then, since it is precisely through the internalisation of threat – the constitution of the threat that is now from the dangerous 'others' that exist within – that societies reproduce at the level of life the ontological commitment to secure the subject, since everybody is now possibly dangerous and nobody can be exempt, for political modernity to function one always has to be capable of killing in order to go on living:

> Wars are no longer waged in the name of a sovereign who must be defended; they are waged on behalf of the existence of everyone; entire populations are mobilized for the purpose of wholesale slaughter in the name of life necessity; massacres have become vital ... The principle underlying the tactics of battle – that one has to become capable of killing in order to go on living – has become the principle that defines the strategy of states.[14]

When Foucault refers to 'killing', he is not simply referring to the vicious act of taking another life:

> When I say 'killing', I obviously do not mean simply murder as such, but also every form of indirect murder: the fact of exposing someone to death, increasing the risk of death for some people, or, quite simply, political death, expulsion, rejection and so on.[15]

Racism makes this process of elimination possible, for it is only through the discourse and practice of racial (dis)qualification that one is capable of introducing 'a break in the domain of life that is under power's control: the break between what must live and what must die'.[16] Having said this, while killing does not need to be physically murderous, we should not lose sight of the very real forms of political violence that *do* take place in the name of human progress. As Deleuze duly noted, when notions of security are invoked in order to preserve the destiny of a species, when the defence of society gives

13 Foucault, *Society Must Be Defended*, p. 62.
14 Michel Foucault, *History of Sexuality*, vol. 1, *An Introduction* (London: Penguin, 1990), p. 137.
15 Foucault, *Society Must Be Defended*, p. 256.
16 Foucault, *Society Must Be Defended*, p. 256.

sanction to very real acts of violence that are justified in terms of species necessity – that is, when the capacity to legitimate murderous political actions in all our names and for all our sakes becomes altogether more rational, calculated, utilitarian, hence altogether more frightening, and

> when a diagram of power abandons the model of sovereignty in favour of a disciplinary model, when it becomes the 'bio-power' or 'bio-politics' of populations, controlling and administering life, it is indeed life that emerges as the new object of power. At that point law increasingly renounces that symbol of sovereign privilege, the right to put someone to death, but allows itself to produce all the more hecatombs and genocides: not by returning to the old law of killing, but on the contrary in the name of race, precious space, conditions of life and the survival of a population that believes itself to be better than its enemy, which it now treats not as the juridical enemy of the old sovereign but as a toxic or infectious agent, a sort of 'biological danger'.[17]

Auschwitz for many remains the most grotesque, shameful and hence meaningful bio-political example of 'necessary killing' – the violence that is sanctioned in the name of life necessity. Indeed, for Agamben, since one of the most 'essential characteristics' of modern bio-politics is to constantly 'redefine the threshold in life that distinguishes and separates what is inside from what is outside', it is within those sites that 'eliminate radically the people that are excluded' that the bio-political racial imperative is exposed in its most brutal form.[18] The camp can therefore be seen to be the 'defining paradigm of the modern' insomuch as it is a 'space in which power confronts nothing other than pure biological life without any mediation'.[19] While lacking Agamben's intellectual sophistry, such Schmittean-inspired approaches to violence – that is, sovereignty as the ability to declare a state of juridical exception – gained widespread academic currency in the aftermath of 9/11. The field of international relations, for instance, was awash with works that tried to theorise the 'exceptional times'

17 Gilles Deleuze, *Foucault* (London: Continuum, 1999), p. 76.
18 Agamben, *Homo Sacer*, p. 171.
19 Agamben, *Homo Sacer*, p. 179.

in which we live. While some of the tactics deployed in the 'global war on terror' undoubtedly lent credibility to these approaches, in terms of understanding violence they have subsequently proved to be of limited use. Violence was only rendered problematic here when it was associated with acts of unmitigated geopolitical excess (e.g., the invasion of Iraq, Guantánamo Bay, use of torture and so forth). This proved unfortunate as the war effort was reduced to outdated twentieth-century geo-strategic frames of analysis. Precluding, then, any critical evaluation of the contemporary forms of violence that take place *within* the remit of humanitarian discourses and practices, there was limited engagement with those forms of violence that continue to define the liberal encounter. Indeed, as we moved into post-interventionary phases of engagement in zones of crises and instability, the politics of exceptionalism had little to say about both the governance of populations in post-conflict environments that were still experiencing low-intensity violence and about the micro-physics of war in the homelands, especially concerning the violence of veterans for whom the neat demarcations between times of war and peace held no meaningful distinction.

One lesson, however, is clear: racism is not what it used to be. As a number of critical theorists understood some time ago, cultural fitness has now replaced biological heritage to contour the new lines of political struggle.[20] This shift from notions of biological supremacy to cultural difference has not been incidental. While liberals would agree that the former is abhorrent, they nevertheless govern through the latter.[21] There is an important history to this. Initially, for the post-war liberal fraternity, claiming that Nazism was some aberration or failure of modernity proved to be essential to this process.[22] With modernity's bio-political capacities for species manipulation therefore left firmly intact, alternative judgements on the human species could be made. Importantly, as Étienne Balibar has pointed out, in the light of the fact that the history of modern thought has always shown some affinity with cultural prejudice (albeit because they have been

20 On this see in particular Étienne Balibar, 'Is there a Neo-racism?', in Étienne Balibar and Immanuel Wallerstein, *Race, Nation, Class: Ambiguous Identities* (London: Verso, 1991), pp. 17–28.
21 Mark Duffield, *Development, Security and Unending War: Governing the World of Peoples* (Cambridge: Polity, 2007).
22 Zygmunt Bauman, *Modernity and the Holocaust* (Cambridge: Polity, 1991).

inexorably intertwined), what concerns us today has already existed beneath the surface for some considerable time:

> We now move from the theory of the races or the struggle between the races in human history, whether based on biology or psychological principles, to a theory of 'race relations' within society, which *naturalizes not racial belonging but racial conduct*.[23]

It should be stressed here that, while these concerns with the conduct of 'others' have been used for decades by right-wing governments to warn of the dangers of global migration flows, liberals more generally have also upheld the overriding concern that radically different ways of life are a principal source of society's ills. Marked divisions based on cultural difference have therefore ensured that a culturally coded racism striates the world of peoples, separating good from bad, useful from useless in terms of their contribution to international security. Based on the political interpretation of the genuine fears of ordinary people, this racism, as Mark Duffield has observed, 'decides the sovereign boundary between the included and excluded, between those exempted from the zone of exception and those destined to disappear within it'.[24]

The liberal war thesis   Imposing liberalism has often come at a price. That price has tended to be a continuous recourse to war. While the militarism associated with liberal internationalisation has already received scholarly attention,[25] Foucault was concerned more with the continuation of war once peace has been declared. Denouncing the illusion that 'we are living in a world in which order and peace have been restored',[26] he set out to disrupt the neat distinction between times of war, or military exceptionalism, and times of peace, or civic normality. War quite simply conditions the type of peace that follows. Nobody has been more ambitious in mapping out this war–peace continuum than Michael Dillon and Julian Reid.[27]

23 Balibar, 'Is there a Neo-racism?', p. 22.
24 Duffield, *Development, Security and Unending War*, p. 277.
25 Michael Howard, *War and the Liberal Conscience* (New York: Columbia University Press, 2008).
26 Foucault, *Society Must Be Defended*, p. 53.
27 Michael Dillon and Julian Reid, *The Liberal Way of War: Killing to Make Life Live* (London: Routledge, 2009).

Their Foucault-inspired 'liberal war thesis' provides a provocative insight into the bio-politically driven lethality of making life live. With the very idea of 'liberal peace' predicated on the pacification or elimination of all forms of political difference in order that liberalism might meet its own globally ambitious political objectives, the more peace is commanded, the more war is declared in order to achieve it: 'In proclaiming peace ... liberals are nonetheless committed also to making war.' This is the 'martial face of liberal power' that, contrary to the familiar narrative, is 'directly fuelled by the universal and pacific ambitions for which liberalism is to be admired'.[28] Liberalism thus stands accused here of universalising war in its pursuit of peace:

> However much liberalism abjures war, indeed finds the instrumental use of war, especially, a scandal, war has always been as instrumental to liberal as to geopolitical thinkers. In that very attempt to instrumentalize, indeed universalize, war in the pursuit of its own global project of emancipation, the practice of liberal rule itself becomes profoundly shaped by war. However much it may proclaim liberal peace and freedom, its own allied commitment to war subverts the very peace and freedoms it proclaims.[29]

This invariably poses a direct challenge to the more conventional and well-rehearsed 'liberal peace thesis' as advanced by Michael Doyle, among others. Indeed, it offers a purposeful and rigorous counter to Steven Pinker's much lauded *Better Angels of Our Nature*.[30] Reworking the self-serving claim that liberalism and peace march hand in hand, for Pinker the reason we have become less war-like today can be account for in terms of our liberal maturity. Interrogated, however, through a Foucauldian lens, we might argue that not only does Pinker's book offer a fundamental misreading of the historical relationships between liberalism and violence but it also pays no service whatsoever to the logic of bio-politics. John Gray is rightly suspicious:

28 Dillon and Reid, *The Liberal Way of War*, p. 2.
29 Dillon and Reid, *The Liberal Way of War*, p. 2.
30 Steven Pinker, *The Better Angels of Our Nature: Why Violence Has Declined* (London: Viking, 2011).

The idea that a new world can be constructed through the rational application of force is peculiarly modern, animating ideas of revolutionary war and pedagogic terror that feature in an influential tradition of radical Enlightenment thinking. Downplaying this tradition is extremely important for Pinker. Along with liberal humanists everywhere, he regards the core of the Enlightenment as a commitment to rationality. The fact that prominent Enlightenment figures have favoured violence as an instrument of social transformation is – to put it mildly – inconvenient ... No doubt we have become less violent in some ways. But it is easy for liberal humanists to pass over the respects in which civilisation has retreated. Pinker is no exception. Just as he writes off mass killing in developing countries as evidence of backwardness without enquiring whether it might be linked in some way to peace in the developed world, he celebrates 're-civilisation' ... without much concern for those who pay the price of the re-civilising process.[31]

While Dillon and Reid's thesis makes only veiled reference to the onto-theological dimension (something all too evident in the title of Pinker's volume), they are fully aware that bio-political rule depends upon a certain religiosity in the sense that war has now been turned into a veritable human crusade with only two possible outcomes: 'endless war or the transformation of other societies and cultures into liberal societies and cultures'.[32] Endless war is underwritten here by a new set of problems. Unlike Clausewitzian confrontations, which at least provided the strategic comforts of clear demarcations (them/us, war/peace, citizen/soldier and so on), these wars no longer benefit from the possibility of scoring outright victory, retreating or achieving a lasting negotiated peace by means of political compromise. Indeed, deprived of the prospect of defining enmity in advance, war itself becomes just as complex, dynamic, adaptive and radically interconnected as the world of which it is part. That is why 'any such war to end war becomes a war without end ... The project of removing war from the life of the species becomes a lethal and,

31 John Gray, 'Delusions of Peace', *Prospect* (21 September 2011), www.prospectmagazine.co.uk/magazine/john-gray-steven-pinker-violence-review.
32 Dillon and Reid, *The Liberal Way of War*, p. 5.

in principle, continuous and unending process'.[33] Duffield, building on these concerns, takes this unending scenario a stage further to suggest that, since wars for humanity are inextricably bound to the global life-chance divide, it is now possible to write of a 'global civil war' into which all life is openly recruited:

> Each crisis of global circulation ... marks out a terrain of global civil war, or rather a tableau of wars, which is fought on and between the modalities of life itself ... What is at stake in this war is the West's ability to contain and manage international poverty while maintaining the ability of mass society to live and consume beyond its means.[34]

War by other means   Liberals have continuously made reference to humanity in order to justify their use of military force.[35] War, if there is to be one, must be for the unification of the species. This humanitarian caveat is by no means out of favour. Most recently it underwrites the strategic rethink in contemporary zones of occupation, which has become bio-political ('hearts and minds') in everything but name.[36] While criticisms of these strategies have tended to focus on the naive dangers associated with liberal idealism,[37] insufficient attention has been paid to the contested nature of all the tactics deployed in the will to govern illiberal populations. Foucault returns here with renewed vigour. He understood that forms of war have always been aligned with forms of life. Liberal wars are no exception. Fought in the name of endangered humanity, humanity itself finds its most meaningful expression through the battles waged in its name:

> At this point we can invert Clausewitz's proposition and say that *politics is the continuation of war by other means* ... While it

---

33 Dillon and Reid, *The Liberal Way of War*, p. 32.

34 Duffield, *Development, Security and Unending War*, p. 162.

35 Michael Ignatieff, *Empire Lite: Nation-Building in Bosnia, Kosovo and Afghanistan* (London: Vintage, 2003).

36 See David Kilcullen, *The Accidental Guerrilla: Fighting Small Wars in the Midst of a Big One* (Oxford: Oxford University Press, 2009); Rupert Smith, *The Utility of Force: The Art of War in the Modern World* (London: Penguin, 2006).

37 See especially John Gray, *Black Mass: Apocalyptic Religion and the Death of Utopia* (London: Penguin, 2008).

is true that political power puts an end to war and establishes or attempts to establish the reign of peace in civil society, it certainly does not do so in order to suspend the effects of power or to neutralize the disequilibrium revealed in the last battle of war.[38]

In other words, what occurs beneath the semblance of peace is far from politically settled:

Political struggles, these clashes over and with power, these modifications of relations of force – the shifting balances, the reversals – in a political system, all these things must be interpreted as a continuation of war. And they are interpreted as so many episodes, fragmentations, and displacements of the war itself. We are always writing the history of the same war, even when we are writing the history of peace and its institutions.

In a remarkable address on the Future of NATO, former British Foreign Secretary David Miliband, without perhaps knowing the full political and philosophical implications, appears to subscribe to the value of this approach, albeit for an altogether more committed deployment:

NATO was born in the shadow of the Cold War, but we have all had to change our thinking as our troops confront insurgents rather than military machines like our own. The mental models of 20th century mass warfare are not fit for 21st century counter-insurgency. That is why my argument today has been about the centrality of politics. People like quoting Clausewitz that warfare is the continuation of politics by other means ... We need *politics to become the continuation of warfare by other means*.[39]

Miliband's 'Foucauldian moment' should not escape us. Inverting Clausewitz on a planetary scale – hence promoting the collapse

---

38 Foucault, *Society Must Be Defended*, p. 15.

39 David Miliband, 'NATO's Mission in Afghanistan: The Political Strategy', speech at NATO Headquarters, Brussels, 27 July 2009, www.davidmiliband.info/speeches/speeches_09_09.htm (accessed 22 April 2010) (emphasis added).

of all meaningful distinctions that once held together the fixed conceptions of political spatiality (i.e., inside/outside, friend/enemy, citizen/soldier, war/peace and so forth), he firmly locates the conflict among the 'world of peoples'. With global war therefore appearing to be an internal state of affairs, vanquishing enemies can no longer be sanctioned for the mere defence of things. A new moment has arrived, in which the destiny of humanity as a whole is being wagered on the success of humanity's own political strategies. No coincidence, then, that authors such as David Kilcullen – a key architect in the formulation of counter-insurgency strategies in Iraq and Afghanistan – argue for a global insurgency paradigm without too much controversy.[40] Viewed from the perspective of power, global insurgency is after all nothing more than the advent of a global civil war fought for the bio-political spoils of life. Giving primacy to counter-insurgency, it foregrounds the problem of populations so that questions of security governance (i.e., population regulation) become central to the war effort.[41] Placing the managed recovery of maladjusted life into the heart of military strategies, it insists upon a joined-up response in which sovereign and militaristic forms of ordering are matched by bio-political and developmental forms of progress.

What is being proposed here challenges conventional understandings of civil war. While the well-established Eurocentric narrative starts with the question of sovereignty, colonised peoples have never fully accepted the inevitability of the transfixed utopian prolificacy upon which sovereign power increasingly became dependent. Neither have they been completely passive when confronted by colonialism's own brand of warfare by other means. Foucault was well aware of this history. While Foucauldian scholars can therefore rightly argue that alternative histories of the subjugated alone permit us to challenge the monopolisation of political terms – not least 'civil war' – for Foucault in particular there was something altogether more important at stake: there is no obligation whatsoever to ensure that reality matches some canonical theory. Despite what some scholars may insist, politically speaking there is nothing that is necessarily *proper*

40 Kilcullen, *The Accidental Guerrilla*.
41 RAND Corporation, *War by Other Means: Building Complete and Balanced Capabilities for Counter Insurgency* (Santa Monica: RAND Corporation, 2008).

to the sovereign method. It holds no distinct privilege. Our task is to use theory to help make sense of reality, not vice versa. While there is not the space here to engage fully with the implications of our global civil war paradigm, it should be pointed out that, since its bio-political imperative removes the inevitability of epiphenomenal tensions, nothing and nobody is necessarily dangerous simply because location dictates. With enmity instead depending upon the complex, adaptive, dynamic account of life itself, what becomes dangerous *emerges* from within the liberal imaginary of threat. Violence accordingly can only be sanctioned against those newly appointed enemies of humanity – a phrase that, immeasurably greater than any juridical category, necessarily affords enmity an internal quality inherent to the entire species, for the sake of planetary survival.

Confronting violence in the world

During the wars of the past decade or so, two visions of battle have emerged. The first is premised on the logic of technology, where it was assumed that high-tech sophistry could replace the need to suffer casualties. The second is premised upon a more humanitarian ethos, which demanded local knowledge and engagement with dangerous populations. The narcissistic violence of the global war on terror has put this secondary vision into lasting crisis as the violence of the liberal encounter has fatefully exposed the lack of any universal commitment to rights and justice. Not only have liberal societies appeared to be the principal authors of violence, thereby challenging the notion that underdevelopment was the true cause of planetary endangerment, but also populations within liberal consumer societies are more reluctant to support war efforts and publicly support engagements in zones of crises and instability. If there has been one notable casualty of the wars on terror, it has been precisely our belief that we might engage and transform the world and its peoples for the better. So what does this mean for the relevance of Foucault's work today?

Foucault's work has undoubtedly allowed us to raise necessary questions concerning the violence of humanitarian wars. We must, however, now take this a stage further. Further, the idea that citizens in the metropolitan homelands are radically endangered by threats from terror to weather and everything in between is reshaping the logic of liberal rule, as the politics of catastrophe becomes a central and defining feature of contemporary political discourses and practices.[42] The outcome has been the normalisation of terror as premised on the ubiquitous promise of violence to come. We see this played out most evidently in the United States as the embrace of weapons to be used on enemies abroad has taken a new turn and these weapons are now openly used on those considered dangerous at home. As the police become more militarised, the legacy of killing recalcitrant populations abroad becomes an element of domestic policy. None of this would have been lost on Foucault, who once noted:

> While colonization, with its techniques and its political and juridical weapons, obviously transported European models to other continents, it also had a considerable boomerang effect on the mechanisms of power in the West, and on the apparatuses, institutions, and techniques of power. A whole series of colonial models was brought back to the West, and the result was that the West could practice something resembling colonization, or an internal colonialism, on itself.[43]

So is there political life after Foucault? In a remarkable essay entitled 'Speech Begins after Death', he offers perhaps his most cutting of critical interventions. 'Writing means', he explains, 'having to deal with the death of others, but it basically means having to deal with others to the extent that they're already dead … I'm in the situation of the anatomist who performs an autopsy.'[44] To which he adds: 'I also understand why people experience my writing as a form of aggression … They feel there is something in it that condemns them to death.' But, as he further qualifies:

> I don't condemn them to death. I simply assume they're already dead. That's why I am so surprised when I hear them cry out. I'm as astonished as the anatomist who became suddenly aware that the man on whom he was intending to demonstrate has

42 See Brad Evans, *Liberal Terror* (Cambridge: Polity, 2014); Brad Evans and Julian Reid, *Resilient Life: The Art of Living Dangerously* (Cambridge: Polity, 2015).
43 Foucault, *Society Must Be Defended*, p. 103.
44 Michel Foucault, *Speech Begins after Death*, ed. Philippe Artières (Minneapolis: Minnesota University Press, 2013), pp. 40–41

woken up beneath his scalpel. In short, 'I don't claim to kill others with my writing. I only write on the basis of the other's already present death.'

Perhaps we too need to heed that warning in respect to the bio-politicised Foucault, who seems to have reached his final state in the resiliently minded subject. There is, after all, nothing beyond the unending states of catastrophe. This certainly does not imply laying Foucault to rest. And it certainly doesn't mean mourning the passing of a conceptual persona whose time is being outlived. It is to breathe new life into modes of subjectivity that are not content with having the human condition reduced to the level of some biological species stripped of those irreducible qualities that make life worth living. If speech truly begins 'after death', as Foucault insisted, maybe it is the case that political life begins after the death of a once vital bio-political Foucault, which is also to declare the already present death of liberalism.

Further reading

Campbell, Timothy and Adam Sitze, *Biopolitics: A Reader* (Durham, NC: Duke University Press, 2013).

Debrix, François and Alexander Barder, *Beyond Biopolitics: Theory, Violence, and Horror in World Politics* (Milton Park: Routledge, 2012).

Dillon, Michael and Andrew Neal (eds.), *Foucault on Politics, Security, War* (New York: Palgrave Macmillan, 2008).

Duffield, Mark, *Development, Security and Unending War: Governing the World of Peoples* (Cambridge: Polity, 2007).

Foucault, Michel, *Discipline and Punish: The Birth of the Prison* (London: Vintage Books, 1995).

Foucault, Michel, *Security, Territory and Population: Lectures at the Collège de France 1977–1978* (New York: Macmillan, 2007).

Foucault, Michel, *Society Must be Defended: Lectures at the Collège de France 1975–1976* (New York: Picador, 2003).

Gregory, Derek, *The Colonial Present: Afghanistan, Palestine, Iraq* (Oxford: Blackwell, 2004).

Stoler, Ann Laura, *Carnal Knowledge and Imperial Power: Race and the Intimate in Colonial Rule* (Berkeley: University of California Press, 2010).

Stoler, Ann Laura, *Race and the Education of Desire: Foucault's History of Sexuality and the Colonial Order of Things* (Durham: Duke University Press, 1995).

6 | JACQUES DERRIDA

Gregg Lambert

Biographical details

Jacques Derrida (1930–2004) was born in El-Biar, a suburb of Algiers, into a Sephardic Jewish family. Algeria at this time was a French colony, and Derrida recounts how, when he was in the local *lycée* (high school), the Vichy regime in France proclaimed certain interdictions concerning the native languages of Algeria, in particular Maghreb and Berber, and offered Arabic as a foreign language. Derrida calls his experience of the interdiction 'unforgettable and generalizable'.[1] In 1941 the 'Jewish laws' passed by the Vichy regime interrupted his high school studies at the Lycée Ben Akoun, and Derrida later recounted with bitter resentment the story of one day being called into the head of school's office and then abruptly sent home with no explanation, an incident that had a lasting effect on his psychology, forming the basis of a seemingly telepathic attunement to the faintest signs of anti-Semitism and xenophobia throughout his later life and writings. The experience also informed a fundamental suspicion of any institution, but particularly of educational institutions and the university. Derrida found them historically suspect, given their complicity with the policies of the modern state (as in the case of the French educational institutions under the colonial system, but also in the case of the universities under National Socialism). He found universities to be too pliable and to conform too much with state directives. This is in open contradiction to any prescription of Enlightenment rationality, and he was later the most severe critic and controversial reformist in relation to the idea of the university in France.

After the Allied landing in 1943, Derrida returned to Lycée Ben Akoun, where he began reading Nietzsche, Rousseau, Camus

---

1 Derrida, quoted in M. Chérif, *Islam and the West: A Conversation with Jacques Derrida* (Chicago: University of Chicago Press, 2008), p. 37.

and especially Gide, whom he idolised and sought to emulate in his personal journals. At the same time, Algiers became a French literary capital in exile, and many important writers of Algerian origin, including Camus, as well as writers in Maghrebian literary movements, created a flourishing culture of new journals and schools. In 1949 Derrida completed his studies at the Lycée Gauthier in Algiers and moved to Paris to enrol at the Lycée Louis-le-Grand, where he prepared for the entrance exam in philosophy to the prestigious École normale supérieure (ENS). Derrida failed his first attempt at this exam but passed it on his second try, in 1952. After entering ENS he completed his *aggrégation* in 1956, and he received a scholarship to conduct research at Harvard University in 1957. In the same year he married and was called back to military service during the Algerian war, in which he asked to be assigned to a post as a teacher of French and English to Algerian students and children of French servicemen. In 1962 his family left Algiers and settled in Nice. Derrida was employed at the Sorbonne in Paris, where he became assistant to Gaston Bachelard and Paul Ricoeur, until he later returned to ENS, where he soon became close friends with the French Marxist and fellow Algerian Louis Althusser. The two never talked of philosophy or theory when they met, only what Derrida would later describe as his *nostalgerie* for the southern shores of the Mediterranean, which he revisited briefly just once before his death from pancreatic cancer on 9 October 2004.

Theorising violence

In this brief biography I have highlighted Derrida's Jewish and Algerian origins, because this helps to explain his sensitivity to all forms of racism and his criticism of bureaucratic and administrative logics of modern institutions. These are the two topics of violence that became the hallmarks of a deconstructive style of criticism, but Derrida's biography can also help us to understand his tendency to critique any system (linguistic, cultural, political or religious) from a position on the periphery, or from the perspective of a repressed and marginalised representative. For example, both tendencies inform the basis of his most systematic work, *Of Grammatology*, published in 1967, where the method of deconstruction first appeared and was announced in the preface as a critique of Western logocentric and ethnocentric reason. Finally, events from Derrida's childhood in

Algiers might also explain the severity of his critique of any system of totalisation and any form of authority that is based on an identifiable and supposedly 'proper identity'.

At least part of the mythology that surrounds Derrida's meteoric rise in the institutions of higher learning in North America through the 1970s, and in the rest of the world throughout the 1980s (including Africa, China, Japan, Palestine and South America), derives from an earlier controversy. In 1966 Derrida was invited to a conference at Johns Hopkins University along with several other French intellectuals (including Roland Barthes, Lucien Goldmann, Jacques Lacan and Jean-Pierre Vernant) on an occasion that became the beachhead for what was described in the anglophone media as the 'French invasion'. After this moment, Derrida was frequently invited to teach in American institutions and later to hold visiting positions at Cornell University, the University of California, Irvine (where I studied with him through the mid-1990s) and the Benjamin N. Cardozo School of Law of Yeshiva University in New York City.

The 1980s also mark the beginnings of the most severe reaction against Derrida and deconstruction, mostly from departments of philosophy in the United States and the United Kingdom. As is well known, most of the public attacks were focused on the 'revelations' of complicity and anti-Semitism of Derrida's colleague Paul de Man, and, more importantly on the European continent, on the revelation of Heidegger's involvement with national socialism during the period when he was rektor of the University of Freiburg. On both counts, Derrida was charged with guilt by association and was called to make public responses on the relationship between deconstructive philosophy and Nazism. It is important to note, in this regard, that the knowledge of Heidegger's involvement and partial endorsement of the national socialist ideology was well known beforehand in academic circles, and even the subject of a severe critique by Derrida's friend and mentor Emmanuel Levinas in his 1947 article 'The Philosophy of Hitlerism', but these comments had been ignored or dismissed by the French academic establishment, in particular, as 'an episode'.

Derrida was attacked as an 'obscurantist and a terrorist', a phrase that American philosopher John Searle reported to the *New York Times* but unverifiably ascribed to a private comment made by Michel Foucault. Derrida's philosophy was also suspected of harbouring an unconscious or implicit nihilist, apolitical and anti-moral agenda (that is, when it was not charged with simply being decadent). This became especially vicious and personal and reached a peak in an incident that took place in spring 1992 when the award of an honorary degree by Cambridge University was challenged by a number of academics on both sides of the Atlantic. The protestors took out advertisements in the *New York Times* and the *Times Literary Supplement*, venerable journalistic institutions, excoriating both Derrida and his philosophy.

Thus commenced a brief period that has been described as Derrida's war against the journalists, who launched a media blitz, fuelling the controversy over the Heidegger affair and Derrida's relation to the 'philosopher of national socialism'. After this Derrida agreed to several interviews and wrote letters to the editors of the *New York Review of Books*. He realised that issues of translation and accurate reporting were no longer time-honoured codes of modern journalistic culture and that journalism had rather succumbed to a calculated feeding frenzy around the creation of media events that consumed serious philosophical issues in scandal and anecdotal evidence. Just as in the case of Derrida's experiences of anti-Semitism and state-sponsored racism from his early years, which informed an ambivalent relationship with official French academic culture throughout his life, this incident foreshadowed the degree of suspicion and overt caution he expressed in response to the 'major event' of the 9/11 attacks on the 'twin towers'.

In an interview with Giovanna Borradori forty days after 9/11, Derrida cautioned:

> We must try to know more, to take our time and hold onto our freedom so as to begin to think this first effect of the so-called event: From where does this menacing injunction itself come to us? How is it being forced upon us? *Who* or *what* gives us this threatening order (others would already say this terrorizing if not terrorist imperative): name, repeat, rename 'September 11', 'le 11 septembre', even when you do not yet know what you are saying and are not yet thinking what you refer to in this way. I agree with you: without any doubt, this 'thing', 'September 11', 'gave us the impression of being a *major event*'. But what is an impression in this case? And an event? And especially a '*major event*'? Taking your word – or words – for it, I will underscore

more than one precaution. I will do so in a seemingly 'empiricist' style, though aiming beyond empiricism. It cannot be denied, as an empiricist of the eighteenth century would quite literally say, that there was an 'impression' there, and the impression of what you call in English – and this is not fortuitous – a '*major event*'. I insist here on the English because it is the language we speak here in New York, even though it is neither your language nor mine; but I also insist because the injunction comes first of all from a place where English predominates. I am not saying this only because the United States was targeted, hit, or violated on its own soil for the first time in almost two centuries – since 1812 to be exact – but because the world order that felt itself targeted through this violence is dominated largely by the Anglo-American idiom, an idiom that is indissociably linked to the political discourse that dominates the world stage, to international law, diplomatic institutions, the media, and the greatest technoscientific, capitalist, and military power. And it is very much a question of the still enigmatic but also *critical* essence of this hegemony. By *critical*, I mean at once decisive, potentially decisionary, decision-making, and *in crisis*: today more vulnerable and threatened than ever.[2]

It was around this period that Derrida's writings became more overt and seemingly less ambiguous on the subject of politics. This is particularly true of a series of works and public addresses that appeared throughout the early 1990s, after the first Gulf War, and includes his published interview, two years after 9/11, with Islamic intellectual Mustapha Chérif, which took place on the day that Derrida was diagnosed with pancreatic cancer. In 2004, in his last published interview with *Le Monde*, Derrida even talked openly of his hope for Europe to become separated from its alliance with the United States militarily and to begin to become an active proponent globally of international laws and of the different forms of 'democracy to come' (*a venir*), a term that he often employed to designate the difference between the possibility of democracy and the democratic form of

2 Giovanna Borradori, *Philosophy in a Time of Terror: Dialogues with Jürgen Habermas and Jacques Derrida* (Chicago: University of Chicago Press, 2003), p. 88.

the state that currently exists (especially in the United States). This current democratic form of the state, he argued, must be submitted to a constant deconstruction of its institutions and particularly of its relationship to religion and Christianity, to militarism and to a new order of imperialism and unprecedented global violence. This critique was especially addressed to the United States in the Bill Clinton and George W. Bush eras and to its domination of the global economic markets, from which an increasing proportion of the world's populations are excluded. This is despite the misleading equality that is often implied in the terms 'free market' and 'globalisation', especially in the mouths of Republican politicians and conservative economists.

In the interview with Chérif, which dealt with the post-9/11 'war on terror' and the concomitant rise in racism against Muslim populations around the world, Chérif exclaims that the idea of a universal democracy is the only saving response, even though it would bear no resemblance to the one that President George W. Bush and Vice President Dick Cheney had planned for Iraq and Afghanistan. Derrida replies:

> What you call the universalism of democracy, a concept that is very difficult to define, presupposes that democracy is conceived in a way other than as a fixed model of a political regime. I believe that what distinguishes the idea of democracy from all other ideas of political regimes – monarchy, aristocracy, oligarchy, and so on – is that democracy is the only political system, a model without a model, that accepts its own historicity, that is, its own futures, which accepts its self-criticism, which accepts its perfectibility ... This is why I always speak of a democracy to come, it is a promise that one can always criticize, and question that which is supposed to be de facto democracy.[3]

It is ironic to hear Derrida's critics in the United States call him and his philosophy 'Eurocentric', since in many of his later writings he expounds an understanding that 'deconstruction is America', meaning that the history of the United States leading up to the present

3 Chérif, *Islam and the West*, pp. 42–43.

political regime represents the deconstruction of all European ideology and political institutions. This is for the very reason that many of its earlier settlers and immigrant communities were castaways from Europe – political refugees, failed and persecuted reformists, illiterate populations and even radical intellectuals and activists, who came to places such as New York and Los Angeles. As with the flight of Jewish–German intellectuals to the United States before the Second World War, here Derrida may also be alluding to the destination or what he calls *destinerrance* of his own philosophy in US institutions. They had formerly welcomed it, though they later reacted to expel it, after it had been rejected by the academic hierarchies of France and Germany. At the same time, Derrida always spoke of the limited concept of democracy that defines the United States, of new forms of racism and discrimination that have been bred by its settler communities against 'non-Western others', of a market capitalism that dominates the entire polity and even today its universities, and a new order enforced globally through militarism and violence. In its own 'territory', the United States institutionalises a legal system of extortion and intimidation through populations voluntarily giving up their political rights and freedoms in exchange for bio-political security. As Derrida suggests, it is almost impossible to think of a viable form of democracy when, on a daily basis, every one of its citizens can be at any moment, in the most routine conduct of their daily lives and often through the most accidental and arbitrary of circumstances, under *a priori* suspicion of being an enemy of the state.

Derrida's most severe criticisms of the United States came in the George W. Bush era, especially his 2002 lectures published later under the title *Voyous* (translated as *Rogues*), where the United States is defined as a 'rogue state'. In this context we should recall the arguments first made by Kant in *Perpetual Peace* (1795) concerning barbarous states that routinely violate international law and thus become a threat to the security of all nations on earth through their lawlessness and violence, as opposed to the establishment of a universal cosmopolitan society. Kant also outlines a situation in which legally formed nations are within their rights to ally themselves against the appearance of what political theorists call the 'super-state', in order to maintain their own freedom and security against a stronger opponent. In a parallel manner, perhaps Derrida was suggesting in this last work that Europe and the other nations that comprise the United Nations should form an alliance against the United States, one that would enforce a new determination of international law that would no longer serve an imperial order. This is also hinted at in the earlier writings collected in *Specters of Marx* (1993), which concern what he calls 'the new International'. It is in this sense that the statement 'America is deconstruction' has a second meaning, understandable only by Europeans and other nations globally, in which the deconstruction of the idea of democracy in its latest historical instance brings forth a universal emancipation of the concept. This is to be repeated and re-established in new models, given that democracy is the only political form that exists without any specific model or 'proper' form.

Who is the real enemy today? In the late 1980s, Derrida began a series of seminars in Paris and Irvine, California, around the question of friendship (including consideration of a number of figures such as Walter Benjamin, Martin Heidegger, Friedrich Nietzsche, Franz Rosenzweig and Carl Schmitt), all of whom took as their point of departure a phrase from Aristotle: 'Oh my friends, there is no friend.' These were collected in *The Politics of Friendship* in 1994, the principal thesis of which is outlined in the conclusion. This was an attempt

> to think and to implement democracy, all the while keeping
> the name, in the process of uprooting from it all the figures
> of friendship (philosophical or religious) which prescribe
> fraternity (either through blood or territory, the family or the
> anthropocentric group).[4]

It is here that one finds Derrida's most pointed encounter with Carl Schmitt, whose concept of 'political theology' was recovered by the Italian philosopher Giorgio Agamben in his book *Homo Sacer* (1998). This concerned the friend–enemy distinction and the claim that the modern political state is founded on this concept.

In *The Concept of the Political* (1932), Schmitt focuses almost exclusively on what he calls 'concrete situations' in order to arrive at

4 Jacques Derrida, *The Politics of Friendship*, trans. George Collins (London: Verso, 1997), p. 306.

what he claims to be a pure concept of the political as being. This is founded upon the need to determine the friend – enemy distinction (i.e., the need to identify the enemy of my friend and the friend of my enemy) as a point of certainty that structures the social field. In his reading of Schmitt, Derrida is completely accurate in determining the character of this certainty. He sees it not as an epistemological certainty but rather as a practical certainty (praxis), which is why Schmitt calls this a 'concrete situation'. Schmitt refers to the subject who knows and is capable of acting, and, in this case, he is referring to a subject capable of knowing and acting upon the answers to the questions 'who is the enemy?' and 'who is the friend?' As Derrida writes,

> If the political exists [in Schmitt's sense], one must know who everyone is, who is a friend and who is an enemy, and this knowing is not a mode of theoretical knowledge but one of practical identification: knowing consists in knowing how to identify the friend and the enemy.[5]

This is the very problem that Derrida invokes in the following passage from the chapter 'In Human Language, Fraternity':

> If a politics of friendship rather than war were to be derived, there would have to be agreement on the meaning of 'friend'. But the signification of 'friend' can only be determined from within the friend/enemy opposition.[6]

What Derrida is calling our attention to in this passage is that the signification of the term 'friend' is itself fated to remain abstract within a system – linguistic as well as social – that is ordered by a nearly univocal agreement on the term 'enemy' (*der Feind*). In other words, the friend suffers not from a lack of signification but rather from too much signification, which is determined in various manners, such as individualistic, subjective, intuitive, culturally relative, probabilistic, spontaneous and overdetermined.

5 Derrida, *Politics of Friendship*, p. 116.
6 Derrida, *Politics of Friendship*, p. 246.

With regard to the praxis demanded by a Marxist determination of knowledge or 'scientific materialist practice', the recognition of the 'enemy' becomes an acute political problem that, in some ways, lends credence to Schmitt's analysis. In other words, something striking occurs when we realise that in both concepts of the political – that of Schmitt and that of Marx – the fundamental order of determination is focused upon the enemy. The enemy comes first, prior to the friend, in this distinction; it is only after the enemy is determined that the relations to friends (or comrades) is made possible. It is the practical certainty of the identity of the enemy that allows for the 'political recognition' of the friend: that is, *the enemy of my enemy is my friend*. In a certain manner, this already fulfils Schmitt's argument that the concept of the political is determined as a pragmatic or concrete situation of alliances in a more or less generalised situation of war, something that can also be found in Marx's concept of the political and the generalised situation of class warfare or 'war between estates'.

In the case of Schmitt's concept of the political, however, this allows for the emergence of the modern state to appear as the purest and most instrumental determination of the friend–enemy distinction; in a Hegelian sense, we are conscious of the certainty of state identity and 'the political' by the right to wage war on the basis of this distinction. It is in relation to the state and its power to determine the enemy that the subject becomes conscious of the political as such. The importance of Marx was that he recognised the certainty of this identity and its power, and he worked to turn this instrumental function into a weapon that could be wielded by the working classes in their own national spheres. Marx 'demythologised' this identity by revealing that 'the state' was itself only an instrument that was invented by a certain class, which could in turn be turned against it. In order for this to happen, a new class consciousness needed to emerge that would find itself directly in opposition to the certainty of the political in the nation-state. The certainty of national identity, by which the friend–enemy distinction was determined by various national bourgeois classes competing for their own particular class interests through the political instruments they had invented, would need to be replaced by the 'concrete situation' of a new universal class at war against all national elites. In the end these would be revealed to be only different bourgeois classes, each in their own spheres of influence, all having an integral role to play in the states they had instituted in order to pursue their own particular interests.

However, what is important to see in this is a radical overturning of the original Greek concept of the *polis* as the common or open space (*agora*) that is shared by friends who must organise the form of conflict (*stasis*) into generalised forms of competition (*philotimia*) that do not approach the extreme division implied by war (*polemos*). In the original Greek, *stasis* indicates both homogeneity and strife, and it is the identity of the two opposing and contradictory meanings that form a specific dialectical trajectory for the history of the *polis* to resolve. Let us be clear on this point: war (*polemos*) is still a distribution or partition of space (even when this distribution takes the form of occupation or colonisation) and of the economic distribution of goods (even through their destruction). However, it was this distribution or economy that Plato wanted to keep outside the *polis*, wishing to admit only those forms of antagonism that belong to the term *stasis*.

As Leo Strauss observed in his epilogue to the 1976 edition of *The Concept of the Political*, one of the distinctive characteristics that he finds in Schmitt's analysis of the political is that, unlike other regions of culture and society, the political has no sphere of its own. In other words, the friend–enemy antithesis can be found in other spheres and regions of culture (civil society), such as the religious, economic, legal, scientific and ethical. However, it is only the political that names the point of actuality and 'concrete determination' of a particular friend–enemy grouping at a given historical moment. Religious conflicts can intensify within or between societies, but they become political only to the extent that they become actualised as lethal conflicts, providing each side with the power to kill or to sacrifice the members of its own association. Although it would seem that Schmitt is founding the political on the actuality of war – a thesis that is more in keeping with Foucault – he reminds us many times that it is not the actuality of war that proves to be most decisive in determining the political, but rather its pure possibility, which takes the form of a 'right to kill', or *jus belli*. The political, then, would be the purest expression of a decision to kill, and it is for this reason that it enjoys no separate sphere of its own. Rather, it exists below every sphere of culture, every religious argument, every quarrel between neighbours, every encounter with a stranger, in every murderous impulse or thought. However, in all these expressions what is absent is the power to actualise it – that is, to become decisive.

The political would then be the name for the 'concrete situation' of a decision once it has been made; it would come after the thought of killing but before the actual act of killing. It would become not only possible but also a potentiality that can be realised at any moment afterward, and in this sense we can understand the decision as something that divides time into a 'before' and an 'after' and institutes itself as a 'ground'. It is only in this way that we might understand Schmitt's clarification that 'the State must presuppose the political' in the sense that the state emerges from the ground of a decision to kill, which then subsequently must be deprived of its simple moral meaning for the individual (i.e., it must be sanctioned, legalised, condoned, excused, ordered etc.). And yet, if Schmitt derives his theory of the state from Hegel, he clearly departs from Hegel by defining the character of the decision upon which the personality of the state is grounded so narrowly. In this sense, Schmitt is thinking as a jurist and not as a philosopher, and thereby determines what is the deciding issue or the precedent that will function as a rule in determining the case of each 'concrete situation' in which the political appears as the condition of existence of the state. As we noted earlier, the rule that Schmitt endorses is *jus belli*: 'the right to demand from its own members the readiness to die and to unhesitatingly kill its enemies'.[7] It is on the basis of this ruling that the concept of the political can be clarified, in its purest expression, from all the murkiness that it has been subjected to by romantic philosophy and by liberal humanists.

Perhaps this would go a long way in explaining the contamination between the two senses of conflict noted above, between *polemos* and *stasis*, as well as various confusions that occur between the determinations of public and private enemy, or internal and external precincts of the *polis*, the former being subject to the dialectic of the political and the latter being circumscribed as belonging to the conditions of total war against anyone who is determined to be 'a natural enemy of the State'. For example, in a post-9/11 world, this might serve to outline the archaic imperial grounds of the various

---

7 C. Schmitt, *The Concept of the Political*, trans. George Schwab (Chicago: University of Chicago Press, 1996), p. 46.

justifications made by the George W. Bush administration to invoke *jus belli* against an 'enemy' according to the definition offered above. Ironically, according to Schmitt's own logic, if the concept of the political can be understood to appear in its purest and most threadbare sense in the current 'global war on terror', it is because any moral sense of evaluation (i.e., that of a 'just war') must be assumed to inherently express a polemical or oppositional meaning and cannot be employed theoretically or scientifically in order to grasp the truth of the situation.

It is at this point that we turn to Derrida's relentless attack on Schmitt's purity of the concept, in his deconstruction of all of Schmitt's claims to purify the term 'politics' from every weakened, mixed, abstract and metaphorical sense (economic, religious, aesthetic, even moral). In the several commentaries on Schmitt in *The Politics of Friendship*, Derrida argues that these claims are to be founded on an impure presupposition (if not prejudice) of 'the political as such' in a Platonic sense. This is most clearly argued in a note that appears in his chapter 'On Absolute Hostility', where he recounts the transcript of Schmitt's interrogation by the American prosecutor at Nuremburg, Professor Robert Kempner. Referring to a sentence in which Schmitt asserts that 'Jewish authors' were not responsible for the creation of a theory of space (*der Raum*), nor, indeed, for 'the creation of anything at all', Kempner asks, 'Do you deny that this passage is in the purest Goebbels' style?' Schmitt responds: 'in its intent, method, and formulation, it is a pure diagnosis … a scholarly thesis that I would defend before any scholarly body in the world'.[8] Here we see the word 'pure' employed in Schmitt's own discourse in a manner similar to how it is used in *The Concept of the Political* with regard to the intent, method and formulation in his scholarly work. It would seem that this scene, to Derrida's mind at least – and here I am only speculating – has so contaminated the usage of this term as to make suspect any claim to the neutrality or scientifically objective, or 'purely diagnostic', status of Schmitt's discourse. As Derrida writes: 'He [Schmitt] would wish – it is his Platonic dream – that this "as such" should remain pure at the very spot where it is contaminated.'[9]

8 Derrida, *Politics of Friendship*, p. 134.
9 Derrida, *Politics of Friendship*, p. 116.

Recalling the passage from *The Republic* where Plato attempts to exclude the *hostis* (enemy) from the boundaries of the *polis*, Derrida alludes to the long tradition of historical scholarship on this passage in order to show that Plato is here himself engaged in a polemic or diatribe, one that seeks to remove the political possibilities of real war (*polemos*) from 'civil war'. As Schmitt himself acknowledges in a note on the passage, 'civil war is only a self-laceration and does not signify perhaps that a new state or people is being created'.[10] As Derrida rightly observes, 'The purity of the distinction between *stasis* and *polemos* remains in the *Republic* a paradigm, accessible only to discourse.'[11] Furthermore, the conceptual distinction is only accessible through the metaphors that Plato employs in order to establish the difference between 'killing the enemy' and 'self-laceration'. In other words, for Plato, civil war was tantamount to an act of misrecognition or misidentification in which one thinks one is aiming at an enemy only to shoot oneself instead. In politics, just as in war, the problem of 'friendly fire' is an ever-present threat, and it is crucial to know 'who the enemy is' and practically 'how to recognize the other who is the enemy' in order to avoid mistaking the enemy for oneself (or one's friend). To help out in this identification, Plato employs the analogy of the barbarian (or one 'who is an enemy by nature') in order to orient this distinction outward in an appropriate direction, away from the *polis*, towards the outside, but also metaphorically or poetically away from one's own body or the body proper of the people itself towards the foreign body of the *hostis*.

In other words, Plato employs the paradigm of barbarian versus Hellene in order to assist his contemporary audience in conceptually orientating this distinction between proper and improper identification, even though at the same time he will then worry about the metaphorical properties of this analogy when applied to antagonisms internal to the *polis*. Returning to Schmitt's use of this identification, and to the mechanism of identification at the basis of the political decision as to 'who is the enemy?', how can this purely political determination be made on the basis of an analogy to one 'who is an enemy by nature', which is to say, on the basis of an impure, pre-political or non-political determination? Race is only one

---

10 Schmitt, *Concept of the Political*, p. 29.
11 Derrida, *Politics of Friendship*, p. 114.

concept today that has emerged on the basis of this analogy, perhaps in order to orient social antagonisms towards a foreign body, but others no less problematic have preceded it. In fact, we know that the entire history of the concept of the political is plagued by the inappropriate or metaphorical uses of this analogy, especially in the politico-strategic uses of 'the natural enemy' up to and including the strategic usage deployed by Marx and Engels when they identified the bourgeoisie as the natural enemy of the proletariat. Perhaps this is enough to throw into sharp relief Derrida's criticism of Schmitt's constant claim to purify the concept of the political from all abstractions (by which he means of all weak analogies), and the friend–enemy concepts from all metaphor and symbol, when the concept of the enemy is impure from the start.

What I have just outlined is the structure of what Derrida calls 'the worst' (*le pire*). In other words, 'in a time of terror' there is no identifiable enemy in the form of a state against which one would wage what could still be called a war, even if we think of this as a war on international terrorism. The Cold War's balance of terror, which ensured that no escalation of nuclear weapons would lead to a suicidal operation, is over. Instead,

> a new violence is being prepared and in truth has been unleashed for some time now, in a way that is more visibly suicidal or auto-immune than ever. This violence no longer has to do with *world* war or even with *war*, even less with some right to wage war. And this is hardly re-assuring – indeed, quite the contrary.[12]

Confronting violence in the world

In conclusion, I refer to Derrida's 1994 article 'Faith and Knowledge: The Two Sources of Religion within the Limits of Reason Alone'. There Derrida challenges us to think about the meaning of 'the return of religion and of the religious' under two horizons, which he reminds us are always complex and overdetermined, by posing the following question: how is it possible to understand the form of absolute peace announced under the first horizon, of 'religion without religion', without also announcing (at least as the condition

---

12 Jacques Derrida, *Rogues: Two Essays on Reason*, trans. Pascale-Anne Brault and Michael Haas (Stanford: Stanford University Press, 2005), p. 156.

of this new horizon) the total pacification of another sense of *religio* that is still embodied by a majority of the world's populations?

What then is 'globalatinisation', or what Derrida called the current age of the Anglo-American 'return of religion' (i.e., the global war on terror)? Firstly, according to Derrida, it belongs to an apparatus that emerged initially in the Roman empire and took a detour through the United States, an apparatus of global international law *and* of a global political rhetoric that will determine the meaning of public conduct and citizenship. These will be the requisite conditions of access to territory in the name of 'security and the public peace' and will also define the virtues of fidelity and confidence, which will become conditions of access to the world market. As the result of both determinations, not all cultures will be guaranteed to have equal access to the same world market.[13]

Secondly, this rhetoric also imposes the meaning of religion and religiousness upon things it designates by quasi-imperial decree and claims sovereignty over other forms of life, including cultural life, or even bio-political life. As Derrida writes, concerning the first so-called apparatus, the imperial law of Rome, it is also accompanied by a global rhetoric that is historically incarnated in 'the dominant juridical system and the concept of the State'[14] but also in the most 'Latiniglobal and cederomized' rhetoric. This concerns the universality of a certain concept of religion that one hears in relation to the 'certain death of God'.[15] As Derrida writes,

> Inasmuch as it comes from Rome, as is often the case, it would first try, and first in Europe, upon Europe, to impose surreptitiously a discourse – i.e. a global rhetoric – a culture, a politics, and a right, to impose them on all the other monotheist religions, including non-Catholic Christian religions.[16]

Finally, Derrida concludes his observations on both aspects of this apparatus, making what is perhaps the most acute prognosis of

13 Jacques Derrida, 'Faith and Knowledge: The Two Sources of Religion within the Limits of Reason Alone', in *Religion: Cultural Memory in the Present*, ed. Jacques Derrida and Gianni Vattimo (Stanford: Stanford University Press, 1998), p. 18.
14 Derrida, 'Faith and Knowledge', p. 72.
15 Derrida, 'Faith and Knowledge', p. 72.
16 Derrida, 'Faith and Knowledge', p. 43.

the problems surrounding the increase of 'religious violence' today. He writes:

> The task seems all the more urgent and problematic (incalculable calculation of religion for our times) as the demographic disproportion will not cease henceforth to threaten external *hegemony*, leaving the latter no other *stratagem* than internalization.[17]

In quoting this passage, I emphasise the use of the words 'hegemony' and 'stratagem' in order to signal a theologico-political sense of war in response to what Derrida calls 'a gesture of pacification', which is not a neutral phrase but rather a stratagem or tactic invented by modern technological warfare.

Following this final observation, one might find a similarity between Foucault's earlier remarks on historical transformation of the nature of sovereignty associated with the birth of 'the rights of man' and the emergence of what he calls 'bio-power' in relation to Derrida's observation concerning what he calls the 'double horizon' of the death of God. In other words, the first horizon announced in the self-destructive affirmation of religion (which proclaims the essence of *religio* as pacifist, ecumenical or Catholic) may also conceal another horizon associated with an overt gesture of pacification, that is, with the hidden and no less violent nature of globalatinisation itself.

According to the sense of this unprecedented double bind, or of an affirmation that conceals its hostility towards another meaning, paradoxically hidden in the form of the affirmation of religion itself, we might also be reminded of an enigmatic statement made by Deleuze, who remarked that today the rights of man can both preserve bio-political life and, at the same time, authorise another holocaust. In commenting on this passage in relation to Derrida's reference to a 'pacifying gesture', I would point out that the qualities of 'insanity' or 'madness' could also be treated as bio-political dangers, and I would consider the pages in 'Faith and Knowledge' that specifically concern the double bind of immunity and auto-immunity of religion and science to be perhaps the most acute and profound reflections on

17 Derrida, 'Faith and Knowledge', p. 43 (emphasis added).

the same phenomena that were observed earlier by Foucault under the concept of 'bio-political life'.

Further reading

Bennington, Geoffrey, *Jacques Derrida* (Chicago: Chicago University Press, 2002).

Derrida, Jacques. *Points: Interviews 1974–1994* (Palo Alto: Stanford University Press, 1995).

Kamuf, Peggy (ed.), *A Derrida Reader: Between the Blinds* (New York: Columbia University Press, 1991).

Mikics, David, *Who Was Jacques Derrida? An Intellectual Biography* (New Haven: Yale University Press, 2009).

Naas, Michael, *Taking on Tradition: Jacques Derrida and the Legacies of Deconstruction* (Palo Alto: Stanford University Press, 2002).

7 | GILLES DELEUZE

Ian Buchanan

Biographical details

Gilles Deleuze (1925–1995) was a French philosopher who was born in Paris and, following a long, incapacitating illness, took his own life in the same city. Deleuze's *oeuvre* is difficult to classify. He described his work as philosophy, 'nothing but philosophy', even when it looked like something else – anthropology, art history, social theory, politics, film theory and so on. As this brief litany suggests, his work ranges far beyond the usual concerns of the discipline. His work is read equally widely – indeed, it tends to be most influential outside philosophy. He has devoted readers in art, architecture, anthropology, cultural studies, film studies, gender studies, politics and sociology. Deleuze introduced both a new way of writing philosophy and a new way of thinking about philosophy that contributed in profound ways to the construction of the new discursive form known today simply as theory.[1] His friend Michel Foucault, a towering intellectual figure in his own right, recognised the significance of Deleuze's contribution to twentieth-century thought very early and in 1969 mischievously went so far as to suggest the century would be named after him.[2]

Violence was a central concern for Deleuze, though he rarely talked about it directly. As I will discuss in more detail below, one cannot understand his social theory – particularly the works he wrote with Félix Guattari – without considering his account of violence. In capsular form, it can be said he followed Nietzsche in thinking that all forms of government, from the most primitive to the most

---

1 I disagree with the various attempts, such as Cusset's, to discredit 'theory' as a lesser form of philosophy – I think Jameson is correct in recognising that theory came into being precisely because philosophy of the formal logical variety that existed in the 1950s was incapable of accounting for the new social forms that emerged alongside late capitalism.

2 Michel Foucault, 'Theatrum Philosophicum', in *Language, Counter-Memory, Practice* (Ithaca: Cornell University Press, 1977), p. 165.

sophisticated, are inherently violent. For Deleuze, government is a 'grey zone' (a concept he borrowed from the Italian Auschwitz survivor and author Primo Levi) because it entails both the direct violence of coercion and the indirect violence of something he called 'control' (a concept he borrowed from the American Beat writer William Burroughs).[3] Deleuze tended to focus on the problem of the violence of control. He was particularly fascinated by control mechanisms that rendered submission voluntary. His key example of this is television, which he acidly describes as a form of machinic enslavement.[4] Today the same must be said, a fortiori, of social media enterprises such as Facebook, which literally profits from the 'free' labour its users contribute to making the site attractive, thereby eliding the distinction between production and consumption. Deleuze often cited Wilhelm Reich's question: 'Why do men fight *for* their servitude as stubbornly as though it were their salvation?'[5] His answer, provocatively enough, was that at some level people desire it – they don't merely submit to 'power'; they want what it offers them, even at the price of their subjection.

It has been said, by critics such as Alain Badiou and Slavoj Žižek, that Deleuze was neither political nor politicised and that it was only when he started working with Guattari that his work took on any kind of a political hue.[6] Others, such as Peter Hallward, have gone even further and said that his thinking was disconnected from the realpolitik of everyday life. The title of Hallward's book, *Out of This World*, is as much a calculated insult as it is a summation of his

3 Gilles Deleuze, 'Postscript on Control Societies', in *Negotiations* (New York: Columbia University Press), pp 177–182.
4 Gilles Deleuze and Félix Guattari, *A Thousand Plateaus: Capitalism and Schizophrenia* (Minnesota: University of Minneapolis Press, 1987), p. 458.
5 Gilles Deleuze and Félix Guattari, *Anti-Oedipus: Capitalism and Schizophrenia* (London: Athlone Press, 1983), p. 29.
6 Slavoj Žižek's book *Organs without Bodies: On Deleuze and Consequences* (London: Routledge, 2004) is so bad I'm surprised he hasn't disavowed it. It is highly reliant on secondary sources, some of which are profoundly questionable, such Manuel DeLanda's work, and, more especially Alain Badiou's. Moreover – in my view, embarrassingly – the book exhibits a very limited understanding of Deleuze's work. Badiou's book *Deleuze: The Clamour of Being* (Minnesota: University of Minneapolis Press, 2000) is problematic because it flattens Deleuze's concept of multiplicity into a monotonous one-all, thus denying him his most important conceptual advance, the creation of a form of thinking equal to the complexity of our times.

thesis.[7] One has only to read Deleuze's impassioned defences of the Palestinian cause, however, to see the falsity of these caricatures of his thought. In a piece first published in Arabic in the journal *al-Karmel*, Deleuze writes: 'One hears that Israeli intelligence is much admired by the entire world; but what kind of democracy is that whose political life is too much entwined with the activity of its intelligence service?'[8] His comments here anticipate the 1990 essay 'Postscript on Control Societies' mentioned above and highlight a constant theme in his work: anything that curtails the real and practical autonomy of the subject is violence as far as Deleuze is concerned. He concedes, at times, that it is a necessary violence, that the subject would be lost and adrift without the structures that constitute society, but he remains adamant that the processes that bind people together into a collective should be understood as violence. 'There is always social repression [*refoulement*], but the apparatus of repression varies.'[9]

It would be wrong to suggest that Deleuze's views are coloured by personal experience, but the fact is that, like many people of his generation, Deleuze's formative years were marked by the violence of the Second World War. Although his early life was comfortable – his parents were middle class but not wealthy, he attended good schools and he vacationed in the fashionable seaside resort town of Deauville – that idyll was shattered when Germany invaded and occupied France. As Camus, Ionesco and Sartre illustrated with their creative works, the long occupation led to a suffocation of thought, or what we might also think of as a violence of the mind. It was probably this experience, the loss of the freedom of thought, that Deleuze felt most acutely, but, that said, his life was not untouched by actual violence. Fortunately for Deleuze he was in Deauville, far from the front line, when the German army crossed the border in the summer of 1940, so he did not experience the so-called shooting war. His parents sought to spare him the danger and violence of war by keeping him on the coast until after the armistice was signed. However, Deleuze's elder brother, Georges, did not want to be sheltered in this fashion

---

7 Peter Hallward, *Out of this World: Deleuze and the Philosophy of Creation* (London: Verso, 2006).
8 Gilles Deleuze, 'Wherever They Can See It', *Discourse* 20(3) (1988), p. 35.
9 Deleuze and Guattari, *Anti-Oedipus*, p. 184.

and immediately put himself in harm's way by joining the resistance. He was quickly captured and died en route to a concentration camp. According to Deleuze's biographer, François Dosse, Deleuze's parents never recovered from Georges' death, and Gilles was made to feel insignificant in their eyes because he couldn't match his dead brother's heroism.[10]

Outwardly, at least, Deleuze's academic career followed a predictable path. He went to the 'right' junior schools – Lycée Carnot and Lycée Henri-IV – and studied for his first degree at the Sorbonne, where he proved to be a precocious talent. Badiou writes admiringly of the notice Deleuze was already attracting at this young age.[11] His first book, *Empiricism and Subjectivity: An Essay on Hume's Theory of Human Nature* (1953), was written while he was still a student. Deleuze later repudiated everything he wrote in this period, largely because of its theological themes, but not this book. Deleuze began as he meant to continue because Hume was anything but a safe and predictable choice with which to launch one's career in philosophy. Kant's critique of Hume was considered by most scholars at the time to be definitive, and Hume had been effectively cast into the dustbin of history[12] From these inauspicious beginnings, Deleuze followed a path that, to borrow his own phrase, might best be described as a witch's flight. His next book, which he worked on for eight years, the longest he ever went without publishing something, was on Nietzsche. The fruit of those long labours, *Nietzsche and Philosophy* (1962), is regarded by many as his most important book. It is often credited with sparking French theory's 'return to Nietzsche'. Deleuze overturned the gloomy image of a nihilist Nietzsche and replaced it with a joyous Nietzsche. He also expunged the calumnies of Nietzsche's sister Elisabeth, who tried to recruit her brother's works for the Nazi cause.

Deleuze's Nietzsche is a diagnostician and in many ways this is what he tried to become himself. The books that followed, on Proust and Sacher-Masoch, pursued this idea that great authors can be read

10 François Dosse, *Gilles Deleuze and Félix Guattari: Intersecting Lives* (New York: Columbia University Press, 2010), pp. 88–90.

11 Badiou, *Deleuze*, p. 1.

12 For an account of Deleuze's defence of Hume in response to Kant, see Jeff Bell, *Deleuze's Hume: Philosophy, Culture and the Scottish Enlightenment* (Edinburgh: Edinburgh University Press, 2009).

as symptomatologists. His collaborative work with Félix Guattari makes extensive use of literary texts as diagnostic tools. Beckett, Büchner, Céline, Gombrowicz, Lawrence, Lowry, Nerval, Poe, Sade and countless other writers are called upon as 'seers', Deleuze's word for people who can see past the façade and capture a 'deeper truth'. His first major work using literature in this way was *Logic of Sense*, which he worked on while teaching philosophy at the University of Lyon between 1964 and 1969. In this period he also prepared the requisite two theses for his *doctorat d'état*, *Difference and Repetition* and *Expressionism in Philosophy*, both of which appeared in the watershed year of 1968. Recovering from the removal of a lung, Deleuze did not participate in the events of May 1968. He was in any case ambivalent about its results. He never agreed with the conservative assessment that 'nothing happened', but he was concerned by the manifestation of what he would later call micro-fascism that it seemed to occasion. He was impressed by the fact that such a large number of people, some 10 million students and blue-collar workers, had coordinated their action to show their dissent, but, on the other hand, he detested the factionalism of the so-called *groupuscules*.[13]

Undoubtedly the most important event in Deleuze's career happened in the summer of 1969. At the insistence of a friend and former student from the University of Lyon, he agreed to meet Félix Guattari, a young psychoanalyst and political activist. It proved to be a meeting of true minds. He and Guattari agreed to work together and over the next several months they met, shared ideas and developed a work that was simultaneously a critique and a rethinking of both Marx and Freud (particularly the Lacanian interpretation of the latter) that they proposed to call 'schizoanalysis.' Their first of four collaborations, *Anti-Oedipus*, was published in 1972. It was an immediate sensation in France, where it was generally well received. In the anglophone world it divided opinion quite sharply between those such as Fredric Jameson, who heralded it as a radical intervention, and those such as Perry Anderson, who dismissed it as irrational nonsense. It was, however, the second instalment, *A Thousand Plateaus* (1980), that cemented the place of both Deleuze

13 For a more detailed account of Deleuze's reaction to May 1968, see Ian Buchanan, *Deleuze and Guattari's Anti-Oedipus* (London: Bloomsbury, 2008), pp. 7–19.

and Guattari in the pantheon of the twentieth century's most important intellectuals.

Theorising violence

In his Auschwitz memoir, *The Drowned and the Saved* (1958), Primo Levi distinguishes between two kinds of violence: that which serves a purpose and that which does not. This second kind of violence he speaks of, which he pointedly calls 'useless violence', is the violence of the endless and ultimately senseless indignities that the Nazis imposed on their captives, as though murder were not enough. The tattoo, for instance, which they administered even to people they intended to kill more or less immediately, was a calculated insult to Jewish sensibilities, which prohibit tattooing. Similarly, shaving heads and forcing people to walk to their deaths naked is a useless violence, a pure gratuity. Useful violence, by contrast, is the violence that a governing body determines it must exercise in order to bind a people together and maintain order. In the case of the camps, roll calls and electric fences clearly served a purpose. They imposed order and made escape difficult. Somewhere in between these two orders of violence is something Levi called the 'grey zone'. This is where ethics becomes difficult to determine. As Levi writes, one cannot really pass judgement on the camp collaborators, who simply did what they had to do in order to survive.[14] The existence of the situation is itself an indictment, not just of the Nazis but of humanity itself. In *What Is Philosophy?* (1991), Deleuze and Guattari argue, with reference to Levi's work, that the very existence of grey zones teaches us the shame of being human. And they go on to say that there is no other reason for the existence of philosophy.[15]

Deleuze and Guattari's analysis of violence follows similar lines. It is inherent in the nature of government to exert violence, to enact social repression, but the means and method of that violence vary considerably according to the situation. The third chapter of *Anti-Oedipus*, 'Savages, Barbarians, Civilized Men', is Deleuze and

14 Agamben is surely correct to argue that refugee camps are part of the same spatial order. See Giorgio Agamben, *Means without End* (Minneapolis: University of Minnesota Press, 2000), pp. 37–45.

15 Gilles Deleuze and Félix Guattari, *What Is Philosophy?* (London: Verso, 1994), pp. 106–107.

Guattari's attempt to schematise the various socially repressive apparatuses that have existed throughout history. It is written in a linear fashion, progressing from the so-called 'savage' through the 'barbarian' to the 'civilised', but that is just a matter of convenience. They are careful to insist both that these three apparatuses can and do exist side by side and that one is not necessarily a precursor to the other. Similarly, they are also careful to clarify that the later-appearing forms should not be construed as an improvement on what came before – the civilised form is no less violent than either the barbarian or the primitive forms, even if its methods are less physically brutal. Nevertheless, a trajectory may be discerned in their history. On the one hand, there is the necessary or purposeful violence of primitive peoples, who mobilise pain in order to inscribe government on the skin of the people. On the other hand, there is the unnecessary and purposeless violence of the state, which achieves control over the population by other means. The difference between primitive 'anti-state' modes of government and the so-called civilised state regime is that the latter form does not require our belief either in it or in the god who perhaps licences it. The state controls our situation through regulation. It does not need to inscribe itself on our bodies. And yet it does not trust its regulations; it must deform us too. It does this not only by attacking the body – mutilating us, as Deleuze and Guattari put it – but also by enslaving our subjectivity.

For Deleuze, writing with Guattari and on his own, all social and cultural events and practices are particular to a machine. In this regard, schizoanalysis, the label Deleuze and Guattari applied to their jointly created method, can be summarised in a single question: 'Given a certain effect, what machine is capable of producing it?'[16] Here they follow Nietzsche in thinking humans are constituted as social beings by means of repression:

All the stupidity and the arbitrariness of the laws, all the pain of the initiations, the whole perverse apparatus of repression and education, the red-hot irons, and the atrocious procedures have only this meaning: *to discipline* man [*dresser l'homme*], to mark him in his flesh, to render him capable of alliance, to form him

16 Deleuze and Guattari, *Anti-Oedipus*, p. 3.

within the debtor–creditor relation, which on both sides turns out to be a matter of memory – a memory straining toward the future.[17]

This system of cruelty (as Deleuze and Guattari put it, following Nietzsche) ensures that the organs are 'hewn into the socius' (imaginary body of society) in such a way that 'man ceases to be a biological organism and becomes a full body, an earth, to which his organs become attached, where they are attracted, repelled, miraculated, following the requirements of a socius'.[18] Organs here and elsewhere in Deleuze and Guattari's work are not simply parts of the body; they are the points of contact between the individual and the collective. Take the obvious example of the eyes: as Sartre and Lacan (among others) have theorised, in contemporary society, the eyes are subsumed by 'the gaze', a way of seeing that is primarily social. When we make visual distinctions between genders, races, classes and so on, our eyes are not merely 'seeing' what's in front of them; they are operating according to a set of social principles and conditions. Deleuze and Guattari's social theory attempts to explain how this type of capture takes place. They identify three types of machine – the territorial, the despotic and the civilised – as responsible.

Deleuze and Guattari's thesis is that communities are formed in the same way as subjects: an aggregate of processes of capture gives rise to a 'whole' that in turn acts on its constitutive elements to produce an entity qualitatively different from its component parts. This is why today we can think of ourselves as 'individual' subjects, despite the fact that it is only under very particular social conditions that obtain now in the West that 'individuals' can exist. In brief, their thesis is consistent with the constructivist view that the social 'whole' does not subsume us; it produces us. But it differs from the standard constructivist view of things by maintaining that beneath the surface there rumbles the possibility of change. Desire for Deleuze and Guattari is something like the gene; even under strict regulation it remains capable of mutation and transformation, which is why no regime lasts forever.

17 Deleuze and Guattari, *Anti-Oedipus*, p. 190 (translation modified).
18 Deleuze and Guattari, *Anti-Oedipus*, p. 144.

The territorial machine   Deleuze and Guattari's conception of the territorial machine challenges two of twentieth-century anthropology's paradigmatic assumptions: that the incest taboo is universal and that all social relations are exchange relations. In their view, neither of these hypotheses holds up. Their counter-argument is, firstly, that the incest taboo is an instrument of socialisation that captures desire by forcing it into feeling guilty for imaginary desires; and, secondly, that society is inscriptive not exchangist.

Socialisation in this context implies that desire has been captured and made to function according to the rules of a given society. This does not mean we should look for a single or universal repressing agent. Instead we should search for an affinity or co-efficiency between the subjective desire of persons and the collective desire of social machines.[19] Social machines consist of a combination of two different kinds of relationship between people in groups, according to Deleuze and Guattari: filiation and alliance. The former is linear in composition (uniting father and son to form a lineage) while the latter is lateral (uniting brothers and cousins to form a tribe).[20] The social machine mobilises both types towards its own ends. Each is violent in its own way: there is the violence of the blood ancestry, which haunts us like destiny, and the violence of a lateral bond formed by the extraction of blood.

Rarely if ever mentioned in the secondary literature on Deleuze and Guattari, filiation and alliance are absolutely central to any understanding of the political dimension of their work. Filiation and alliance are likened to 'primitive capital', one fixed (filiative) and the other circulating (in the form of capital or debt).[21] It is the fixed capital of his lineage that gives the chief the right to rule, but he could not maintain his position as ruler nor rule effectively if he did not mobilise circulating capital and form alliances outside his immediate family. Through elaborate feasts and gift-giving, the chief mobilises his wealth to induce others to be in his debt. He thereby converts perishable wealth – for example, food, skins and weapons – into imperishable prestige, namely the mandate to rule.

---

19 Deleuze and Guattari, *Anti-Oedipus*, p. 184.
20 Deleuze and Guattari, *Anti-Oedipus*, p. 152.
21 Deleuze and Guattari, *Anti-Oedipus*, p. 147.

This disequilibrium in the machine is fundamental to its operation.[22] Violence in this system is directed at the threat that arises from within, namely accumulated wealth (i.e., a stockpile of food, skins and weapons), which, if it were allowed to grow, would become capital in the capitalist sense of the word and unleash flows of its own that would neither cement filiative relations nor consolidate alliances.

Potlatch rituals, which often include the deliberate destruction of accumulated wealth either by feasting, festive bonfires or throwing objects off cliff tops into the sea, purposely put a tribe into the debt of its neighbours and at the mercy of the elements, thereby ensuring by power of necessity that all members of the tribe work together to avoid starvation. Tribe members wear the signs of their tribe on their flesh in acknowledgement of this common cause and their individual indebtedness to the tribe for providing for them. Primitive inscription is the instrument whereby the filiative relations of descent are bonded with the mobile alliances of tribe and inter-tribe. Alliances do not derive from filiation. They function as a counterweight to the concentrated power of filiation. By the same token, alliances are not the product of an exchange whereby the chief trades his wealth for allegiance. Rather he must convert his wealth into allegiance. But this is not straightforward, because there is no general model of equivalence – such as money – to enable the calculation. Consequently, the giver tends to give more than is strictly necessary, but has to do so in such a way that the gift-giving ritual makes the gift seem like a theft (what is stolen must be repaid).[23]

This is the purpose of primitive inscription: it transforms the gift into theft and records the ensuing debt on the body of the debtor in the form of a mark of allegiance. But the mark itself is merely mnemonic. It is the process of marking, which is intentionally painful, that performs the real work of social transformation. This is purposive violence in its purest form. The flesh must be torn, not sliced – the rock mustn't be too sharp – and the pain witnessed by select members of the tribe, for it is 'the terrible equivalence between the voice of alliance that inflicts and constrains, and the body afflicted by the sign that a hand is carving in it', that produces the desired socialisation. The pain is 'like the surplus value that the eye extracts, taking hold of the effect of active speech on the body, but also of the reaction of the body insofar as it is acted upon'.[24] The resulting mark attaches a name to a person, and, by forcibly expelling the child from the world of the 'biocosmic', creates a subject whose body and soul have been pledged to the collective. So what brought about the downfall of the primitive machine? 'Some pack of blond beasts of prey', as Nietzsche put it, meaning the founders of the state.[25]

The despotic machine The essential ingredients of the despotic machine (by which Deleuze and Guattari mean the so-called *Urstaat*) were always already present in the territorial machine. But the primitive rituals binding tribe members laterally and vertically prevented them from becoming operational. So the despotic machine remained latent in the primitive machine. In this sense, it can even be said that the territorial machine presupposes the despotic machine.[26] This thesis, which is central to Deleuze and Guattari's account of the despotic regime, is that the state did not come into being in stages. It is not the result of a process of aggregation whereby something begins in a small way and steadily grows into something both larger and different, as in standard accounts of the growth of villages into cities. On Deleuze and Guattari's view of things, the state, like language, was born fully formed.[27] 'The State was not formed in progressive stages; it appears fully armed, a master stroke executed all at once; the primordial *Urstaat*, the eternal model of everything the State wants to be and desires'.[28]

This is only possible – both theoretically and historically – because the despotic machine was virtual, a necessary abstraction.[29] It conditioned both what came before (the primitive territorial machine) and what followed (the modern capitalist machine) but never actually

24 Deleuze and Guattari, *Anti-Oedipus*, p. 189.
25 Deleuze and Guattari, *Anti-Oedipus*, p. 192.
26 Deleuze and Guattari, *Anti-Oedipus*, p. 219.
27 It is worth noting here that Manuel DeLanda's account of Deleuze and Guattari in *A New Philosophy of Society* (London: Continuum, 2006) overlooks this key point altogether and proposes a model of the assemblage that is cumulative rather than instantaneous.
28 Deleuze and Guattari, *Anti-Oedipus*, p. 217.
29 Deleuze and Guattari, *Anti-Oedipus*, p. 220.

existed in its own right. Our experience of the modern capitalist state cannot therefore be used to guide us in our understanding of the despotic machine. It functions differently from its (never extant) predecessor. Indeed, its function is purely theoretical: it is a passage that follows the path of the knight's move, zigzagging from its point of departure to its destination without stopping at any of the points in between. Given that the despotic machine remains abstract throughout this process, it can usefully be described as a 'vanishing mediator' (in Jameson's sense of the word).[30] It is a catalytic agent that enables the transmission of energies between various mutually incompatible social regimes.[31] Deleuze and Guattari insist that the despotic machine is not a transitional stage, but that doesn't stop it from being a mediator of the vanishing type. So how does the despotic machine work?

> The founding of the despotic machine or the barbarian socius can be summarised in the following way: a new alliance and direct filiation. The despot challenges the lateral alliances and the extended filiations of the old community. He imposes a new alliance system and places himself in direct filiation with the deity: the people must follow.[32]

Moses, Saint Paul, Saint John and even Christ are for this reason counted among the despots, according to Deleuze and Guattari, for what their visions entailed was precisely a new alliance with God based on filiation to a chosen people.[33] The despot, or his God, replaces the territorial machine's association with the earth, from which the people are usually said to belong. In doing so, a new social hierarchy is installed with the despot at the top and the villagers at the bottom. Bureaucracy replaces inter-tribal alliance and, most importantly of all, stock is now allowed to accumulate unchecked. Debt is thereby rendered infinite in the form of tribute to the despot that can never be fully or finally rendered – God does not accept one-off final payments.[34]

30 See Fredric Jameson, *The Ideologies of Theory*, vol. 2 (Minneapolis: University of Minnesota Press, 1988), p. 25.
31 Deleuze and Guattari, *Anti-Oedipus*, p. 193.
32 Deleuze and Guattari, *Anti-Oedipus*, p. 192.
33 Deleuze and Guattari, *Anti-Oedipus*, p. 193.
34 Deleuze and Guattari, *Anti-Oedipus*, p. 194.

The despotic machine, like the primitive machine, feared the socially corrosive effects of uncoded flows, particularly the flows of money its merchants unleashed. But, having said that, money is the invention of the state, primarily for the purposes of taxation, by means of which the state rendered debt infinite.

> The infinite creditor and infinite credit have replaced the blocks of mobile and finite debts. There is always a monotheism on the horizon of despotism: the debt becomes a *debt of existence*, a debt of the existence of the subjects themselves. A time will come when the creditor has not yet lent while the debtor never quits repaying, for repaying is a duty but lending is an option.[35]

As with the territorial machine, it is debt that holds the despotic machine together. The difference is that there are no lateral bonds of mutual debt and obligation binding people together. Now they are bound by the fact they all exist under one god.[36]

The civilised capitalist machine   Capitalism only broke free from its latency period (the despotic age) when it appropriated production itself. There is, of course, a whole series of vigorous historical debates as to when precisely this took place, but Deleuze and Guattari are only interested in those debates insofar as they inform the ontological point they want to make about the precise nature of this new machine. Once again their analysis turns on the transformation of the relation between fixed (filiative) and mobile (alliance) stock. For Deleuze and Guattari, the defining contradiction at the heart of the modern capitalist machine, which is nothing less than an obscenity in their view, is the shameful difference in kind between the money of the wage earner and the money of the financier, between a type of money that functions purely as payment (alliance) and money that functions as finance (filiation).

It may be surprising that Deleuze and Guattari should think in such apparently vulgar Marxist terms, but, as they insist throughout *Anti-Oedipus*, contradictions are *not* what bring social systems down (contrary to vulgar Marxism). Rather, they are the dynamic motors of society. Social machines feed off

---

35 Deleuze and Guattari, *Anti-Oedipus*, pp. 197–198.
36 Deleuze and Guattari, *Anti-Oedipus*, p. 198

the contradictions they give rise to, on the crises they provoke, on the anxieties they *engender*, and on the infernal operations they regenerate. Capitalism has learned this, and has ceased doubting itself, while even socialists have abandoned belief in the possibility of capitalism's natural death by attrition.[37]

Capitalism thrives on the crises it induces – Deleuze and Guattari describe this process as 'schizophrenisation', which is why they refer to their methodology as a form of schizoanalysis. Again, it is not the actual economic changes capitalism occasions that are decisive as far as Deleuze and Guattari are concerned. It is the nature of the social machine it unleashes that is crucial.

The capitalist machine has two main characteristics. It stimulates over-production via a radical process of decoding (setting aside all the codes society imposes via culture and tradition), then it retards that over-production by insinuating anti-production into every level of society (creating new hyper-vigilant forms of neo-traditionalism). The primitive territorial machine established the social unit by coding the flows of desire, giving them a precise meaning; the despotic machine unchained these codes but also bonded them to its own regime by over-coding them. It emptied the codes of their sacred content and at the same time spiritualised them (in Weber's sense), making them part of what defined 'good society'. Capitalist decoding evacuates the meaning out of all codes – that is to say, all the rules, regulations, laws, codes of conduct and so forth – rendering them completely arbitrary, or rather purely functional. The codes work, but they have no meaning and require only our obedience, not our belief. Deleuze and Guattari designate this resulting decoded machine 'the axiomatic'.

The axiomatic is unavowable:

there is not a single economic or financial operation that, assuming it is translated in terms of code, would not lay bare its own unavowable nature, that is, its intrinsic perversion or essential cynicism (the age of bad conscience is also the age of pure cynicism).[38]

37 Deleuze and Guattari, *Anti-Oedipus*, p. 151.
38 Deleuze and Guattari, *Anti-Oedipus*, p. 247.

Capitalism is not something we can believe in. In contrast to the territorial and despotic machines, the capitalist machine does not require our belief to function. It nevertheless continues to solicit our belief, but only in order to contain the uncoded flows it unleashes. Capitalism is secular about money but utterly orthodox when it comes to civic order – people are free to believe whatever they like so long as they don't stop buying things. Belief is in this context a form of anti-production, or what Deleuze and Guattari also call the manufacture of stupidity. 'The State, its police, and its army form a gigantic enterprise of anti-production, but at the heart of production itself, and conditioning this production.'[39]

In effect, modern societies are torn in two directions: 'archaism and futurism, neoarchaism and ex-futurism, paranoia and schizophrenia'.[40] What is crucial to understand in all this is that the relations of alliance and filiation that structure all types of society no longer apply to people, as they did in the previous territorial and despotic regimes. In the modern state, these relations apply to money. In this situation, 'the family becomes a microcosm, suited to expressing what it no longer dominates'.[41] The family becomes an object of consumption in the modern system.

Confronting violence in the world

Deleuze's short paper on 'Control Societies' (1995) has received an inordinate amount of attention. This is not to say that it is not important but to stress that his thinking about the contemporary situation is much richer than this work, which was effectively an unrevised conference paper. It is suggestive precisely because it is brief and speculative. His central claim that we have moved on from Foucault's 'disciplinary society' has, perhaps unsurprisingly, been resisted by Foucauldians, who insist that disciplinary apparatuses continue to exist. This misunderstands Deleuze's claim – he simply says that control mechanisms (by which he means axiomatic systems) are steadily overtaking disciplinary mechanisms as the dominant form of social coercion. Deleuze was of the view that Foucault himself thought the same way. We are moving in a direction whereby the

39 Deleuze and Guattari, *Anti-Oedipus*, p. 235.
40 Deleuze and Guattari, *Anti-Oedipus*, p. 260.
41 Deleuze and Guattari, *Anti-Oedipus*, p. 264.

direct monitoring of the person is less relevant than monitoring their digital shadow. Given the revelations of WikiLeaks, this observation now seems irrefutable: privacy has all but disappeared in the twenty-first century: our calls, emails, searches, purchases and so on are being monitored, aggregated and returned to us in the form of 'predictive' marketing.

The disagreement between Foucauldians and Deleuzians with regard to the continued existence of disciplinary apparatuses is a distraction from the real points of difference between the two thinkers, namely their respective positions on power and desire. Deleuze rejected the concept of power, and Foucault rejected the concept of desire. Why? For Deleuze, power was too all-encompassing, too one-dimensional – this isn't just a matter of there being no room left for resistance, since Foucault was quite explicit on this front. Rather it has to do with complexity and the need to think of political allegiances as complicated compounds of mixed ideas, or what Deleuze and Guattari called 'assemblages'. By the same token, Foucault mistrusted desire because it seemed too ephemeral to him. Pleasure was more solid. One could understand pleasure as a motive, whereas desire seemed to be directed at what one didn't have. Here Foucault's lens was rather too Lacanian, and he failed to see that Deleuze and Guattari's concept of desire is far more Kantian than Lacan ever allowed himself to be. For Deleuze and Guattari, desire is a mode of production; it is the process whereby all affects, ideas, emotions, feelings and ultimately thoughts are produced. They only disagree with Kant inasmuch as they are unwilling to dismiss fantasies and hallucinations as 'psychic reality' not worthy of further consideration.

The importance of these points can be seen most clearly in their analysis of fascism in *Anti-Oedipus*. Foucault was so impressed by this analysis that he described the whole book as a handbook for non-fascist living in his preface to the English translation. Foucault rightly observes that 'fascism' in this context not only refers to the events in Germany and Italy during the Second World War but also to an entire way of thinking that has survived the war. He defines it in terms of a love of power, and, speaking to future generations of activists, cautions against it. Given his later rather negative comments about desire, it would seem that Foucault failed to appreciate the degree to which Deleuze and Guattari's analysis of fascism turns on the question of desire. For Deleuze and Guattari, fascism is ultimately a very particular formation of desire, one that seems to beckon its own destruction (a thesis they borrow from Paul Virilio). To begin with, they take up Reich's claim that the German people weren't duped by fascism; they knew what it was, and they wanted it. But then they ask: how is it possible for a people to desire against its interest, for that is finally what fascism amounts to – desire against one's interest. The German people well knew that another war would be a disaster – the memory of the previous war was as fresh as an open wound when Hitler came to power – yet they embraced fascism all the same.[42] Thus, as Foucault recognised, fascism is always within. It is strange that he couldn't see that this meant that fascism is a mode of desire.

Thus we re-encounter Spinoza's question regarding how the masses learn to desire their oppression as though it were their liberation. But what does this mean for thinking about the forces of fascism today? How can we critique fascism without retreating back into questions of ideology or even pure race? From the perspective of desire, what forms of mobilisation are taking place so that people learn to desire that which should otherwise appear suffocating? Deleuze certainly warns us about the dangers of simply retreating back into authoritarian state-centric models. Or, to put it another way, the focus upon authoritarian personalities (of which we can cite many in the contemporary period) distracts us from the broader and more intimate social phenomena of fascism, those manipulated desires, which encourage us to desire power and through which fascistic forms of violence are recreated anew.

Further reading

Bell, Jeff, *Deleuze's Hume: Philosophy, Culture and the Scottish Enlightenment* (Edinburgh: Edinburgh University Press, 2009).

Buchanan, Ian, *Deleuze and Guattari's Anti-Oedipus* (London: Bloomsbury, 2008).

Evans, Brad and Julian Read (eds), *Deleuze and Fascism* (London: Routledge, 2013).

Holland, Eugene, *Deleuze and Guattari's A Thousand Plateaus* (London: Bloomsbury, 2013).

Nail, Thomas, *Returning to Revolution: Deleuze, Guattari and Zapatismo* (Edinburgh: Edinburgh University Press 2012).

Protevi, John, *Life, War, Earth: Deleuze and the Sciences* (Minnesota: University of Minneapolis Press, 2013).

Widder, Nathan, *Political Theory after Deleuze* (London: Bloomsbury 2012).

42 For an extensive account of Deleuze and Guattari's thinking on fascism, see the excellent collection *Deleuze and Fascism*, ed. Brad Evans and Julian Read (London: Routledge, 2013)

8 | JUDITH BUTLER

Jelke Boesten

Biographical details

Judith Butler (1956–) was born in Cleveland, Ohio, to parents of Hungarian and Russian–Jewish descent. She attended Hebrew school, where, as punishment for being 'too talkative' at age fourteen, she engaged in private classes in Jewish ethics at the synagogue. On her own account, Butler's interest in philosophy and ethics stems from this period and formed the beginning of an ongoing career in the fields of queer and gender theory, philosophy, literary theory and arguably, or perhaps increasingly, political theory.[1] Her latest work returns to those early years with a defence of nonviolence and a critique of state violence – particularly of Israel's use of violence – grounded in Jewish ethics. But, before she published *Parting Ways* in 2012, she published eleven single-authored books, six co-authored works, two edited volumes and a range of chapters, articles and interviews – an as yet unfinished *oeuvre* of great diversity within critical social and political theory.

Butler received her BA (1978) and PhD (1984) in philosophy from Yale University on the reception of the philosopher G. W. F. Hegel in France, which formed the basis of her first book, *Subjects of Desire: Hegelian Reflections in Twentieth-Century France* (1987). Since then she has taught at a range of universities in the United States and elsewhere, and currently holds the Maxine Elliot Chair in Rhetoric and Comparative Literature at the University of California, Berkeley. Butler has won many prizes, visiting professorships, honorary degrees and awards, among which recently (2009–2013) was the Andrew Mellon Award, which allowed her to work on a critical theory programme at Berkeley.

---

1 'As a Jew, I was taught it was ethically imperative to speak up', Butler quoted in Aloni Udi, *Haaretz* (24 February 2010), www.haaretz.com/news/judith-butler-as-a-jew-i-was-taught-it-was-ethically-imperative-to-speak-up-1.266243.

Butler gained popular acclaim, and even fame (a rare feat for a professor of philosophy – bar Žižek), for her work on gender: for troubling, untying, deconstructing, denaturalising and undoing gender. Her book *Gender Trouble: Feminism and the Subversion of Identity* (1990) responded to the identity politics of the 1970s and 1980s, in which those who felt marginalised by society claimed a group identity from which to fight for their rights as citizens – as feminism did through a politics of 'sisterhood' and even later with a focus on intersectionality and multiple cross-cutting markers of identity and inequality. The gay liberation movement and the civil rights movements also relied on identity politics as the grounds for collective action.[2] *Gender Trouble*, and many of Butler's writings that came after that (especially *Bodies that Matter* from 1993 and *Undoing Gender* from 2004), unsettle our common understandings of what gender, sex and desire might mean. Butler's analysis denies a direct or natural link between (biological) sex and gender, and thereby undermines the idea that there is such a thing as a collective identity based on gender or sexuality. Butler's troubling of gender as a category aims to destabilise gender identities as in any way given, or even resulting from, biological sex. Rather, Butler sustains, gender is a performance that responds to the expectations and norms of society. *Gender Trouble* was not only theoretically innovative and important but also had very concrete political consequences in that it inspired and legitimised an 'anti-identarian turn of queer politics'.[3] Indeed, Butler became an icon of radical feminism, queer studies and queer politics and a basher of anything perceived as 'common sense' about gender and sexuality.

Butler's work is concerned with the philosophy of *how we become*, considering the social restrictions that govern our imagination, and indeed our consciousness. Thus, while sexual politics might seem far removed from Hegelian and Continental nineteenth- and twentieth-century philosophy, Butler's main sources of analysis were not only Hegel but also Friedrich Nietzsche, Walter Benjamin and Hannah Arendt, and French and German existentialism. In addition, she drew on psychoanalysis (Sigmund Freud, Jacques Lacan, Jacques Derrida); feminist thinkers such as Simone de

2 Moya Lloyd, *Judith Butler: From Norms to Politics* (Cambridge: Polity, 2007).
3 Slavoj Žižek, cited in Lloyd, *Judith Butler*, p. 1.

Beauvoir, Luce Irigaray, Julia Kristeva and Monique Wittig; and of course the sociologist Michel Foucault. In practice, her work on subject formation is very much grounded in thinking about sex, sexuality and gender as well as on considering theoretical notions of subjectivity, subversion and power. Butler's more recent work on 'livable life' extends the idea of the constraining power of normative frameworks in the context of gender to grief and violence. In *Undoing Gender* (2004), livable life as a concept is embedded in the experience of gender and sexuality in a heteronormative society. In *Precarious Life*, published in the same year, Butler expanded the question of livability to an analysis of post-9/11 warfare and grief. Her theoretical work and her conceptual journey tie her ethics and her politics together, as most clearly discussed in *Frames of War* (2009). Her politics seeks to minimise the precariousness of life, the always lingering possibility of the subjection to a suspension or undoing of life. So, while according to some Butler's writings are too far removed from reality (Martha Nussbaum famously ridiculed and dismissed her as the 'professor of parody')[4] or linguistically too difficult (she won a first prize in 1998 for 'bad writing'), there is a real desire for social justice in her thinking.

More recently, Butler's politics with regard to Zionism and the politics of the state of Israel formed the centre of controversy over her work: when she was offered the Theodor Adorno Prize in 2012 for her contribution to critical social theory, a storm of protest emerged because of her – what Gerry Kearns calls – 'geopolitics of identity'. Butler is a staunch critic of Israel and takes an anti-Zionist position vis-à-vis the Israeli state as well as Jewish identity. She partly supports the boycotts, divestments and sanctions movements, and then, in 2012, published *Parting Ways*, a theoretically underpinned defence of a one-state multiple-identities politics. German, Israeli and US Jews who equate anti-Zionism, or even critique of Israel as a state, with anti-Semitism felt that she was not worthy of the Adorno Prize, as a 'self-hating' Jew. But Butler has long defended her right to be critical of the state of Israel, once responding to the then president of Harvard University, Lawrence Summers, that

4 Martha Nussbaum, 'The Professor of Parody', *New Republic* (22 February 1999).

A criticism of Israel is not the same ... as a challenge to Israel's existence ... A challenge to the right of Israel to exist can be construed as a challenge to the existence of the Jewish people only if one believes that Israel alone keeps the Jewish people alive or that all Jews invest their sense of perpetuity in the state of Israel in its current or traditional forms.[5]

Butler's politics, then, is a politics of ethical living and nonviolence in the face of various levels of normative, ethical and state violence and always seems to propose a radical departure from what some persistently construct as common sense.

Theorising violence

In her 2004 book *Undoing Gender*, Butler elaborates on her ideas around subject formation in relation to the normative frameworks that guide our lives. She builds on a Foucauldian bio-political view in order to argue that rules, regulations and norms set out the meanings and limits of physical and social life. Hence norms are enabling, they provide context and regulate our interdependency and they make subject formation intelligible, but they also restrict the possibilities of how life can be lived. Butler refers to the

norms and conventions that permit people to breathe, to desire, to love and to live, and those norms and conventions that restrict or eviscerate the conditions of life itself. Sometimes norms function both ways at once, and sometimes they function one way for a given group and another way for another group.[6]

Norms are fields of power, and they provide the cultural frameworks in which we *become*; through the productive power of repetitive performance, norms provide the implicit standard for *normalisation* – that is, the process whereby the norm 'is acted out in social practice and re-idealized and reinstituted in and through the daily

---

5 Judith Butler 'No, It's Not Anti-Semitic', *London Review of Books*, 25(16) (2003), www.lrb.co.uk/v25/n16/judith-butler/no-its-not-anti-semitic, cited in Gerry Kearns, 'The Butler Affair and the Geopolitics of Identity', *Environment and Planning D: Society and Space*, 31(2) (2013), pp. 191–207.
6 Judith Butler, *Undoing Gender* (New York: Routledge), p. 8.

social rituals of bodily life'.[7] Some norms are of course set in law, and a discussion of law and accountability before the law is Butler's concern in *Giving an Account of Oneself* (2005), as well as in her work on understanding what she calls 'precarity' and war. Many laws that govern gender relations – inheritance law, marriage, paternity and so on – are actually subject forming; they set the limits on what gendered being means. But, at the same time, following Foucault, there is a recognition that many norms that inform our subject formation are not written into law but, rather, are produced and reproduced, owned and maintained by society at large; norms are reproduced by 'regulative discourses'.[8]

Thus Butler asks 'what, given the contemporary order of being, can I be?'[9] Her questions emerges from thinking about gendered subject formation: how (what mechanisms?) are we pushed into being someone according to pre-existing understandings of what it is to be human? What is a coherent gendered being; what counts as a citizen? But she also asks crucial questions about resistance to the hegemonic order: 'What happens when I begin to become that for which there is no place within the given regime of truth?'[10]

This is the point at which the concept of normative violence becomes relevant. On the one hand, Butler sees violence in the restrictions imposed on being – when norms tell us what we can and cannot do at the most personal and intimate level of life, and we are not 'allowed' to become what we might be. But Butler also refers to violence as emerging from that which might happen if one becomes that for which there is no place within a given regime of truth. Those who *become* beyond and outside existing normative frameworks or understandings of truth become unintelligible to wider society and therefore need to be corrected by that society – or eliminated. In *Undoing Gender*, one of her most accessible books, Butler uses a range of examples to underpin her arguments. One of her main examples concerns the intersexed body, which has long been treated as an impossibility. The impossibility or unintelligibility of the intersexed body means that the norm imposes surgical adaptation to become

7 Butler, *Undoing Gender*, p. 48.
8 Michel Foucault, *Discipline and Punish: The Birth of the Prison* (New York: Pantheon, 1977).
9 Butler, *Undoing Gender*, p. 58.
10 Butler, *Undoing Gender*, p. 58.

an intelligible body: a man or a woman, both anatomically as well as socially adapted to conform to prevailing understandings of gendered being.[11] To Butler, intersexuality is not a biological or medical problem, but rather a social problem that is violently policed.

So, with normative violence, Butler points to the violence of the norm – that is, it may or may not be physical violence; it may or may not lead to physical injury. Normative violence refers to violence by restriction and may result in actual physical violence. Normalisation not only justifies such violence but also turns the blame for such violence upon its victim. Those who experience violence in response to their own transgression have provoked it, turning the vulnerability, and thus putative protection against violence, on its head. The perpetrator becomes the victim, the victim the perpetrator. How violence against LGBT people is justified, or how wife-battering or rape of women is often justified, mirrors such an argument whereby violence becomes socially justified, and thus invisible, against the normative framework in which society is immersed. The imposed boundaries of being that provide the parameters of personhood 'make persons according to abstract norms that at once condition and exceed the lives they make and break'.[12] These boundaries of being make certain lives unlivable in specific given social environments – for example, gay lives, divorced lives, intersexed lives or any other lives that transgress the norms set in the socio-political context in which one happens to be born. Only a few are able to turn transgression into subversion, in open resistance to imposed norms, putting their life at stake in order to subvert those norms. So, considering all this, when is life livable?

In her work on the post-9/11 world, Butler uses the same concepts – normative violence, subversion, livable life – to analyse public grief, a line of thought she started in *Undoing Gender*. Her point about the grievability of life is that, by examining our ceremonies of public grief, who is grieved and who is not, we can identify who is seen as included and who is not, who is deserving of a 'lived' life. This implies that those who are not grieved have not lived a life that fits the normative framework. Taking this a step further, Butler asserts that those who are not grieved are subject to culturally viable notions of

11 Butler, *Undoing Gender*, pp. 59–65.
12 Butler, *Undoing Gender*, p. 56.

the human:[13] they do not deserve to be grieved, nor is grief possible, simply because they are non-existent as full human beings in a particular cultural context. Only full human beings can be grieved. As Moya Lloyd emphasises, this is an active process of dehumanisation, which serves political purposes.[14] In *Undoing Gender*, Butler uses the example of the contrast in the second Gulf War between the lives of the thousands of killed Iraqis and the high visibility of public grief over American lives. The second example she uses are AIDS victims in Africa; they are not grieved as full, individual human beings. If anything, they are recognised as a mass of unaccounted-for poor and worthless beings summarised in statistics. Many other examples exist, of course: women and children trafficked and killed in the sex industry, immigrants dying in containers, migrant labourers anywhere, organ 'donors' in remote and poor areas of the world and so on.

The questions Butler poses in *Precarious Life* are 'Whose lives count as lives? Who counts as human? What *makes for a grievable life*?'[15] Her starting point is the personal experience of mourning, the realisation of our own embodiment through the attachment to others – and the possibility of loss. Our physical vulnerability is constituted in 'our being socially constituted bodies, attached to others, at risk of losing those attachments, exposed to others, at risk of violence by virtue of that exposure'.[16] Butler argues that personal loss may feel privatising, 'that it returns us to a solitary situation' and is often seen as depoliticising, but actually shows us the complex constitution of political community, of the 'we' in which we live our lives. Seen in such a way, grief – that is, public grief – is a political act and actively shows patterns of inclusion and exclusion, hence the question: what makes life grievable? Public grief, and the denial of grief, are then political acts that purposefully produce and reproduce an 'us' and 'them'. Butler fails to mention, possibly because it is irrelevant to her argument, that private grief, whether at an individual, family or community level, is still grief and being grieved, and that such 'private' forms of grief have their own political meaning in any

13 Butler, *Undoing Gender*, p. 24.
14 Lloyd, *Judith Butler*, p. 95.
15 Judith Butler, *Precarious Life: The Powers of Mourning and Violence* (London: Verso), p. 20 (emphasis in original).
16 Butler, *Precarious Life*, p. 20.

particular setting. However, for the sake of the argument that grief serves to recognise lived lives in a post-9/11 world, grief is analysed from the point of view of the powerful: the powerful determine whom to grieve and whom to deny grief to, thereby showing the world whom they perceive as important – that is, US soldiers yes, Iraqi civilians no. Thus hegemonic orders and hierarchies can be analysed through the politics of public grief as a 'mechanism of power through which life is reproduced'.[17]

By asking which lives are publicly grieved, Butler asks us to look at which lives are not grieved. She asks us to make visible the dehumanising effect of othering that makes violence possible and life ungrievable. Butler seeks to highlight the gross injustice of the violence perpetrated in the name of conceptions of humanity that are not only exclusive but also seem to legitimise a continuous violence upon certain groups of people. This continuity of violence, Butler suggests, is the result of a perception of bodies that will not die – an endless battle against a perceived other. The ungrievable life is not necessarily dead but is undone, is made 'unreal'.[18] This means that violence 'fails to injure' and that such lives must be negated again and again. The rhetoric that portrays the war on terror as an unending war does just that: it pronounces the 'infinity of its enemy'.[19] In this context, the result is a generalised racism that is rationalised through a discourse of threat and self-defence: the dehumanisation of all lives that vaguely look Arab and Muslim.

State of emergency, state of exception   In discussing the so-called global war on terror, Butler asks how power is used to make possible excesses such as those perpetrated in Guatánamo Bay.[20] She uses Foucault and Giorgio Agamben to discuss the suspension of law and the use and abuse of sovereignty in the creation of an infinite enemy. In her essay 'Indefinite Detention',[21] she discusses Foucault's

17 Judith Butler, *Frames of War: When Is Life Grievable?* (London: Verso, 2009), p. 1.
18 Butler, *Undoing Gender*, p. 33.
19 Butler, *Undoing Gender*, p. 34.
20 This is based on her essay 'Indefinite Detention' in *Precarious Life*, pp. 50–100. In *Frames of War*, Butler discusses the meaning of the abuses at Abu Ghraib and their visuality.
21 Butler, 'Indefinite Detention'.

understanding of governmentality, in which political power manages and regulates populations. Foucault saw governmentality as characteristically late modern, in that it is clearly distinct from earlier understandings of state power – that is, sovereignty. Butler points out that sovereignty has come back, emphasising that it has not replaced governmentality but that 'sovereignty, under emergency conditions in which the rule of law is suspended, [re-emerged] in the context of governmentality with the vengeance of an anachronism that refuses to die'.[22] Writing in the context of the discussion about Guantánamo Bay, Butler observes how the concentration of power in the executive branch of the US government suspended the separation of powers and vested judiciary power in the president – suggesting a 'return' to the times when a monarch had sovereign power over his or her subjects. Yet, Butler asserts, decision-making about who gets a trial and who will be detained indefinitely lies with 'managerial officials', which suggests that they make these decisions within a field of governmentality. Modern governmentality is bound up with contemporary sovereignty in the officials who rule via delegated power, deciding over life and death in a paralegal setting. Agamben notes that sovereignty, understood as an extra-legal authority, establishes conditions for the exceptional suspension of law – that is, the sovereign has the power to grant exceptional status. In doing so, the state creates a 'para legal universe that goes by the name of law'.[23] This does not mean that the bureaucrats who exercise power over life and death do so in a context of lawlessness but that they operate on the basis of an *exception to* the law. Such a construction of a state of emergency, Butler suggests, makes all life vulnerable to be assigned exceptional status – that is, to be stripped of rights in an indefinite state of emergency. This vulnerability we have in relation to others is what Butler calls the precarity of life.

It is sovereignty that makes possible the state of emergency and the suspension of law. As Butler asserts, 'the law is suspended in the name of the "sovereignty" of the nation where "sovereignty" denotes the task of any state to preserve and protect its own territoriality'.[24] Of course, the notion of nation and territory helps to set the parameters

22 Butler, 'Indefinite Detention', p. 54.
23 Butler, 'Indefinite Detention', p. 61.
24 Butler, 'Indefinite Detention', p. 55.

for exclusion, for defining the other. The process of imagining the nation shows that the 'other' can be internal and that a nation does not necessarily include all who live in its territory. Nevertheless, sovereign power does cover territory, and the suspension of law within its territory means that those who are not perceived as forming part of the nation enter a freefall, are suspended themselves and become vulnerable to the visions of the infinite enemy – in other words, they become a state of exception.

Butler calls upon Agamben to reflect on the meaning of the infinite enemy. According to Agamben, the state that invokes its sovereign power to declare an exception to the law, or an emergency, strips certain lives from their 'ontological status as subjects'.[25] Agamben distinguishes between the political being and bare life. The political being, or *bios*, is a life valued with rights, a citizen. Bare life, or *zoē*, consists of life, but not rights. It is life devoid of value, life that does not deserve to live. It is life as biological minimum.[26] Bare life is the exception, a situation where law does not rule or protect. Butler is interested in bare life in the context of the suspension of law in cases that fit the vision of the infinite enemy according to a sovereign state, in this case 'animated by an aggressive nostalgia that seeks to do away with the separation of powers'.[27] Bare life refers to those kept in indefinite detention: it is life, but ungrievable, unreal, disposable in the political context as perceived by the sovereign power in a state of emergency.

The notion of bare life is powerful as it invokes processes of dehumanisation and the possibility of horrendous violence perpetrated upon bodies. However, bare life is a philosophical notion that describes a state of ontological suspension; it does not allow for subtleties that may keep people at the margins of the *polis*, in the permanent uncertainty of becoming subject to such extreme exception. Agamben himself, in his discussion of crimes against humanity in general and the holocaust in particular, urges that

> instead of asking the hypocritical question of how crimes of such atrocity could be committed against humans we must investigate

25 Butler, 'Indefinite Detention', p. 67.
26 Giorgio Agamben, *Homo Sacer: Sovereign Power and Bare Life* (Stanford: Stanford University Press, 1998).
27 Butler, 'Indefinite Detention', p. 61.

carefully the juridical procedures and deployments of power by which human beings could be so completely deprived of their rights and prerogatives that no act committed against them could appear any longer as a crime.[28]

A careful questioning of the normative truths that guide and restrict life helps to visibilise violence that is otherwise tolerated, normalised and, in some cases, legitimised. This is a powerful approach to analysing forms of violence and dispossession in the everyday, such as gender-based violence, as well as the analysis of the mechanisms of institutional violence related to vectors of inequality such as race, class, sexuality, religion, age, nationality and indeed gender.

Considering this analysis of the power of governance and normativity in subject formation, Butler is concerned with the possibility of agency. In *Giving an Account of Oneself*, she discusses the opacity of the self, given our emergence as related to the other. Does this opacity, or the limits of self-knowledge, not make it impossible to be a responsible and accountable human being? Underlying questions here seem to concern what is accountability? And what is punishment for one's actions if one's actions cannot be fully accounted for? *Giving an Account of Oneself* is an attempt at understanding the capacity for agency in a world that, according to Adorno, depends on self-identity as opposed to universalism. Butler interrogates the nature of agency and how agency is shaped by the normative framework in which we live (i.e., society) and the personal relations we have (i.e., with the 'other'). How can we become people of good judgement, or, as she formulated it in her Adorno Prize lecture, how 'can one lead a good life in a bad life?'[29] Considering the prevailing normative and institutional restrictions upon being, 'the flourishing of diverse people is simply impossible and many are denied the possibility of a good life',[30] but that, however precarious, does not undo agency. To be an accountable human being, or to exercise a 'politics of a good life', is then, in Kearns' words, about 'biopolitics, nonviolence, and the preconditions of mutual flourishing'.[31]

28 Agamben, *Homo Sacer*, p. 171.
29 Judith Butler, 'Can One Lead a Good Life in a Bad Life?', Adorno Prize lecture, *Radical Philosophy* 76 (2012), pp. 9–18, cited in Kearns, 'Butler Affair', p. 191.
30 Kearns, 'Butler Affair', p. 191.
31 Kearns, 'Butler Affair', p. 192.

In her book *Parting Ways: Jewishness and the Critique of Zionism*, Butler expresses the ideals of nonviolence and mutual flourishing in a carefully argued critique of Zionism and the politics of Israel. Butler draws on Arab intellectuals (e.g., Edward Said and Mahmood Darwish) and also on Jewish intellectuals (e.g., Benjamin, Arendt and two Israeli post-Zionist intellectuals, Amnon Raz-Krakotzkin and Yehuda Shenhav) in order to develop a sophisticated argument against a political, philosophical or religious adherence to Zionism, because it is Israel's ethno-nationalist Zionism that justifies and promotes state violence against Palestinians. Butler's 'geopolitics of identity'[32] draws heavily on her earlier ideas about subject formation in relation to 'others', but from a perspective that makes one's identity imaginable, possible, mouldable. She advocates binationality, or postnationality, whereby being part of a nation-state is inherently beyond the nation-state. Citizenship should be beyond religion, race, ethnicity or any identity markers that separate and prevent solidarity: both Palestinians and Jews in Israel should be able to feel Jewish, or Palestinian, as well as part of a compound identity that includes the 'other' and the other's rights and responsibilities. The only way to overcome the ethno-nationalist violence that persists in and dominates over Israel–Palestine is for each party to recognise the other as worthily human and to incorporate that worthy 'other' into their own identity. The reliance on Jewish ethics and Jewish intellectuals to make this argument allows her to foreground the objection that the historical and religious or ethnic nature of identity is already given and therefore justifies the ethno-nationalist separation from the 'other' – culturally and physically. Butler argues that co-habitation, binationality and diasporic identity are at the heart of Jewish ethics, and hence ultimately this disqualifies Zionism as in any way central to Jewish identity.

Parting Ways is very much a critique of the criticism that anti-Zionism equals anti-Semitism – or Jewish self-hatred. But some progressive critics also reject Butler's objectives: Chaim Gans[33]

---

32 Kearns, 'Butler Affair', p. 192.
33 Chaim Gans, Review of Butler, *Parting Ways: Jewishness and the Critique of Zionism*, in *Notre Dame Philosophical Reviews* (13 December 2012), https://ndpr.nd.edu/news/36335-parting-ways-jewishness-and-the-critique-of-zionism.

and Miro Daniel Garasic,[34] in similar vein, argue that Butler's understanding of Zionism is too limited and that her end goal precludes her theoretical investigation; hence, the activist argument informs the philosophy, instead of the other way around. This, then, leads to unattainable or unrealistic proposals with regard to a binational Israeli–Palestine future. However, Butler does consider her own proposals somewhat utopian, and considers this also a necessary political counterpoint against prevailing Zionism:

> Although it is commonly said that a one-state solution and an ideal of binationalism are impractical goals ... it is equally true that a world in which no one held out for a one-state solution and no one thought anymore about binationalism would be a radically impoverished world. I take it that we might say the same about pacifism. It might be discredited as lacking all Realpolitik, but would any of us want to live in a world in which pacifists no longer existed? What kind of world that would be?[35]

Indeed, whether particular utopian outcomes are attainable or not, Butler's politics of nonviolence demands a continuous questioning and unsettling of the everyday common sense that feeds into a violent social and political world of precarious living. And such questioning of who we are and what we do – that is, not only giving an account of oneself but also actively striving for a socially just world – informs her political activism.

Confronting violence in the world

Considering the above, there should be no doubt about Butler's contemporary relevance, be that for thinking about gender and sexuality, subject formation, (state) violence or contemporary modes of resistance. Her contributions to the fields of critical social and political theory are immense. But her political views are not only theoretical; her theories undoubtedly aim to unsettle the way we tend

34 Miro Daniel Garasic, Review of Butler, *Parting Ways: Jewishness and the Critique of Zionism*, in *Plurilogue* (8 October 2013), www.plurilogue. com/2013/10/parting-ways-jewishness-and-critique-of.html
35 Judith Butler, *Parting Ways: Jewishness and the Critique of Zionism* (New York: Columbia University Press, 2012), p. 28.

to see the world, and thereby help to transform violent or restrictive social–political configurations of power. Butler's understanding of subject formation as an inherently interdependent social process that is highly influenced by prevailing normative frameworks constitutes the groundwork for understanding both how norms restrict what we can be and how we can formulate agency and hence resistance. If violence itself is an important part of how and what we become, then our response to violence is potentially the source of change. Nonviolence, Butler asserts, is not necessarily useful or possible as a principle in all circumstances, but must be identified and considered each and every time that 'non-violence makes a claim on us'.[36] It is our ability to challenge normative frameworks that is subversive; responding with violence to violence will entrench violence as norm, while it is the aggression in ourselves that demands the ethical necessity of nonviolence. Hence nonviolence is a struggle against normative or normalised structural or contingent violence, as well as a struggle against the rage within.

Butler is increasingly outspoken about the politics of the world we live in, and actively opposes the common sense of war and oppression that has emerged after 9/11. Again, these positions are not only theoretical; her critique of Israel's Zionist politics has concrete consequences, generates very real opposition and causes her to be barred from public lectures as well as to withdraw from them. According to Kearns, she is known for taking a stand, supporting activist groups and supporting others in developing particular standpoints.[37] He tells how Butler 'has been exemplary in her support of others working out how to respond to' the calls for boycotts of academic institutions in Israel that do not explicitly support an end to the occupation, advising Slavoj Žižek to talk at a film festival but as a participant rather than as a funded invitee, and advising Sarah Schulman, in connection with Schulman's intent to talk about LGBT studies at Tel Aviv University, to talk to grassroots activists and Palestinian communities instead of to speak formally at the university. Butler's advice was 'to use the academic boycott [as] an education tool'.[38]

---

36 Butler, *Frames of War*, p. 165.
37 Kearns, 'Butler Affair', p. 196.
38 Kearns, 'Butler Affair', p. 196.

At the heart of Butler's activism lies the idea of solidarity, as opposed to, or contrasted with, activism that is based on identity. Butler's adherence to solidarity reaches back to her understanding of Jewish ethics, as a commitment to social justice and ethical living in recognition of the 'other', but also to her analysis of how our vulnerability is grounded in mutual precarity. For Butler, the livability of life is not a medical or even a biological issue, but a social and political one: our physical vulnerability is ultimately conditioned by social and political exposure, and that means that life needs to be protected against ever-looming precariousness. It is that interdependency, as Butler states, that 'establishes our vulnerability to social forms of deprivation'.[39] Thus a Leftist politics of solidarity should start by recognising our individual precarity as a shared problem, even if it is clear that not all are equally exposed to such precarity.[40] Butler insists that precarity is politically relevant and should be translated into policy:

> Policy needs to understand precariousness as a shared condition, and precarity as the politically induced condition that would deny equal exposure through the radically unequal distribution of wealth and the differential ways of exposing certain populations racially and nationally conceptualized, to greater violence.[41]

Of course, the practice of a 'normative commitment to equality … to minimize precariousness in egalitarian ways',[42] would need to be preceded by a political understanding of how policy – and geopolitics – actively sustain unequal exposure to precarity. And this, then, is part of Butler's political activism: she has spoken at several 'Occupy' encampments and 'Slut Walk' events, allying herself to contemporary social movements fighting against hegemonic neoliberal, sexist and racist logics.

Butler understands neoliberal governance as a global economic system that exposes the majority of the vulnerable to the capital-

39 Judith Butler and Athena Athanasiou, *Dispossession: The Performative in the Political* (Cambridge: Polity, 2013), p. 5.
40 Butler, *Frames of War*, p. 28.
41 Butler, *Frames of War*, p. 28.
42 Butler, *Frames of War*, pp. 28–29.

accumulating few and also shapes modes of rationality, morality and subject formation that make precarity seemingly legitimate, and even the only way forward. The common sense of neoliberal economic practice rises far beyond economics: it undermines and reshapes democratic relationships.[43] Such a Foucauldian understanding of contemporary neoliberal governance is essential for our understanding of the relation between feminism, contemporary gender relations and neoliberalism, and has been debated widely.[44] But Butler is not known for her analysis of neoliberal governance (her partner, Wendy Brown, is, of course). Nevertheless, the debate between Nancy Fraser and Butler in the late 1990s in the journal *Social Text* about the economic/cultural distinction was important in understanding feminist forms of resistance to neoliberalism.[45] Fraser differentiates between the economic and cultural spheres in order to suggest ways to overcome the harm that contemporary neoliberalism causes – redistribution has to be accompanied by a politics of recognition in order to improve well-being and reduce vulnerability and exploitation. Butler, in turn, finds that reasserting the economic/cultural distinction has a political function that works to dismiss political claims as 'merely cultural'. What is at stake here, ultimately, is the question of how the neoliberal logic has become internalised by the very agents of resistance we tend to look for in order to subvert the logic: are contemporary feminists indeed

---

43 Judith Butler, 'Fiscal Crisis or the Neoliberal Assault on Democracy?' *Greek Left Review* (November 2011), http://greekleftreview.wordpress.com/2011/11/12/1718.

44 Michel Foucault, *The Birth of Biopolitics: Lectures at the Collège de France 1978–79* (Basingstoke: Palgrave Macmillan, 2008). Foucault's neoliberalism as governance has found resonance in many left-leaning analyses of contemporary economic and political regimes, such as Wendy Brown, 'Neoliberalism and the End of Liberal Democracy', *Theory & Event* 7(1) (2003), https://muse.jhu.edu/article/48659; Aihwa Ong, *Neoliberalism as Exception: Mutations in Citzenship and Sovereignity* (Durham, NC: Duke University Press, 2006).

45 Nancy Fraser, *Justice Interruptus: Critical Reflections on the 'Postsocialist Condition'* (London: Routledge, 1997); Judith Butler, 'Merely Cultural', *Social Text*, 52/53 (1997), pp. 265–277; Nancy Fraser, 'Heterosexism, Misrecognition, and Capitalism: A Response to Judith Butler', *Social Text*, 52/53 (1997), pp. 279–289. See also Joanna Oksala, 'Feminism and Neoliberal Governmentality', *Foucault Studies*, 16 (2013), pp. 32–53.

agents of capitalism, as Fraser has asserted?[46] Now Butler never has been much of a mainstream feminist, actively opposing the idea that there is a singular identity on which to base such activism, so her interpretation of resistance to the mainstream – neoliberal and/or feminist – will perhaps always be troubling.

In a series of conversations with Athena Athanasiou published in 2013, Butler elaborates on her understandings of precarity, dispossession and resistance. The conversations intend to engage with the concrete violence of contemporary forms of dispossession and vulnerability from a leftist-queer-feminist perspective, engaging with the logics of how the contemporary geopolitics of dispossession within the neoliberal order – 'accumulation by dispossession', as David Harvey calls such logic[47] – are what Butler has analysed as moralised forms of violence. In *Precarious Life* and *Frames of War*, Butler interrogates the ways in which war is framed using moralistic arguments around the liberation of others, who are, simultaneously, discarded as human beings; the conversations with Athanasiou focus on the one hand on the analysis of dispossession without resorting to counter-arguments around what is lost and, on the other hand, they are intended to reflect on contemporary protest. In these protests[48] Butler sees the survival of democracy and collective action in the face of overwhelming dispossession and injustice as loosely defined social movements occupying public space. This collective voicing of discontent with the powers that be may be an attractive vision of global crowds defending 'our collective precarity and persistence in the making of equality and the many-voiced and unvoiced ways of refusing to become dispossible'.[49] Alternatively, such an interpretation reflects Butler's tendency to utopian visions in relation to the violence of the political: perhaps not entirely realistic, but certainly inviting us to the struggle.

46 Nancy Fraser, 'How Feminism Became Capitalism's Handmaiden – and How to Reclaim It', *The Guardian* (14 October 2013), www.theguardian. com/commentisfree/2013/oct/14/feminism-capitalist-handmaiden-neoliberal.
47 David Harvey, *The New Imperialism* (Oxford: Oxford University Press, 2003).
48 Both Butler and Athanasiou tend to group all protest of the past five years or so together under the banner of 'new protest', from the revolutions that started in Tunisia to Occupy Wall Street and the London riots of summer 2011.
49 Butler and Athanasiou, *Dispossession*, p. 197.

Further reading

Butler, Judith, *Frames of War: When Is Life Grievable?* (London and New York: Verso, 2009).

Butler, Judith, *Gender Trouble: Feminism and the Subversion of Identity* (New York and London: Routledge, 1990).

Butler, Judith, *Parting Ways: Jewishness and the Critique of Zionism* (New York: Columbia University Press, 2012).

Butler, Judith, *Precarious Life: Powers of Violence and Mourning* (London and New York: Verso, 2004).

Butler, Judith, *Undoing Gender* (New York and London: Routledge, 2004).

Butler, Judith and Athena Athanasiou, *Dispossession: The Performative in the Political* (Cambridge: Polity, 2013).

Chambers, Samuel A. and Terrell Carver, *Judith Butler and Political Theory: Troubling Politics* (Milton Park: Routledge, 2008).

Lloyd, Moya, *Judith Butler: From Norms to Politics* (Cambridge: Polity, 2007).

Schippers, Birgit, *The Political Philosophy of Judith Butler* (Milton Park: Routledge, 2014).

9 | ZYGMUNT BAUMAN

Keith Tester

Biographical details

Zygmunt Bauman (1925–) was born to a Jewish family in Poznań in Poland. With his parents he escaped the 1939 Nazi invasion of Poland by fleeing to the Soviet Union.[1] In 1943 he joined the Polish army and fought on the Eastern Front. He ended up taking part in the siege of Berlin in 1945. After the Second World War he remained in the Polish army but in 1953 he was expelled during an anti-Semitic purge. He then reinvented himself. He started a career in academia and studied at the University of Warsaw with two of the most important figures in twentieth-century Polish sociology and political thought: Stanisław Ossowski and Julian Hochfeld. In 1963 Hochfeld was offered a post at UNESCO in Paris, and Bauman assumed his chair at Warsaw, becoming professor of sociology. He remained at the University of Warsaw until 1968, when he was expelled during another anti-Semitic purge. He was one of six professors to be accused by the Polish state and media of 'corrupting youth', and was forced into exile. In 1971 he became professor of sociology at the University of Leeds in the United Kingdom.

This potted biography immediately raises a question: *why* was Bauman expelled? Of what did his alleged corruption of youth consist? It wasn't *just* because Jewishness was then identified by the communist state as a kind of 'cosmopolitanism' threatening to

---

1 As Bauman rarely talks about his life, there have been discussions previously about whether this move to the Soviet Union was flight or deportation. While probability suggests forced deportation to Siberia by the Soviets is more likely, historical research shows this not to be the case for Bauman and his family. For information about deportations, see Maciej Sikierski and Feliks Tych, *Widziałem aniola śmierci: Losy deportowanych Żydów polskich w ZSSR w latach II wonjny światowej* (Warsaw: Rosner & Wspólnicy, 2006).

Poland, as had previously been the case in 1953.[2] It was also because of the positions he adopted in his work. It is quite important to have insight into Bauman's intellectual concerns when he was in Poland because they run through to his subsequent work.[3] By the early 1960s, Bauman was associated with what the state called revisionism and the West called Marxist humanism. Marxist humanism made an argument that diametrically opposed the official Stalinist theory that history is made by law-like processes scientifically revealed and understood by dialectical materialism. Marxist humanism instead stressed human creativity and action.[4] Bauman's work in the 1960s was typical in this regard and emphasised praxis: the creativity of human agency and the creation of the human world. From this perspective, praxis is also a practical declaration of what it means to be human – it is to be free and is therefore in conflict with the managerial interests of the state. The state is identified as a giant apparatus seeking to manipulate human creativity and responsibility so that we are all subjects who *act* – and ideally from the point of view of the state also *think* – in regulated and orderly ways.[5]

These positions can be seen to carry through to the book that is the focus of attention of the first part of this chapter. Before the late 1980s, Bauman was largely unknown, certainly in the British academic world in which he had been working since his arrival at Leeds. This ignorance began to abate when he published *Legislators and Interpreters* (1987), one of the first attempts by a sociologist to think seriously about the then influential postmodernity debate. But the ignorance completely disappeared with the publication of

---

2 For an engaging and deep insight into communist Poland's relationship with Jewishness, see Marci Shore, *The Taste of Ashes: The Afterlife of Totalitarianism in Eastern Europe* (London: Windmill Books, 2014).

3 In other words, it is important always to remember that Bauman did not first start writing in the late 1980s – he has a Polish history, too, and the work for which he is known cannot be understood sufficiently deeply if the Polish roots are not acknowledged; see Keith Tester, *The Social Thought of Zygmunt Bauman* (Basingstoke: Palgrave, 2004).

4 For some of the best contributions to Marxist humanism, see the essays in Leszek Kołakowski, *Marxism and Beyond: On Historical Understanding and Individual Responsibility*, trans. Jane Zielonko Peel (London: Pall Mall, 1969).

5 Zygmunt Bauman, 'Image of Man in the Modern Sociology (Some Methodological Remarks)', *Polish Sociological Bulletin*, 1 (1967), pp. 12–21.

Modernity and the Holocaust in 1989.[6] The second part of this chapter surveys Bauman's essays responding to 9/11.

Theorising violence

Prior to 1989 and Bauman's contribution, sociologists did not talk about the Holocaust. The sociological orthodoxy had already – and easily – settled accounts with it. The Holocaust was identified as either just another – albeit terrible – instalment in the history of the persecution of Jews or the deed of pathologically evil deviants, or it was identified as a throwback to a condition from which the rest of us had been freed thanks to the civilising process.[7] *Modernity and the Holocaust* was important because it refused any of these rather easy 'explanations'.[8] It put the Holocaust at the centre of the understanding of modernity. As Bauman put it, the Holocaust does not at all stand to one side of the main story of modernity; rather it is better treated as '*a significant and reliable, test of the hidden possibilities of modern society*'.[9] In *Modernity and the Holocaust*, Bauman sees the Holocaust as a window through which we can see modernity; it sharpens the vision of aspects of modernity. As he wrote:

> The Holocaust was an outcome of a unique encounter between factors by themselves quite ordinary and common ... the possibility of such an encounter [of the ordinary factors leading

6 *Modernity and the Holocaust* was actually quite shattering. I can vividly remember reading it at the time, and, although it sounds stupid to say so now, actually being shocked and startled that sociology could talk about important things. The book did not just set an agenda – it opened minds.

7 Zygmunt Bauman, *Modernity and the Holocaust*, 2nd ed. (Cambridge: Polity, 2000), p. 3. In this chapter, all citations of this book are of the second edition; it is identical to the first edition except for the addition of an extra couple of chapters at the end.

8 It should be noted that Bauman's *Modernity and the Holocaust* thesis has generated considerable debate. Some authors have pointed to the longer processes for the violence, of which the 'bureaucratic' element was more of a subsequent outcome. Others would still maintain that 'historic fascism' was an aberration or failure of modernity. It is also noted that Bauman's work is more indebted to Adorno and Horkheimer than it acknowledges. There are compelling arguments to challenge these. While there are numerous volumes that deal with the broader debates on the causes of genocide and mass violence, a very accessible account is provided by Martin Shaw in *What Is Genocide?* (Cambridge: Polity, 2015).

9 Bauman, *Modernity and the Holocaust*, p. 12 (emphasis in original).

to a very extraordinary result – the Holocaust] could be blamed
to a very large extent on the emancipation of the political state,
with its monopoly of means of violence and its audacious
engineering ambitions, from social control – following the step-
by-step dismantling of all non-political power resources and
institutions of self-management.[10]

The main theme to be pulled out of this passage is clear: the Holocaust
was a product of ordinary and common factors. The factors leading
to the Holocaust were not unique or an aberration from modernity.

Bauman is a sociologist, but he is not a sociologist who does what
most sociologists do. It is very rare to find statistics in his work, and,
if they are there, they are given in passing and purely for illustrative
purposes. His work is light on empirical evidence (and none of what
there is can stake a claim to originality), and he rarely carries out
literature reviews in order to contextualise his arguments. Instead
Bauman's work operates through suggestive metaphors to make us
think. The metaphor he offered in order to clarify and stimulate
thought about the political state in modernity is that of the 'gardening
state'. Let's think with the metaphor – but also think all the time of
the Holocaust.

What is a gardening state? Well, quite simply, just think of what we
do when we garden. When we garden, we take a plot of land and we
impose our own design upon it. Nature, or what is found, is assumed
to require intervention if it is going to be able to meet the demands
we impose upon it. We have the design; the land itself does not have
it. We impose it, and we then engage in practices to ensure that the
design eventually appears in the ground. We engage in practices to
make the two coincide, and we believe that, without our imposition
of order, without us going around rooting up the weeds, the garden is
going to collapse into chaos and become completely unruly.[11]

Now Bauman argues that modernity can be understood as a
gardening project in precisely this way: 'Modern culture is a garden
culture. It defines itself as the design for an ideal life and a perfect

10 Bauman, *Modernity and the Holocaust*, p. xiii (emphasis in original).
11 Bauman first offered the metaphor of the gardening state in *Legislators and
Interpreters: On Modernity, Post-modernity and Intellectuals* (Cambridge: Polity,
1987), pp. 51–67. It is used to help us think about the Holocaust in Bauman,
Modernity and the Holocaust, pp. 91–93.

arrangement of human conditions. It constructs its own identity out of distrust of nature.' Bauman continues to say of modern culture: 'In fact, it defines itself and nature, and the distinction between them, through its endemic distrust of spontaneity and its longing for a better, and necessarily artificial, order.'[12] So modernity, for Bauman, is built on the historical presumption that order is neither natural nor inevitable. Rather, order has to be created and imposed upon an unruly world. The state is the gardener that imposes order on its territory. Anything that is out of place, anything that does not fit the order, is subject to either or both of two forms of treatment. It might be *assimilated* into the design, or, if it is defined as a weed, it is more likely to be *uprooted* and *annihilated*. 'If garden design defines its weeds, there are weeds wherever there is a garden. And weeds are to be exterminated.'[13] The garden is tidied up by getting rid of everything that is defined as having no legitimate place within it, because, if left to prosper, those elements would become a danger to the orderly scheme of things. With this argument it is possible to see some of the debts that Bauman's work owes to Mary Douglas' *Purity and Danger* (1966).[14] What the gardening state is doing, therefore, is engaging in a completely purposive and deliberate activity of tidying up the human world. It's not that the human world needs tidying up of itself; it only needs tidying up in terms of the ideal of the orderly world. The human world is made to fit the order imposed upon it. Bauman identifies gardening as the typical practice of the Nazi state. There is nothing unique about this; all modern states do it. The only difference is that the Nazi state operated in – and created – a situation in which there were no social, cultural or institutional brakes on its ambitions. Consequently the Nazis took gardening to its logical conclusion: 'The Holocaust is a by-product of the modern drive to a fully designed, fully controlled world, once the drive is getting out of control and running wild.'[15]

But what is the means of gardening? How is the gardening carried out? If the gardening metaphor is extended, it can be argued that the state goes about its business in much the same way as I go about

---

12 Bauman, *Modernity and the Holocaust*, p. 92.
13 Bauman, *Modernity and the Holocaust*, p. 92.
14 Mary Douglas, *Purity and Danger: An Analysis of the Concepts of Pollution and Taboo* (London: Routledge & Kegan Paul, 1966).
15 Bauman, *Modernity and the Holocaust*, p. 93.

gardening. I do what the final plan demands and seek to do it as efficiently as possible. Action is carried out according to principles and procedures of instrumental rationality. Here Bauman's argument begins to run parallel to Weber.[16] The practice of gardening is essentially the practice of a Weberian rational bureaucracy. As Bauman put it: 'It so happened in Germany half a century ago that bureaucracy was given the task of making Germany *judenrein* – clean of Jews.'[17] This Weberian rationality operates according to two principles. Firstly there is the legitimacy of the ends. All action becomes defined as a means to an end. In this case all action is a means to the end of establishing the orderly garden. Secondly, and consequently, any specific instance of action is morally neutralised, and, indeed, the actor merely becomes a cog in a much bigger machine that is concerned only to deliver the desired end as quickly and as well as possible. The bureaucracy will be all the more efficient where the political state has been emancipated from having to take other considerations, such as democratic accountability, into account and can therefore dictate what 'must be done', what orders must be obeyed. Where it has monopolised power, the state is able to establish what has to be done and is also able to silence any dissenting voices. Instrumental rationality requires institutions. Institutions ensure that the ends are pursued with rigour and efficiency. An action isn't good or bad; it is efficient or inefficient:

> Bureaucracy is programmed to seek the optimal solution. It is programmed to measure the optimum in such terms as would not distinguish between one human object and another, or between human and inhuman objects. What matters is the efficiency and lowering of costs of their processing.[18]

This activity is also carried out, as Weber put it, without regard to persons.[19] The emotions of the actor are irrelevant; the point is to carry out an action instrumentally and efficiently. The identity of

16 Compare the discussion of bureaucracy in Bauman, *Modernity and the Holocaust*, with the foundational one in Max Weber, *From Max Weber: Essays in Sociology* (London: Routledge & Kegan Paul, 1948), pp. 196–266.
17 Bauman, *Modernity and the Holocaust*, p. 104.
18 Bauman, *Modernity and the Holocaust*, p. 104.
19 Weber, *From Max Weber*, p. 215.

the victim does not matter either – they are just the object of the bureaucratic process. The human consequences of the instrumental rationality of the Holocaust are explored in novels and films such as *The Garden of the Finzi-Continis* (1962), where the audience is encouraged to identify with the Jewish characters and think through what is slowly yet inexorably happening to them, thanks to process and not their own actions.

According to Bauman's explanatory metaphor, it was gardening practices of this order that made the Holocaust possible as both ambition and act. As soon as this point is made, the impact of Bauman's approach can be felt. Where conventional academic narrative persuades through accumulation, Bauman's metaphorical approach turns the attempt to understand the Holocaust into a punch. As Bauman makes it possible to see, from the point of view of its perpetrators, the Holocaust was actually an activity of tidying up the world, tidying up a world that did not fit the neat categories of order. That tidying up was done by identifying the groups that did not fit the neat categories and getting rid of them, pulling them out, annihilating them. The violence of the Holocaust was, in part, *aesthetically* inspired. 'Modern genocide is ... meant to bring about a social order conforming to the design of the perfect society.'[20]

But how was it possible to get men and women to go about the business of the Holocaust? A significant part of the answer to this question has already been glimpsed in Bauman's debt to Weber. But Bauman pushes the point further. He tackles the question of how it was possible for people to work in the bureaucracy of genocide and still sleep at night. His answer is that the Holocaust could be perpetrated because, through instrumental rationality, the state was able to dismantle the moral sensibility of actors. The action of individual actors was made 'adiaphoric'. The word adiaphoric comes from the debates of medieval theologians. Something was defined as adiaphoric when the Church had no view about it, when the Church was indifferent about it. Bauman argues that instrumental rationality is a generator of the adiaphoric. Instrumental rationality makes some actions *indifferent*: 'neither good nor evil, measurable against technical (purpose-oriented or procedural) but not moral values'.[21]

20 Bauman, *Modernity and the Holocaust*, p. 91.
21 Bauman, *Modernity and the Holocaust*, p. 215.

In the specific circumstance of the Holocaust, there are three ways in which the actions of the political state were rendered adiaphoric in relation to any possibility of social control. But once again the point needs to be made that here the Holocaust reflects possibilities of modernity itself. The conditions exploited by the prosecution of the Holocaust were quite common and ordinary.

Firstly, through instrumental bureaucratic action, there is a stretching of the distance between an action and its consequences. With this stretching, the action is taken out of the moral sphere and the action of itself does not have moral consequences.[22] A prime example of this situation is provided by the case of Adolf Eichmann, the actor who organised the railway system that took the victims to the camps. Eichmann of course became famous because of his trial in Jerusalem, a trial that spurred Hannah Arendt to think through the question of responsibility for genocide.[23] One of the odd aspects of Bauman's discussion of the Holocaust is that it does not significantly deal with the questions Arendt poses even though they are, albeit in a philosophical frame, not far removed from his own sociological investigations. Eichmann's defence was twofold. He claimed, firstly, to have simply tried to do his job to the best of his abilities and, secondly, that his job required him to arrange transport logistics. It was not up to him, he said, to raise doubts about what freight the trains were carrying and what happened to it. What Eichmann did was distant from the hell of the camps, even though the camps would have been empty without his skills with a railway timetable. There was a stretching of a distance, then, between his action and its consequences. Eichmann, like everybody else in the bureaucratic system, according to Bauman, was placed in an 'agentic' state; we all become agents acting in a chain, and our actions are neither good nor evil. They are simply instrumental in the maintenance of a chain stretching far beyond us, either efficient or inefficient.

Secondly, according to Bauman, action is rendered adiaphoric because the objects of action – in the case of the Holocaust, gypsies, gays and primarily Jews – were put into a position from which they could not challenge the actors. The objects of action, the victims,

22 Bauman, *Modernity and the Holocaust*, pp. 215–216.
23 Hannah Arendt, *Eichmann in Jerusalem: A Report on the Banality of Evil* (London: Penguin, 1977)

were denied a presence in social interaction; they were denied a participatory role. At the most extreme, this denial meant putting the 'objects' of action totally outside the normal everyday sphere of social relationships. According to Bauman, this strategy

> stretched from the explicit exemption of the declared enemy from moral protection, through the classifying of selected groups among the resources of action which can be evaluated solely in terms of their technical, instrumental value, all the way to the removal of the stranger from routine human encounter.[24]

Although Bauman himself does not make the connection explicit, this strategy of making others indifferent is embodied in the establishment of ghettos cut off from wider surroundings and relationships.

Thirdly, Bauman identifies how the victim as the object of action (as something to which things are done and that is prevented from acting on its own accord) is destroyed as a self.[25] In other words, the victim as object becomes amenable to being treated, from the point of view of the bureaucracy, as a *thing*. The wholeness of the person who has become a victim is parcelled up into a series of traits or behaviours, 'no one of which can conceivably be ascribed moral subjectivity'. Bauman continues

> Actions are then targeted on specific units of the set, by-passing or avoiding altogether the moment of encounter with morally significant effects … As it were, the impact of narrowly targeted action on the totality of the human object is left out of vision, and is exempt from moral evaluation for not being a part of the intention.[26]

For instance, if there is not enough food to feed all of the people in a ghetto, a bureaucratically efficient solution to the problem is

24 Bauman, *Modernity and the Holocaust*, p. 236.
25 This point links back to Bauman's humanism and, more precisely, to his commitment to praxis. If the processes of *adiaphorisation* entail the impossibility of free action, they also imply the destruction of humanity itself. *Adiaphorisation* prevents someone from expressing their free creativity and, therefore, their humanity.
26 Bauman, *Modernity and the Holocaust*, p. 216.

quickly to reduce the number of hungry people there. All the time this instrumental rationality is upheld, there is no need to think about what has happened to those hungry people who have all of a sudden disappeared – they become a problem to be dealt with by someone else in the bureaucratic machine.

According to Bauman, this is how the Holocaust could be prosecuted and indeed how the prosecutors could sleep at night. The implication of this approach is to deny the validity of arguments by people such as Daniel Goldhagen or indeed, in sociology, Norbert Elias, which suggest that there is something specifically German about the Holocaust and that only the Germans could have carried it out.[27] Of course Bauman holds Germans to be guilty for the Holocaust, but he refuses to concede that they were guilty *because* they were Germans. Rather, they were guilty because they were modern and pursued to their end point some of the possibilities of modernity. As he put it:

> I never said (nor thought) that Germany is not guilty of the
> Holocaust crime. I only said, and repeatedly ... that Germany's
> guilt is not a German affair, that Germany did what it did
> because of what it *shares* with the rest of us, not because of what
> makes it different from us.[28]

Those of us who are not German are put back on the hook of thinking about our own action and responsibility. The Holocaust becomes the problem of everyone who is, to whatever degree, *modern.*

From the Holocaust to 9/11   Bauman's understanding of the Holocaust through the explanatory metaphor of gardening presumes what he was later to refer to as the modern trinity of the nation, state and territory.[29] Within this modern trinity, the nation is identified with a territory,

---

27 Norbert Elias, *The Germans: Power Struggles and the Development of Habitus in the Nineteenth and Twentieth Centuries* (Cambridge: Polity, 1997); Daniel Jonah Goldhagen, *Hitler's Willing Executioners: Ordinary Germans and the Holocaust* (London: Abacus, 1997).

28 Zygmunt Bauman and Keith Tester, *Conversations with Zygmunt Bauman* (Cambridge: Polity, 2001), pp. 85–86.

29 Zygmunt Bauman, 'The Fate of Humanity in the Post-trinitarian World', *Journal of Human Rights*, 1(3) (2002), pp. 283–303.

and they are both managed and protected by a state. The three are mutually reinforcing and legitimating. To put this into the terms of the metaphor, the garden is the territory, the plants are the nation and the gardener is the state. If this trinity is borne in mind, it is possible to appreciate the message Bauman draws from 9/11. It was a moment that revealed that the modern trinity is no longer dominant.[30]

If the Holocaust was a window on modernity, 9/11 can be seen as a screen upon which it is possible to see the dramas of the 'liquid modern world'. The liquid modern world is one in which nothing is certain, nothing can be assumed to last, one in which everything is presumed to be fleeting. Liquid modernity, for Bauman, is the world in which we now live.[31] Thus, 9/11 is a screen on this world:

> The terrorist assault on the best-known landmarks of the globally best-known city, committed in front of as many TV cameras as the modern media can gather in one place, easily won the stature of globally legible signifier which other events, however dramatic and gory, could not dream of.[32]

It was the moment of what Bauman calls the 'symbolic end to the era of space'.[33] The era of space was identified with the state possession of territory, and the demarcation of that territory as *ours* not *theirs*. Bauman identifies the era of space with military technologies such as moats and walls, right up to the Berlin Wall.[34] According to Bauman, 9/11 shows that that era of space is no more:

> The events of the 11th September made it obvious that no one can any longer cut themselves off from the rest of the world, no one can hide from blows and blows can be plotted. Places no longer protect.[35]

30 For a discussion of the political implications of the collapse of the modern trinity, see Zygmunt Bauman, 'Theresa May's Plans for Terror Suspects Undermine Democracy', *Guardian* (31 January 2014), www.theguardian.com/commentisfree/2014/jan/31/theresa-may-terror-democracy-british-citizenship-security.

31 Zygmunt Bauman, *Liquid Modernity* (Cambridge: Polity, 2000).

32 Zygmunt Bauman, 'Reconnaissance Wars of the Planetary Frontierland', *Theory, Culture & Society*, 19(4) (2002), p. 81.

33 Bauman, 'Reconnaissance Wars', p. 81.

34 Bauman, 'Reconnaissance Wars', p. 81.

35 Bauman, 'Reconnaissance Wars', p. 82.

Bauman says that space and distance no longer offer protection from the violence of the world out there. Indeed there is no longer a world *out there*. It is always *right here*. This was the truth revealed by 9/11. Or, as Bauman put it,

> The events of 11th September made it obvious that no one can any longer cut themselves off from the rest of the world ... no one can hide from blows, and blows can be plotted from however enormous a distance.[36]

This is an interesting comment because, apart from its explicit content, it shows how Bauman develops his analyses by drawing on a range of material usually ignored by social and cultural theorists. In this case the remark about it being impossible to hide from blows seems to betray a debt to a point previously made by Milan Kundera. Kundera announced that the old philosopher's dream of unified humanity had been achieved. However, the philosophers thought the dream would be achieved in a moment of global peace whereas, as Kundera points out, it has actually been brought about by the possibility of global destruction – there is no longer any escape. Or, in Bauman's terms, there is no longer any space.[37] Bauman goes as far as to talk about a condition of 'mutually assured vulnerability'.[38]

So we can see 9/11 as a screen on the condition of 'mutually assured vulnerability'. In this world everywhere now is a frontier: 'The global space has assumed the character of a frontierland. In the frontierlands, ability and cunning count for more than a stack of guns. In the frontierlands, fences and stockades mark intentions rather than realities.'[39] They mark the intention to put up barriers against the world rather than the reality of such isolation now being quite impossible. There are no firm boundaries separating the inside from the outside, the safe from the dangerous. Instead, and as 9/11 showed, anywhere in the world can now be at the frontier of violence. The room I am sitting in now could be, as could the one you are occupying. We might be vulnerable on the frontier *right now*.

36 Bauman, 'Reconnaissance Wars', p. 82.
37 Milan Kundera, *The Art of the Novel*, trans. Linda Asher (London: Faber & Faber, 1988).
38 Bauman, 'Reconnaissance Wars', p. 82.
39 Bauman, 'Reconnaissance Wars', p. 83.

According to Bauman, this has implications for conflict perpetrated by states. Conflict has stopped being an activity through which states try to protect themselves by securing space, and instead war has become a probing, exploratory activity. War is about probing the risks to which we are subject in order to establish to what and to whom we are vulnerable. Consequently this is a world that is typified by what Bauman calls 'reconnaissance battles'. Once wars were fought to win space, but, in this era of the reconnaissance battle,

> units are not sent into action in order to capture the enemy territory, but to explore the enemy's determination and endurance, the resources the enemy can command and the speed with which such resources may be brought to the battlefield.[40]

These battles are about managing the risk implied by the enemy, and they are not about conquering territory.

When Bauman discusses reconnaissance battles, he inevitably raises the questions 'who fights them?' and 'who takes part in these battles?' He argues that reconnaissance battles are fought by what he calls 'floating coalitions' that come together according to 'confluent enmities'. 'In the frontierland, both alliances, and the frontlines that separate enemies are, like the adversaries themselves, in flux … As far as coalitions go, there are no stable marriages – only admittedly temporary cohabitations of convenience.'[41] As soon as that enemy has been dealt with, the coalition will dissolve – it is *liquid*. A good example of this is provided by the 2012 action against Libya. The forces that came together in this particular performance of the international community were a floating coalition that broke up as soon as that action ceased. But there is a paradox. The reconnaissance battles are fought by the floating coalitions, but these floating coalitions *have* to come together because the global world is under-regulated. There are no institutions that have the capacity to be global actors. Bauman argues that these very floating coalitions enhance and exacerbate the under-regulation and under-institutionalisation of the global world. As Bauman put it:

---

40 Bauman, 'Reconnaissance Wars', p. 88.
41 Bauman, 'Reconnaissance Wars', p. 85.

Keeping the coalitions 'floating' or 'shifting' is itself one of the paramount factors contributing to the perpetuation of the frontierland nature of global space. The strategy of temporary coalitions of transient interest, allied to the concomitant avoidance of firmly institutionalized structures empowered to illicit permanent obedience to universal rules, and to resistance against the establishment of long-term, mutually binding and authoritatively supervised commitments – stands between the present-day frontier land and any prospect of replacing it with a global, politically serviced and controlled order.[42]

In other words, the international community is a floating coalition that actually denies the very possibility of there ever being an international community, and we are always living on the frontier. There are no safe havens any more; we cannot withdraw from the frontier land; we are all in danger in the globalised world.

Confronting violence in the world

The work of Zygmunt Bauman is significant and important because it refuses to see violence as a philosophical or intellectual problem. Bauman instead emphasises how violence has victims and perpetrators. Put another way, violence is something that men and women exactly the same as us experience and carry out. Violence is neither abnormal nor the product of pathology. Violence then is not an abstraction – and neither therefore should it be abstracted from the historical and social conditions in which is it experienced and carried out. This is the importance of Bauman's implication of differences between the gardening strategies that underpinned the Holocaust and the universal frontier that exploded on our television screens on 9/11. The conditions of violence are historically variable. Consequently it can be seen how Bauman's remarks on violence are not at all intended to be the last word on the subject. With his metaphorical approach, Bauman is seeking to encourage and inspire his readers to think about the violence of their world for themselves. His work is best approached as the intimation and stimulation of our own work rather than as a body of answers to be upheld. This is, after all, a point that is implicit to the principle of praxis that was so

42 Bauman, 'Reconnaissance Wars', p. 86.

important to his humanism, and from which he has never departed. Bauman's work on violence – precisely because it is metaphorical, essayistic and frequently light on evidence – is concerned to encourage us to take responsibility for our own understanding of the violence we might endure or, more worryingly, very easily perpetrate.

Further reading

Bauman, Zygmunt, *The Bauman Reader*, ed. P. Beilharz (Oxford: Blackwell, 2001).

Bauman, Zygmunt, *Modernity and the Holocaust*, 2nd edn. (Cambridge: Polity, 2000).

Bauman, Zygmunt, 'Reconnaissance Wars of the Planetary Frontierland', *Theory, Culture & Society*, 19(4) (2002), pp. 81–90.

Bauman, Zygmunt, *Thinking Sociologically* (Oxford: Blackwell, 1990).

Bauman, Zygmunt, *Wasted Lives: Modernity and Its Outcasts* (Cambridge: Polity, 2003).

Bauman, Zygmunt and Leonidas Donskis, *Moral Blindness: The Loss of Sensitivity in Liquid Modernity* (Cambridge: Polity, 2013).

Bauman, Zygmunt and Keith Tester, *Conversations with Zygmunt Bauman* (Cambridge: Polity, 2001).

10 | PAUL VIRILIO

Mark Lacy

Biographical details

Paul Virilio (1932–): son of an Italian communist father and a French mother; childhood in occupied Brittany; a young man involved in the events of May 1968; academic career in Paris observing the dangers of the Cold War as a university professor; a life in retirement observing the high-speed twenty-first-century networked society of terror, crisis and 'globalisation' from an apartment in Nantes, on the coast of Brittany.

These events, often cited in accounts of Virilio's life, appear to inform and shape the preoccupations of his writings, writings that began in the 1960s and have continued through to the second decade of the twenty-first century. Painting a picture of Virilio that draws out the connections between his experience of European history in the twentieth century and his writings provides a compelling narrative. Indeed, Marianne Brausch has built a series of interviews with Virilio on his life and work around the dates 1940, 1950, 1960 and 1980, a narrative or story with an almost cinematic edge: wartime childhood; youthful revolt in 1968 (after which he had to escape to Brittany); the life of the radical and provocative Parisian academic during the Cold War writing books with bold titles such as *Speed and Politics*, *Lost Dimension* and *Negative Horizon*.

This almost cinematic edge to his biography might explain a new generation's attraction to his work: Virilio lived through interesting times.[1] Yet there is clearly more to the interest in Virilio's work than what seems like the ever-present fascination with radical politics in Paris during 1968 or curiosity about a childhood in France during war and occupation. In the often disorientating worlds of

---

1 For example, the fashionable *Vice* magazine conducted an interview with Virilio: Caroline Dumoucel, 'Paul Virilio' (3 September 2010), www.vice. com/en_uk/read/paul-virilio-506-v17n9..

'liquid modernity' that people find themselves in – shaped by new technologies, news crises, new fears and what can feel like an age of perpetual insecurity and uncertainty – thinkers such as Virilio have an aura of authority and legitimacy that other 'experts' or 'authority figures' might lack. But this is not an aura of authority that is official, corporate or institutional. Throughout his career, Virilio has been free to pursue his 'messy' interests – architecture, military history, cinema, geopolitics, information technology, philosophy, cities, art – inside the university system but *outside* clear academic territories and disciplinary borders, a nomadic approach that has allowed him to examine how all aspects of life in the modern world are shaped by our histories of violence.

Virilio has lived through key moments in our history, and – in a time of what he calls the 'information bomb', our constant bombardment with news and information – new generations feel that thinkers like Virilio can help us understand the world, by drawing our attention to what we might see as part of the normal order of things, the things we become habituated to, to help us grasp the significance of the way the world is changing, to identify the trends – technological, economic, social, geopolitical – that might shape our lives in the future. In a time when those who govern us appear to have too much control over us – and too little control over the consequences of the policies deployed to govern and shape the world – a thinker like Virilio feels like someone to whom we should listen.

A common criticism of Virilio is that his writings on politics, society and security are overly pessimistic, unrelentingly bleak about the human condition and the modern world. On this view, he is unable to escape from the trauma of a childhood shaped by war and occupation. Like the English novelist J. G. Ballard, who as a child during the Second World War was imprisoned in an internment camp in Shanghai, Virilio realised at a young age that the 'world around me was just scenery': a young boy watching the power and speed of industrial war transform and control his world, as if the world around him had all the permanence of a film set.[2] As a young researcher after the war, he realised the fragility of the architectures and policies that were designed to create an Atlantic wall of defence: the bunkers that

2 Paul Virilio and Marianne Brausch, *A Winter's Journey* (Calcutta: Seagull Books, 2011), p. 21

he would obsessively explore on the coast he grew up on (as a boy he drew pictures of the bunkers that he would pass on to the resistance), taking photographs, examining the policy documents that shaped their construction. During his childhood, Virilio didn't simply come to the realisation inevitable in most adolescent experience that the adults were not always in control, didn't always make the right decisions, didn't always act responsibly or humanely: Virilio realised that the material world – the world of buildings, towns, cities – was potentially as fragile and transitory as a film set.

In the twenty-first century, Virilio sees fragility and insecurity in the possibility of the 'integral accident' – the accident that could emerge from inside our complex, connected and networked society. Virilio's account of the world is brutal, anxious, troubling – a vision that some critics describe as 'apocalyptic'. Claude Parent describes his former colleague in the project *Architecture Principe* (1966) as Mr Catastrophe.[3] But I will suggest that we need to pay attention to the etymology of the word 'apocalyptic' when we describe Virilio as an apocalyptic thinker, a thinker who leaves us with a hopeless and fatalistic perspective on the world collapsing into disorder or what Jean Baudrillard – one of Virilio's Parisian peers – described as 'exponential instability'.[4] This awareness of the world as a potential film set that could be torn down also left Virilio with the sense that a different world can be reimagined and redesigned.

From what we can pick up from interviews, Virilio's journey into adulthood was not straightforward. He worked as an artist–craftsman. He went to Algiers as a draftee. He studied architecture and philosophy. He played a role in the events of May 1968, part of the occupation of universities, teaching students about different ways to think about architecture and war. But he wasn't the young Marxist-influenced Parisian rebel, certain in his revolutionary desire. One can imagine him surrounded by young men and women rebelling against their privileged bourgeois upbringings. But, as the child of an Italian communist, his rebellious desire took on different forms. Surrounded by his radical peers, Virilio held on to his Catholicism. His work continued to be shaped by his religious beliefs, his concern with

---

3 Edwin Heathcote, 'The Oblique World of Claude Parent', *Financial Times* (31 May 2014), p. 2.
4 Jean Baudrillard, *The Illusion of the End* (Cambridge: Polity, 1994).

the poor, his anxiety about human arrogance and hubris regarding technology, and the geopolitical strategies that are designed to control and improve the world and its inhabitants – but strategies that have a tendency to contribute to the production of chaos and catastrophe.

One of his closest friends was the poet George Perec, who had experienced the loss of both his parents during the war. His writing and poetry were about finding a new way of describing the world around him, as if the events of the war had made all previous ways of writing appear indulgent and redundant.[5] Like Perec, Virilio was searching for a new way of writing and radical new forms of architecture (as we see with his *Architecture Principe* project with Claude Parent in the 1960s), not simply as a reaction to a century that had been fractured by war in Europe but out of a sense that we needed new concepts and terms (chronopolitics, endo-colonisation, integral accidents, dromology) to make sense of the technological and geopolitical changes that were transforming all aspects of life in the twentieth century.

Although there is a great deal of thematic overlap across his work, I think it is possible to divide Virilio's writings into four core areas: technology, acceleration, and global politics and security (*Speed and Politics, The Original Accident, The Futurism of the Instant*); cities and architecture, technology, and security (*Bunker Archaeology, City of Panic, Lost Dimension*); art, technology and (geo)politics (*Unknown Quantity, Native Land, The Accident of Art, Art and Fear, War and Cinema*); and the interviews and short essays aimed at the more general reader (*Landscape of Events, Desert Screen, Crepuscular Dawn, Politics of the Very Worst, Pure War*).

As I have already suggested, Virilio is part of a generation that sought to develop new ways of writing in order to defamiliarise the world around us, to challenge the ways we have been taught to think about progress, technology and politics. For some readers, Virilio's style of writing might provoke lines of thought that are exciting (and disturbing), changing how they see the world around them; other readers might find some of his work too poetic, too 'essayistic' and 'Continental'. So a useful place to begin reading Virilio is the interviews, in which some of the clearest articulations of his research

5 George Perec, *Of Species and Spaces and Other Pieces* (London: Routledge, 2008).

and ideas are found. The interviews in *Pure War* (1983) are the comprehensive overview of his work, but *Crepuscular Dawn* (2002) is equally useful, especially in terms of his thinking on the post-Cold War world. *Landscape of Events* (2000) and *Desert Screen* (2005) are very accessible and wide-ranging collections of essays. But after the interviews and essays, *Speed and Politics* (1986) is arguably the book with which to begin a voyage through Virilio's work, to be followed by *War and Cinema* (1989) and *Bunker Archaeology* (1975). This 'trilogy' captures the range and diversity of Virilio's approach, setting out the key concepts in his work, highlighting a method that draws together a diverse range of 'evidence' and 'case studies' in order to disrupt our perception of the world as it has been taught to us, to leave us with new questions about the world around us.

In terms of the use of Virilio's work by scholars in security studies, international politics and political science, James Der Derian, Michael Shapiro and Timothy W. Luke were the first wave of scholars to really begin to explore what Virilio's writings could contribute to our understanding of geopolitics and security in the post-Cold War world: Der Derian has attempted to place Virilio on the terrain of what can often be a very conservative discipline through his editing of *The Virilio Reader* (2006) and his books *Anti-diplomacy: Spies, Terror, Speed and War* (1993) and *Virtuous War: Mapping the Military Industrial Media Entertainment Network* (2001), along with his provocative documentary film on the paranoia and uncertainties of post-Cold War geopolitics, *Project Z* (2012).

Theorising violence

In 2011, Microsoft produced a short film titled 'Productivity Future Vision'.[6] It depicts how people will get things done 'at work, at home, and on the go' in five to ten years. The film follows a businesswoman visiting Johannesburg. All parts of her trip are made as efficient as possible by the various networked technologies that she is surrounded by – the glasses that translate language in this new city, the various systems that enable her pre-emptive checking-in on route to the hotel (with staff shown her picture and informed of her preferences before she arrives), the smartphones and tablets that enable her to interact with her family in their 'smart', networked

6 www.microsoft.com/office/vision.

house. We see what productivity and creativity look like in the second decade of the twenty-first century, watching a global team interacting enthusiastically on a project through their on-line interactions.

The film could be viewed as an element in what Virilio describes as the 'propaganda of progress', the optimistic depictions of the future that we often find in corporate advertising and in economic forecasts on growth in the coming century. For Virilio, the propaganda of progress that surrounds us is the promise of a better world to come, brought to us through new and improved technology. In the Microsoft film we see how technology can bring us together at the same time as we live more global, deterritorialised lives (the business traveller who is able to interact with her family remotely); we see how safe, clean and efficient the world can become.

The propaganda of progress suggests that the modern age is a time of perpetual improvement in the human condition. There are 'setbacks' (financial crises, unnecessary wars, the resurgence of fascist political movements) – but there will be less of them, and we will become better at managing them. There will continue to be conflicts over identity and territory, remnants from history, but these are problems we are 'working out of the system' on the path to a world of perpetual peace. When violence is deployed to tackle threats to the order and stability of a global society, the response will be shaped by a responsible use of force that attempts to minimise the risk to both civilians and military personnel through the use of technologies that allow the possibility of humane war-at-a-distance, war that is cleaner and more precise. We are just at the beginning of a 'force transformation' or 'revolution' in military affairs that will erase violence and brutality from the human condition. In our everyday life we can feel the propaganda of progress every time we pull out our new smartphone or tablet. We can touch progress. We can *feel* the rapidly evolving technology that will improve the human condition.

The propaganda of progress shows us a world where the inequality and suffering integral to the world economy will be overcome. There has never been a better time to be the global poor. Not only are there new employment opportunities but also living conditions are improving through advances in medicine and education. The globalisation of the middle-class way of life is transforming cities across the planet. The financial markets will learn to manage the type of risk-taking that leads to crisis. Multicultural societies will learn how to negotiate the problems of tolerance and difference in moments of social tension and conflict. We *learn* from our mistakes in war, economics, and religious and social conflict. That is what the liberal democracies do. They allow for a process of reflection to take place. Mistakes are made – but the mistakes are investigated and agonised over. This is an important component in the *resilience* of liberal capitalist society.

But, to return to the Microsoft film, what is missing in this film, which is – as I am suggesting – an example of 'propaganda of progress'? What don't we see? What is left out of sight? Throughout his work, Virilio is concerned with perception – how technology changes our perception of the world (how, for example, the hand-held camera changed our perception of the modern city or the battlefield); how the images and news stories of a 'frightening' otherness shape our perception of the world and other people; how objects (and peoples) are made to disappear in our perception of the world; how we become habituated to certain ways of seeing. My sense is that what is missing in the Microsoft film illustrates one of the core anxieties that has run through Virilio's work since the 1970s – a theme in his work that one can miss if one moves too quickly on to the problems of speed, technology and geopolitics in his writings.

As we drive from the airport to the hotel, some viewers might ask: what is life like outside the hyper-controlled and efficient environments that the business traveller is moving through? Where are the poor? Have the slum areas that you might see out of the window been transformed? Or what about the street kids, who might knock on the window of your taxi? There are no signs of the excluded (or the 'disappeared'). The only signs of the poor are on the underground rail system. We see what looks like a Bangladeshi, Indian or Pakistani man playing a musical instrument. But the man we see is not sitting *in* the underground – we see him on a screen (it is intimated that he can see us, although this is left rather uncertain). This is what charity and poverty look like in Microsoft's vision of the global networked society: poverty at a safe distance. We can make a contact-less payment to a poor person – who is not simply begging but providing us with entertainment – in a distant territory. But, apart from this encounter, the poor and excluded have disappeared in the Microsoft film – either disappeared through their inclusion (growth and progress have generated employment) or simply left out of view (because our technologies and policies to keep the poor at a distance will be so much more efficient).

If reality is a film set, then the reality in the Microsoft film is one where the many technologies that are making the set function are kept carefully out of view. Since the beginning of his work on politics, war and architecture in the 1960s, Virilio has been interested in the various ways policymakers, police and architects create cities and societies where the poor – the potentially dangerous multitude – are managed and controlled: managed and controlled in a way that we often do not notice or pay attention to, tactics that can remain invisible to us, tactics that are seamlessly integrated into everyday life. In this sense, Virilio's work can be understood as a history of control in society. This is a key theme in books such as *Speed and Politics, Lost Dimension* (1983), *Negative Horizon* (2005) and *City of Panic* (2005).

The history of urban planning and the future of cities in a time of technological, economic and political change was an important concern for the generation of French intellectuals and activists, such as Guy Debord and Jean Baudrillard, who experienced the events of May 1968 in Paris. Virilio was interested in how cities such as Paris had been designed to limit and control urban violence in times of unrest. While critical tipping points can be avoided through fear of imprisonment and through the shaping of the ideological 'habitat', there are moments when control can break down. For Virilio, the city – more than the factory – is the critical terrain of revolutionary politics:

> The revolutionary contingent attains its ideal form not in the place of production, but in the street, where for a moment it stops being a cog in the technical machine and itself becomes a motor (machine of attack), in other words a producer of speed.[7]

Virilio is interested in attempts to shape and control the motor of attacks, sources of urban disorder.

The control of urban space ranges from the design of city streets (the desire to prevent blockades – and facilitate the movement of

---

7 Paul Virilio, *Speed and Politics* (Los Angeles: Semiotexte, 2006), p. 29.

police and armies – through the widening of Parisian streets during the nineteenth century) through to the more everyday attempts to control circulation in the city (from subtle but uncomfortable innovations in the design of park benches through to the less subtle studs on pavements designed to deter rough sleepers).[8] Virilio is interested in the management of circulation by the modern state. In terms of our histories of violence, the ability to move troops across a territory by train transformed the potential scale and destructiveness of modern war.[9] The challenge for the state is to control and 'modulate' all the forms of circulation that 'speed up' in the modern age. The state, Virilio suggests, becomes a *brake*: it wants objects and peoples to move but it wants to be able to control movement and circulation. At the same time, the control of circulation is intimately connected to the production of transparency: the state needs to be able to *see* what's in circulation. In an essay titled 'The Big Night' (2010),[10] Virilio writes about the importance of street lights in the development of modern Paris, the city of *light*. The modern state is concerned with making the urban terrain transparent for police and citizens in order to see what is going on, to reduce the danger of the darkness. The use of street lights was vital in terms of policing and safety but also in terms of the city as a space of consumerism, extending the possibilities for people to live and spend in the city.[11] In the twenty-first century, the dream is to make the whole planet as transparent as possible for the military gaze, a global vision machine that closes in on the details of everyday lives anywhere on the earth (or in cyberspace) in order to make threat assessments and risk analyses – and maybe even to hunt and kill at a distance.

While there are anxieties about the extent of the state's management of circulation and transparency (e.g., the public outrage witnessed in London during 2014 over the use of studs to deter homeless sleepers, and global unease about surveillance and the global war on terror), Virilio's concern is that limits can become more porous in

---

8 Selena Savić and Gordon Savičić, *Unpleasant Design* (Rotterdam: Gloria, 2013).

9 Reviel Netz, *Barbed Wire* (Middletown: Wesleyan University Press, 2004), p. 8.

10 Paul Virilio, *A Landscape of Events* (Cambridge, MA: MIT Press, 2000).

11 Wolfgang Schivelbusch, *Disenchanted Night: The Industrialization of Light in the Nineteenth Century* (Berkeley: University of California Press, 1988).

times when populations and policymakers inhabit what he describes as the 'administration of fear' (the constant anxiety over terrorism or crime, the background noise to everyday life, fear as an environment): Virilio is interested in how the politics of security comes to corrupt politics and society, through a process he describes as 'endo-colonisation', the security state turning inwards.

The liberal optimist will argue that the benefits of economic growth will 'trickle down' across the planet in the twenty-first century. But since the late 1970s Virilio has been warning about the emergence of the 'minimum state' – a state that would begin to dismantle the welfare state in order to create ideal environments for business and finance to operate in. Citizens will vote for the party that promises to deliver the people from the immediate and visceral insecurities that are part of the global 'environment' of fear we inhabit: 'Globalization has progressively eaten away at the traditional prerogatives of States (most notably of the Welfare state), and they have had to convince citizens that they can ensure their physical safety'.[12] Virilio and his peers, such as Jean Baudrillard and Gilles Deleuze, could see the danger of societies in which new technologies and policies of social control were emerging at the same time as neoliberalism was contributing to the production of a global (dis)order that leaves states increasingly powerless to manage the chaotic 'flows' of globalisation. In this environment of fear and unease, we become citizens who 'invest first and foremost in security', managing our 'own protection' as best as we can; we will live, according to Virilio (writing in 1977), with a common feeling of insecurity that will lead to a 'a new kind of consumption, the consumption of protection' that will produce a 'whole new merchandising system'.[13] Those fortunate to live the good life in the 'minimum state' veer chaotically and confusedly between fear of those who are different (living with what Virilio describes as 'siege psychosis') and a moral indifference towards those on the margins: fear and voyeuristic fascination coupled with forgetting and contempt. Like the business traveller in the Microsoft film, we want to circulate effortlessly through the urban environment without any encounter with those on the outside of these carefully controlled and

12 Paul Virilio, *The Administration of Fear* (Los Angeles: Semiotexte, 2012), p. 15.
13 Virilio, *Speed and Politics*, p. 139.

managed spaces. But for Virilio – rather than escape unscathed by our histories of violence and exploitation – we inhabit a world that has been 'dehumanising us', shattering our ethical and aesthetic 'bearings' in cities filled with 'accumulated hate'.[14] We need to pay attention, Virilio is suggesting, to the ways in which we become habituated to the world around us, how we become *indifferent to our indifference*: just as societies seek to physically control the 'other', societies have developed ways to control the moral imagination of the self.[15]

So Virilio is interested in the history of control, and encourages us to pay attention to the various ways in which police, policymakers and security experts have attempted to produce order and security, to endo-colonise society through the policies and technologies that promise to refine the arts of control. But there is more to Virilio's work than this history of cities and control (the *domestication* of the citizenry): Virilio is interested in how movement and speed transform geopolitics or world politics.

One of the new generation of French intellectuals writing about violence and society, Grégoire Chamayou, has come to the attention of the Anglo-American world with his book *Manhunts: A Philosophical History*.[16] In this disturbing and compelling book, Chamayou examines how the techniques and justifications for the organised hunting of humans have mutated through history. Decades earlier in *Negative Horizon*, Virilio – who is not referred to in Chamayou's work – began his alternative history of speed and war with a history of hunting, a practice that he sees as vital in refining and developing the arts of escape and capture through various means of extending and intensifying the power of the body. Hunting – along with the domestication of animals – became a 'speed factory'.[17] This history of speed and war moves from the city and the battleground to geopolitics and cyberspace – and from a history of control to a history of the accident, to a century Virilio sees as unstable, confused and precarious.

---

14 Paul Virilio, *Art and Fear* (London: Continuum, 2000), p. 29.
15 Zygmunt Bauman, *Postmodern Ethics* (Oxford: Blackwell, 1993).
16 Grégoire Chamayou, *Manhunts: A Philosophical History* (Princeton: Princeton University Press, 2012).
17 Paul Virilio, *Negative Horizon* (London: Continuum, 2008), p. 43.

The violence of speed In *Speed and Politics*, Virilio declares that 'history progresses at the speed of its weapons systems'.[18] What does Virilio mean in what at first appears to be a rather disturbing statement designed to offend and shock the reader? As strange as the statement sounds, it cuts to the chase of Virilio's sketch of an alternative history of civilisation, war and technology. Virilio is interested in how human beings responded to the need to hunt (and to escape) by using new 'prostheses' and weaponry, ranging from lances, armour and chariots through to tanks, drones and malware. Societies built camps and castles to protect people from predators and the uncertainties of the environment. But, as well as limiting movement, the castle walls, in particular, allowed the defenders to see the enemy before they became an uncontrollable threat. This innovation in the 'logistics of perception' allowed faster action and decision-making. At root, Virilio is interested in how tribes, warlords, empires and modern states have set out to extend the powers of the body – to protect the body or to place it out of harm's way while also enabling what is best described as 'action at a distance' (from the archer on the castle wall through to the drone operator and the designers of 'Stuxnet'). Innovation in the built environment (castles, camps, roads and rail networks), combined with new ways of protecting the soldier, enable you to prolong the war effort, to protect your resources, to use resources (food, people, machinery) as rationally and effectively as possible. You need to find ways to place a 'brake' (the moat, the Atlantic wall) on the movement of your enemy because the technologies and prostheses used to enhance the human body (the arrow, the bullet) make conflict and violence faster. You always need to be one step ahead.

On this view, this desire to extend the power of the body drives innovation, innovation that transforms *all* aspects of life: society progresses at the speed of its weapons systems. As has already been suggested, one of the aspects of Virilio's writings that makes them so fascinating is his use of seemingly mundane and banal everyday examples to illustrate how the world is transformed and shaped by war and policing (e.g., the width of streets in Paris and the use of streetlights). In *Speed and Politics*, Virilio notes how the 'industry' of orthopaedics emerged as a response to the problem of soldiers

18 Virilio, *Speed and Politics*, p. 90.

having to walk long distances.[19] In *Bunker Archaeology*,[20] he points to the influence that the Atlantic wall of bunkers built in France during the Second World War had on both the design and manufacturing techniques used in post-war architecture. We can point to more contemporary examples such as the satnav, which many of us have been become dependent on as we drive around our towns and countries, a technology that emerged from the satellite navigation systems developed by the US military in the 1960s. So what Virilio is suggesting in his provocative statement on society and weapons systems is that our world is transformed by the research and innovation developed by the 'military–scientific complex' in order to make war faster and more efficient: in many ways, this position is a provocation to his Marxist friends, a challenge to the view that it is the various ways of organising economic life that transform societies.

Virilio is interested in how the speed of our weapons systems transforms geopolitics. For Virilio, the fastest states and armies (with 'vehicular power') have been able to dominate international relations: 'Western man has appeared superior and dominant, despite inferior demographics, because he appeared *more rapid*', Virilio writes in a discussion of naval power, colonialism and European history.[21] But a profound shift occurred in the twentieth century that transformed geopolitics. The speed and destructiveness of nuclear weapons – combined with economic interdependence – means that 'pure wars' over territory between the 'great powers' have come to an end. During the 1970s, Virilio saw the Cold War as a precarious, potentially suicidal moment in world history, noting that 'the reason we did not have an atomic war is due more to a miracle of history than the supposed virtues of mutual dissuasion'.[22] But the time of wars when 'great powers' attempted to extend their territory has come to an end, reached a limit. With the end of the Cold War we entered an age of intensifying economic and political interconnectedness and governance: globalisation and the age of security. The concern with national defence has become supplemented by national *security*, a concern with threats *to* our way of life and threats emerging *from* our

---

19 Virilio, *Speed and Politics*, p. 83.
20 Paul Virilio, *Bunker Archaeology* (Princeton: Princeton University Press, 2009).
21 Virilio, *Speed and Politics*, p. 70.
22 Virilio, *Administration of Fear*, p. 23.

way of life. Writing in 1984, Virilio anticipated the post-Cold War world of mutating threats – from terrorist networks to cybersecurity to environmental catastrophe – that began to shape the 'threat horizon' after the fear of 'pure war' faded, with Virilio writing that the 'politically declared reality of the "enemy" now disappears, making way for the indeterminacy of constantly redefined threats'.[23] National defence is about building shields, defending and extending territory in a world where sovereign states are the enemies you need to be worried about; security is about a threat horizon that is both inside and outside the state, threats orchestrated by non-state actors that target the critical infrastructures and technologies of the 'networked society' or 'borderless' economy – or threats that emerge from the way we live and consume (climate change).

Great powers still prepare for apocalyptic wars with other great powers. But the wars that are actually fought by the great powers are policing wars, wars of humanitarian intervention or wars intended to contain conflict that could impact on the order and security of the liberal democratic world. Writing about Western intervention in Kosovo in *Strategy of Deception* (2000),[24] Virilio is troubled about what the conflict revealed about the post-Cold War world:

> With the doctrine of the 'revolution in military affairs', American technology seems to be becoming today, for Bill Clinton, a sort of Wonderland in which the warrior, like a child in its playpen, wants to *try out everything, show off everything*, for fear of otherwise seeming weak and isolated.[25]

What disturbs Virilio is thinking about the world that is driven by fear and panic (the administration of fear) or policy that is overly optimistic (the propaganda of progress) about what is achievable through technologies of war and security, thinking that ignores the messiness and complexity of history and society, thinking that he describes as the 'degradation of political intelligence'.[26] So the response by the United States to the events of 9/11 did not come

---

23 Virilio, *Negative Horizon*, p. 160.
24 Paul Virilio, *Strategy of Deception* (London: Verso, 2000).
25 Virilio, *Strategy of Deception*, p. 10 (emphasis in original).
26 Virilio, *Negative Horizon*, p. 190.

as a surprise to Virilio. Consumed by a belief or faith that technological and political superiority would facilitate 'regime change', the
politicians and policymakers thought they could begin to redesign
Iraqi society and eradicate deterritorialised terror networks through
territorial war and through a spectacle of power that would try out
everything and show off everything.

Virilio had been thinking about the new terrains of media,
terrorism and geopolitics since the 1970s. In 1978 he had argued
that, when the Palestinian people stopped being 'legal inhabitants
of the Earth', they used the one territory they still had: 'the media.
From airport runways to railroad tracks, from highways to television
and press, they could not afford to lose this last advantage, they could
not let the vectors remain neutral.'[27] The Palestinians could become
masters of an 'audio-visual empire'. In 1993 Virilio suggested that
the Cold War balance of terror had been replaced by the imbalance
of terror: the age of territorial wars between great powers might
be over but smaller groups and networks – able to manipulate the
'miniaturisation of charges' (and, as we saw on 9/11, to 'weaponise'
the critical infrastructures of mobility that underpin globalisation)
– are able to intensify their 'molecular terror' through the use of a
media front, 'the clever combination' of a 'strong symbolic dimension'
and 'an urban demolition capability'.[28] In the second decade of the
twenty-first century, the mastering of the 'audio-visual empire' is
shaped by the changes in the miniaturisation of media technologies
and the shift to images cheaply produced, circulated and consumed
by mobile devices, perhaps even framed in a narrative that references
sadistic Hollywood 'torture porn' horror movies and thrillers that
involve a serial killer taunting the police: 'Jihadi John' becomes to
the United States and United Kingdom what the Joker became to
Batman and Gotham City in *The Dark Knight*.

In *Speed and Politics*, Virilio writes about how the dangerous masses
posed a problem for the police in cities such as Paris; now we live
in a time when small groups and networks of 'molecular terror' can
become a deterritorialised motor of attack in a world-city where one
person being filmed beheading another person can circulate fear and

---

27 Paul Virilio, *Popular Defense and Ecological Struggles* (New York: Semiotexte,
1978), p. 57.
28 Virilio, *Landscape of Events*, p. 20.

anger, 'minor' events that can create a 'synchronisation of affect' across populations that can support changes in strategy and foreign policy.

In 2008 Virilio commented on the post-9/11 world with a point that emerged from a concern he had been exploring since the 1980s: the tendency towards miniaturisation in technology – the tendency of technology to become cheaper, smaller, more powerful and *faster*. In a new introduction to the interviews with Sylvère Lotringer in *Pure War* – titled 'Impure War' – he refers to the problems of what he calls 'globalitarianism'. At root, what makes the post-9/11 world so challenging is the 'change in scale':

> The war that grows of Globalitarianism produces a change in scale. Globalitarianism brings us back to the smallest common denominator: one individual equals Total War; and when I say one, it could be ten as well … Just look at the World Trade Center, eleven men brought in twenty-eight hundred dead, just about as many as Pearl Harbour, with its carriers, Japanese torpedo planes, etc. Exactly the same yields. The cost/efficiency ratio was quite amazing! … Until now we've had national civil wars: The Spanish Civil War, the Paris Commune, but today this will be our first worldwide civil war.[29]

What disturbs Virilio is that the policy makers who shaped the war on terror – and the war in Iraq, in particular – were consumed by a faith that their technological superiority could lead to a positive result in Iraq: that epic, territorial 'international' wars were what was needed in a fight against deterritorialised terror networks. Virilio – who since he was a boy has been unable to be consumed by the hubris of the war machine, who has had a sense of the fragility of things, who learned from an early age not to trust the propaganda of the 'official' media around him – saw the unfolding of the war in terms of hubris. And the problem wasn't simply that policymakers and politicians bought into the realities being sold to them by the architects and designers of the war: they began to believe that they were now controlling and shaping 'reality'. As Ron Suskind reported of an aide to George W. Bush:

29 Paul Virilio and Sylvère Lotringer, *The Accident of Art* (Los Angeles: Semiotext(e), 2005).

The aide said that guys like me were 'in what we call the reality-based community,' which he defined as people who 'believe that solutions emerge from your judicious study of discernible reality.' ... 'That's not the way the world really works anymore,' he continued. 'We're an empire now, and when we act, we create our own reality. And while you're studying that reality – judiciously, as you will – we'll act again, creating other new realities, which you can study too, and that's how things will sort out. We're history's actors ... and you, all of you, will be left to just study what we do.'[30]

Virilio's writings are designed like malware released to circulate through the institutions and organisations where what he describes as 'technological fundamentalism' corrupts and distorts thinking about war and the future of our economic and environmental security.

Since 9/11, the concerns with security and war that have been central to Virilio's writings have been superseded by his interest in the 'integral accident'. While Virilio sees the post-Cold War world as a time of deepening chaos and geopolitical confusion, he is now primarily concerned about the possibility of the accidents that can emerge from our fast, interconnected world, the time of the 'flash crash' or the cascading impacts of human-generated climate change. What if history – rather than being the path to greater levels of control of the environment and the overcoming of human suffering – is the path to a world that will exceed our control, a world that Baudrillard described in terms of 'exponential instability'? And what if technological change is moving so fast that we are unable to respond – ethically, legally, politically – to the pace of this disruptive change? The world is a 'speed factory'.

The central anxiety in Virilio's writings on the integral accident relates to the impact of the life sciences on society and uncertainty about the future of the human being, the types of futures imagined by Michel Houellebecq or by Aldous Huxley. Virilio leaves it to us to make sense of the time of 'impure' war that we confront and the impact of 'acceleration' on security and war.

30 Ron Suskind, 'Faith, Certainty and the Presidency of George W. Bush', *New York Times Magazine* (1 October 2004), www.nytimes.com/2004/10/17/magazine/faith-certainty-and-the-presidency-of-george-w-bush.html?_r=0.

Confronting violence in the world

Virilio's work does appear to describe the world we are living in, a world of endo-colonisation, integral accidents and war. Everywhere we look, there appear to be signs of endo-colonisation. In 2014 the streets of Ferguson, Missouri, looked like a war zone after the killing of a young African American man by the police: the police were armed with weapons that were available to them through a programme known as 1033, which allows the military to sell surplus or redundant supplies to local law enforcement agencies. At the same time, the armies of the industrial age are increasingly subject to the demands of the neoliberal economy and minimum state, mutating into the 'lighter' and more 'flexible' 'agile warriors' of the 'networked society'. In 2012 it was reported that China was spending more money on internal security than external security.[31] Each year that passes, the warnings about the impact of climate change become starker. We live with the sense that reality is becoming more and more like Neill Blomkamp's dystopian science fiction movie *Elysium* (2013): a world of accelerating inequality coupled with accelerating technologies of endo-colonisation. The pace of change is so disorientating that we feel like more technical fixes are the only thing that might be able to save us. As Bertrand Richard comments, this 'son of an Italian communist and a catholic from Brittany traces the rules of the game in which we are caught. And that we must escape.'[32]

So Virilio leaves us with a terrifying vision of our past, present and future. But he is not suggesting that a dystopian future where the planet becomes an endo-colonised planet policed by increasingly deadly and pervasive security technologies is inevitable. And he is not suggesting that all 'progress' in technology leads to us being trapped and controlled in new and distinctive ways. He often makes it clear that he is not against the technologies that are transforming life around the planet. But what Virilio *is* suggesting is that we shouldn't underestimate the hubris or arrogance of the people attempting to shape our existence (whether it is the technologists designing the 'smart cities' we will live in, the wars that will transform and reform 'troublesome' states in the international system or the military

31 'China's Military Rise: The Dragon's New Teeth', *The Economist* (7 April 2012), www.economist.com/node/21552193.
32 Bertrand Richard, 'Preface', in Virilio, *Administration of Fear*, p. 11.

technologies that will make war safer and more 'humane'). And we shouldn't underestimate the way that citizens can be consumed and seduced by the 'administration of fear' or the 'propaganda of progress'. Virilio referred to military technology in the context of Kosovo in the 1990s as a 'sort of Wonderland' for policymakers: the concern in the coming century is that the possibilities of this Wonderland might go beyond anything we can currently imagine. So we need to remain vigilant regarding the seduction of this Wonderland of technology – especially in a time when there will be problems where the technical fix of new military and policing technology will promise 'cost-effective' and 'efficient' solutions to the social, political and economic problems of the twenty-first century.

All this is not to suggest that a dystopia of endo-colonisation and societies of control is the only future ahead of us. What Virilio is suggesting is that we need to cultivate a political intelligence: we need to make sure politicians and policymakers do not treat reality like a videogame where we can press 'replay' or 'restart', erasing our histories of war, violence and catastrophe, the 'active forgetting' that makes it possible to repeat past mistakes – and make new ones.

Virilio is not the best writer on the complexities of political theory nor is he the best guide to our geopolitical history (e.g., there is very little on empire and colonialism) or – for all the comments he makes on the importance of Catholicism for his work – the problems of religion and society. But what he does very well is to draw our attention to details in the landscapes we move through (bunkers on the coast, street lights, the development of camouflage) in order to prompt us to think about the desire to produce order and security – and to think about where we are heading with the techniques and technologies designed to produce order and security, to think about what we need to resist and challenge, to draw attention to how we might be changing as people or societies; to think about what is at stake – ethically, politically, strategically – and what possibilities might be left out of the 'propaganda of progress'.

Virilio is often seen as an apocalyptic thinker, a thinker who leaves us without hope. In a sense it is correct to describe him as an apocalyptic thinker, but only if we use the word 'apocalyptic' in its original meaning. Virilio comes from a tradition that acknowledges the etymology of the word 'apocalypse': the *revelation* of something fundamental about the world.[33] For Virilio, we are in a time of revelation, beginning to take seriously the limits of our capacity to control the world through technical fixes and experiencing a resistance to the 'disproportion or excessiveness that is reentering history'.[34] He warns us that, even when we are confronted with signs of disaster, we can retreat into fantasy or denial. But, if there is hope in Virilio, it stems from his suggestion that we might be entering a time of revelation when we are beginning to confront our limits: we see more clearly – in the debates about inequality and the global economy, the anxiety about the surveillance state, the scepticism about plans to 'geoengineer' our way out of catastrophe, our role in the production of chaos and catastrophe – what could be on the horizon in a world confronting environmental degradation, geopolitical uncertainty and technological acceleration. Of course, liberal democratic politics rests on the idea of limits emerging to counter excesses and hubristic policies. But what Virilio is pointing to is more fundamental. We are beginning to recognise our limits – the limits of our modern, technologically advanced society – at a moment when everything seems possible: Virilio's apocalyptic warnings are part of this time of revelation.

Further reading

Der Derian, James (ed.), *The Virilio Reader* (Oxford: Blackwell, 1997).

Lacy, Mark, *Security, Technology and Global Politics: Thinking with Virilio* (London: Routledge, 2014).

Virilio, Paul, *A Landscape of Events* (Cambridge, MA: MIT Press, 2000).

Virilio, Paul, *Speed and Politics* (Los Angeles: Semiotexte, 2006).

Virilio, Paul, *A Winter's Journey: Four Conversations with Marianne Brausch* (Calcutta: Seagul Books, 2011).

Virilio, Paul and Sylvère Lotringer, *Pure War* (Los Angeles: Semiotexte, 2008).

---

33 Virilio, *Administration of Fear*, p. 71; see also Jean-Pierre Dupray, *The Mark of the Sacred* (Stanford: Stanford University Press, 2013), p. 31.
34 Virilio, *Administration of Fear*, p. 74.

11 | GIORGIO AGAMBEN

Marcelo Svirsky

Biographical details

Giorgio Agamben (1942–) was born in Rome and completed his studies at the University of Rome in law and philosophy with a doctorate on the political thought of Simone Weil. Walter Benjamin and Martin Heidegger are undoubtedly his most significant influences. In the late 1960s, Agamben participated in a series of seminars in France led by Heidegger, from whom, as one of Agamben's translators states, he 'picked up the great philosopher's ambition to provide an overarching account of the history of the West, and use that history to shed light on the contemporary world'.[1] Following research at the Bibliothèque nationale de France, Agamben served as editor of the Italian edition of Benjamin's complete works, from whom Agamben embraced not only his compressed and abstract style of writing but also his polyphony of philosophical and political concerns. Though Agamben became particularly well known in the 2000s because of his *Homo Sacer* book series, in which he addresses pressing contemporary issues of sovereignty and violence, his range of topics is richer and wider and includes research into questions of language, theology, ethics and aesthetics, human and animal, and more.[2]

One of Agamben's most alarming diagnoses of western society – that the paradigm of all modern politics is the concentration camp (was arrived at) as is characteristic of his line of work – by way of investigating the present through the lens of classical times and classical philosophy. This diagnosis derives from what Agamben sees as the root of evil, residing in the Greek classical distinction

---

1 A. Kotsko, 'How to Read Agamben', *Los Angeles Review of Books* (4 June 2013), http://lareviewofbooks.org/essay/how-to-read-agamben.
2 *Homo sacer* is a term from Roman law that has come to mean someone who is outside or above the law; *homines sacri* is the plural.

or division between *bios* (social, qualified and proper form of life) and *zoē* (the simple fact of living that humans and animals have in common), which has historically culminated in the modern fascist 'assumption of the burden – and the "total management" – of biological life, that is, of the very animality of man'.[3] For Agamben, the prioritisation of the biological over the social by modern politics is *the* key political problem of our times; hence, he devotes his last works to the articulation of 'a completely new politics – that is, a politics no longer founded on the *exceptio* of bare life'.[4] But, to the dismay of those thinkers and activists 'who would place their hope in greater democratisation or the development of a culture of human rights', Agamben maintains that they 'are unwittingly complicit with the very powers they intend to oppose',[5] and so the only viable political strategy – which Agamben leaves without unpacking it further into political praxis – is to sever the relation between life and sovereign power.[6]

In his dozens of books, articles and essays, along with Benjamin and Heidegger, Agamben engages and converses with other major figures such as Hannah Arendt, Aristotle, Émile Benveniste, Michel Foucault, G. W. F. Hegel and Carl Schmitt, among others. Selecting from the diversity of Agamben's writings and topics, this chapter focuses on the concept of violence and how this concept is linked to what Leland de la Durantaye rightly claims to be the central concern in Agamben's entire *oeuvre*, the idea of potentiality.

Theorising violence

There is in effect something that humans are and have to be, but this something is not an essence, nor properly a thing: *it is the simple fact of one's own existence as possibility or potentiality.*[7]

---

3 Giorgio Agamben, *The Open: Man and Animal*, trans. Kevin Attell (Stanford: Stanford University Press, 2004), p. 77.
4 Giorgio Agamben, *Homo Sacer: Sovereign Power and Bare Life*, trans. Daniel Heller-Roazen (Stanford: Stanford University Press, 1998), p. 11.
5 Jessica Whyte, *Catastrophe and Redemption: The Political Thought of Giorgio Agamben* (New York: State University of New York Press, 2013), pp. 21–22.
6 See Whyte, *Catastrophe and Redemption*.
7 Giorgio Agamben, *The Coming Community*, trans. Michael Hardt (Minneapolis: Minnesota University Press, 1993), p. 39.

We begin on the basis of a common assumption, which is that political philosophers of life seed their repudiation of violence in their preoccupation with a fundamental refrain. For Hobbes it is order, for Foucault the body, for Deleuze and Guattari subjectivity, and for Agamben it is potentiality. Nothing better explains Agamben's literary machine than his preoccupation with the growing erosion of the experience of the potentiality to think and to act.[8] This tendency imperils humanity itself as 'there is no human essence; the human being is a potential being'.[9] Our age's catastrophe reveals itself in the deterioration of the experience of potentiality, and it is the claim of this chapter that in Agamben's *oeuvre* violence becomes ontologically defined in relation to that tendency. The task here, then, is to identify how violence becomes defined as the process that imperils the experience of potentiality. As part of this task, some misconstructions need to be confronted with regard to the role and the agents of violence in Agamben's works. These misconstructions stem mainly from a reading of Agamben's works that is overly focused on the *Homo Sacer* project, ignoring his other writings.[10]

Because of the exactitude and urgency of his diagnosis of politics in the West, it is conventional in the humanities and the social sciences to interpret Agamben's articulation of violence exclusively in relation to the phenomenology of bare life, the camp and the state of exception – and to place this discussion in the context of a continuation of his critical engagement with the intellectual exchange between Benjamin and Schmitt on the question of anomic violence. These concepts are central themes in the *Homo Sacer* series – where Agamben's most thought-provoking judgement arises: 'Today it is not the city but rather the camp that is the fundamental biopolitical paradigm of the West'.[11] In this reading of *Homo Sacer: Sovereign Power and Bare Life* (2004) and *State of Exception* (2005), it is the sign of contemporary modernity that life has become increasingly

---

8 Leland de la Durantaye has captured that essence in his comprehensive book *Agamben: A Critical Introduction* (Stanford: Stanford University Press, 2009). See also Whyte's constructive reading in *Catastrophe and Redemption*.
9 Giorgio Agamben, *Remnants of Auschwitz: The Witness and the Archive – Homo Sacer III*, trans. Daniel Heller-Roazen (New York: Zone, 2002), p. 126.
10 This diagnosis has also recently been presented by Whyte in *Catastrophe and Redemption*.
11 Agamben, *Homo Sacer*, p. 181.

vulnerable as, in our very midst, it is arbitrarily abandoned and exposed to death by sovereign violence. This is the bare life 'relative humans' are exposed to,[12] as 'mere zoological existence, unprotected by philosophical or legal bastions of citizenship and humanity'.[13] Spatially, the sovereign abandonment takes place within the confines of 'the camp', actualised these days in immigration detention centres, torture prisons such as Abu Ghraib and Guantánamo Bay, American black ghettos, the occupied and sieged territories in Palestine, Brazilian favelas and more generally slums, refugee camps, other precarious spaces of non-citizenship, and hidden universes separated off by walls and fences. This controlled and regulated abandonment of bodies is shaped by means of 'securocratic' apparatuses,[14] the production of social insecurity[15] and also lately by eugenics, as in the case of racialised communities in the United States where medical hot-spotting is used to increase profit by preventing universal medical care.[16]

Not that the empirical accuracies of the violence of 'the camp' are unworthy of reflection and detailed accountancy, but, looking at Agamben's spectrum from a more integrative perspective, one finds that the concrete instances of the lived experience of violence in 'the camp' and their associated political institutions and cultural common sense are linked to a more paradigmatic phenomenon, that of *the deterioration of the experience of potentiality*. This claim unpacks Agamben's concern with 'the secret connections that link power and potentiality'.[17] More specifically, the claim here is that the conditions of emergence of the phenomenology of contemporary violence in

---

12 Omar Barghouti, 'Relative Humanity: The Fundamental Obstacle to a One State Solution', *ZNet* (16 December 2003), https://electronicintifada.net/content/relative-humanity-fundamental-obstacle-one-state-solution-historic-palestine-12/4939.

13 Steve Graham, *Cities under Siege: The New Military Urbanism* (London: Verso, 2010), p. 235.

14 Graham, *Cities under Siege*.

15 Loïc Wacquant, *Punishing the Poor: The Neoliberal Government of Social Insecurity* (Durham, NC: Duke University Press, 2009).

16 Shiloh Krupar and Nadine Ehlers, 'Target: Biomedicine and Racialized Geo-Body-Politics', *Occasion*, 7 (2015), http://arcade.stanford.edu/occasion/target-biomedicine-and-racialized-geo-body-politics.

17 Giorgio Agamben, *Idea of Prose*, trans. Michael Sullivan and Sam Whitsitt (Albany: State University of New York Press, 1995), p. 71.

'the camp' are given in the particular ways by which political power links itself to potentiality. This link, in other words, is the plane of composition of violence.

It seems crucial at this point to expand on Agamben's conceptualisation of potentiality. Agamben's theory of potentiality draws on the distinction between *dunamis* (potency) and *adynamia* (impotence), as defined by Aristotle in chapter eight of book theta of the *Metaphysics*. In this view, potentiality is said to impregnate a state of affairs if the forces that impel a becoming are capable of not impelling it by lingering in the dark. Aristotle, and Agamben after him, define the potentiality 'not to become' as impotentiality. Hence, for potentiality to exist, it must comprise a double structure or double modality: potentiality and impotentiality dwell together, the latter granting the former an ontological distance from actuality – a depth excavated by indeterminacy and contingency. If, as a general rule, 'what is potential can pass over into actuality only at the point at which it sets aside its own potentiality not to be',[18] it is only because impotentiality 'represents an energy that has not been exhausted and *cannot* be exhausted in the passing of the potential to the actual'.[19] For Agamben,

> Potentiality ... is the hardest thing to consider. For if potentiality were always only the potential to do or to be something, we would never experience it as such; it would exist only in the actuality in which it is realized ... An experience of potentiality as such is possible only if potentiality is always also potential not to (do or think something), if the writing tablet is capable of not being written on.[20]

In their brief analysis of martial arts, Deleuze and Guattari press on exactly this point: 'one learns to "unuse" weapons as much as one learns to use them',[21] and they link the power of 'not-doing'

18 Kevin Attell, 'Potentiality/Impotentiality', in *The Agamben Dictionary*, ed. Alex Murray and Jessica Whyte (Edinburgh: Edinburgh University Press, 2011), p. 161.

19 De la Durantaye, *Agamben*, p. 331; see also Agamben, *Homo Sacer*, p. 62.

20 Giorgio Agamben, *Potentialities: Collected Essays in Philosophy*, ed. and trans. Daniel Heller-Roazen (Stanford: Stanford University Press, 1999), p. 250.

21 Gilles Deleuze and Félix Guattari, *A Thousand Plateaus: Capitalism and Schizophrenia*, trans. Brian Massumi (Minneapolis: University of Minnesota Press, 1987), p. 400.

(impotentiality) with their ultimate goal of the continuous undoing of the subject. Without the order of impotentiality, potentiality would be just a pre-actual dimension of already identifiable things, a foyer of actuality – in so doing withdrawing life into an array of calculable *possibles*. Devoid of the depth that impotentiality unravels, potentiality would be the doubling of actuality's range and scope simply waiting to be actualised – a reservoir of mere reflections. Impotentiality gives potentiality – and hence life – an ingenious and surprising nature. A world emptied of the double structure of potentiality is a world in which contingency has been negated, a world ruled by 'the primacy of actuality'.[22] Impotentiality, explains Whyte, 'ensures that we are capable of being other that we are'.[23] It is plausible then to claim that Agamben's preoccupation with potentiality is in fact a preoccupation with impotentiality, or with the *privation* of passing into actuality.[24] 'To be free' – he states – 'is … to be in relation to one's own privation'.[25] To be in relation to one's own privation means to be in a critical relation with the conditions, forces and circumstances that might, or might not, impel the movement of potentiality to pass into actuality. It is this relation that lifts potentiality *before and beyond* actuality.

For Agamben, privation arises from a particular relation to a field of opposites or contraries: 'If potentiality were, for example, only the potentiality for vision and if it existed only as such in the actuality of light, we could never experience darkness (nor hear silence, in the case of the potentiality to hear).'[26] However, what darkness gives to light and silence to hearing is not just an antinomy but their problematisation. Darkness problematises vision because it forces the agent of experience to experiment with the boundaries and assumptions of the visible; therefore it introduces an itinerant 'empty square', setting their relation in motion. Hence, *impotentiality inflicts on potentiality a problematic field*. Agamben's double modality of potentiality is, in other words, the realm of problems. Thus, it is not a synthesis of identities of being and nonbeing that characterises the double modality of potentiality – vision and darkness, sensation

22 Agamben, *Homo Sacer*, p. 44.
23 Whyte, *Catastrophe and Redemption*, p. 318.
24 Agamben, *Potentialities*, pp. 181–182.
25 Agamben, *Potentialities*, p. 183.
26 Agamben, *Potentialities*, p. 181

and anaesthesia, knowledge and ignorance, and so on[27] – but a problematic relation between indeterminacy and play. It is precisely at this point that we find the sense of Agamben's likening of his own Aristotelian double structure of potentiality to Deleuze's concept of virtuality as the field of problematic ideas[28] – particularly as articulated in *Difference and Repetition* (1994).[29] 'A problem' states Bogue, 'is not an amorphous muddle, nor a kind of shadowy double of its eventual resolution within a specific solution, but a structured field of potential actualizations'.[30] We therefore equate impotentiality with the indeterminacy of problems.

What form, then, does the deterioration of the experience of potentiality take? From a Deleuzian point of view, the answer is probably the increasing containment of virtual problems and ideas within controllable modulations.[31] Of Agamben's two modes of potentiality – to become and not to become – contemporary life summons us to enjoy the first at the expense of renouncing the second, to never exhausting the first in exchange for draining the second of its strength. Empirically this takes the form of a compulsive enjoyment of the pseudo-pluralities that have become the symptom of our age, *resonating* among themselves as in the experience of the shopping mall or cable television. Power links itself to life to make it habitable within governable ranges of frequencies. In such a life, 'several voices seem to issue from the same mouth'.[32] Under such conditions, we are encouraged not to contemplate alternative possibilities to the present but to nod, as Ghassan Hage claims, to the 'discourses of confirmation':

Unlike critical discourses which challenge people's beliefs, the confirmationist modes of writing and speaking simply speak to

---

27 . Agamben, *Potentialities*, p. 184.
28 'Ideas for Deleuze are in no sense transcendent, essential or eternal entities, but instead virtual problems immanent within the real': Ronald Bogue, *Deleuze's Way: Essay in Transversal Ethics and Aesthetics* (Aldershot: Ashgate, 2007), p. 61 n. 6.
29 Agamben, *Potentialities*, p. 237.
30 Bogue, *Deleuze's Way*, p. 61.
31 Gilles Deleuze, *Difference and Repetition*, trans. Paul Patton (New York: Columbia University Press, 1994).
32 Deleuze and Guattari, *A Thousand Plateaus*, p. 97.

people to tell them 'yes, I confirm to you that you are right', 'yes, you don't need to think any further to know the truth', 'yes, things are exactly as you say they are'. Such a nonchallenging discourse is particularly suitable for the tensed and defensive citizens/conscripts who cling to the security of the domain of the 'what is' and end up perceiving all critical thought as threatening.[33]

We become progressively more familiar with particular sets of solutions to problems. Our obsession is with solutions, with the actual, not with problems and their virtuality. It is *the problematic* that we fear, but, unavoidably, any attack on the conditions of engagement with problematic fields is nothing but an assault on potentiality. However, our 'familiarity' with solutions does not necessarily secure our positioning in relation to 'the camp'. Though some segments are racially and socio-economically bound to enjoy better structural chances, the struggle to remain on the right side of bare life applies to all: 'we are all virtually *homines sacri*'.[34] For instance, in November 2014, an initiative taken by Scott Morrison, Australian Minister for Immigration and Border Protection, led the Federal Parliament to introduce draconian amendments to the Australian Citizenship Act of 2007, which gave the government extended powers to cancel the citizenship of any citizen not born in Australia.[35] Citizenship is not a warranty to be safe from exceptionalism; in fact, it cannot be such as it is in itself an institution built on exceptionalism. 'The camp' bubbles below for all.

If the experience of potentiality is degraded in 'the camp', it is not only because of the misery it inflicts but also essentially because of the continuing regulation of abandonment as part of the double bind involved in the exception.[36] What is at issue is not *abandonment*

33 Ghassan Hage, 'Warring Societies (and Intellectuals)', *Transforming Cultures eJournal*, 1(1) (2006), http://epress.lib.uts.edu.au/journals/index.php/TfC/article/view/202/181.

34 Agamben, *Homo Sacer*, p. 115.

35 See House of Representatives, Parliament of the Commonwealth of Australia, 'Australian Citizenship and Other Legislation Amendment Bill 2014', www.comlaw.gov.au/Details/C2014B00217.

36 On November 2014, Fort Lauderdale, Florida, enacted a regulation that bans people from meal-sharing with the public to prevent feeding the homeless. This law is also about to be adopted in Dallas, Los Angeles, Philadelphia, Phoenix and Seattle.

as such but *to make sure* that life can be abandoned by rule. This form of power leans on, as Agamben claims, a 'general tendency to regulate everything by means of rules'[37] – and, as a result, life becomes increasingly colonised, heavily populated with regulations and their exceptions.[38] This is about 'the expansion of the *oikos* to the point at which it gradually surpassed the *polis*, bringing with it a form of government that is no longer political but economic'.[39] This is a world ruled by 'the organisation of potentiality', of life itself.[40] Simply, potentiality is organised not just by restricting the prospects of life for some but also by structuring a stringent regulation of those restrictions. This is why 'abandon(ment)' is a noun and a verb, a condition and an active operation. The outcomes of this process are 'by no means certain' – but 'the stakes, as Agamben perceives them, could not be higher: it signals the slow disappearance of meaningful political action'.[41] Thus life has not been increasingly politicised, as it is customary to argue, but hyperbolically managed. It is in this managerial quality of our institutions and political culture where Agamben rightly sees the seeds of violence. It is this violence that explains the violence of the camp, and not the other way around.

At times when violence finds an identity in the policing of multifarious connections, or of potentiality's double structure, and political action finds itself battling not to pursue creative avenues but to ontologically impose incompleteness, *politics itself is increasingly conceived as violence* – a sad twist of reason. Ours are the times of 'the primacy of actuality'.[42] Agamben's call for 'new uses',[43] then, becomes officially profiled as violence. In the media and parliamentary politics, in schools and universities, in every public space, all politics are now seen as agitation, provocation and, more

37 Agamben, *Homo Sacer*, p. 39.
38 See also Stephen Humphreys, 'Legalizing Lawlessness: On Giorgio Agamben's *State of Exception*', *European Journal of International Law*, 17(3) (2006), p. 678.
39 Whyte, *Catastrophe and Redemption*, p. 44.
40 Agamben, *Idea of Prose*, p. 71; it is interesting here to juxtapose Agamben's notion of 'the organisation of potentiality' (or just 'power') with Deleuze and Guattari's notion of 'organisation' as regards the 'body without organs'. Both notions point to the tendency to asphyxiate immanence.
41 Humphreys, 'Legalizing Lawlessness', p. 678.
42 Agamben, *Homo Sacer*, p. 44.
43 Agamben, *Coming Community*; Giorgio Agamben, *Profanations*, trans. Jeff Fort (New York: Zone Books, 2007).

exactly, as terror. Perhaps it is because transformative activism never had to face such impediments that Agamben questions the impetus to regenerate democracy and human rights as a viable solution to our predicament.

The question of sovereignty If the first misconstruction in the secondary literature on Agamben's works has to do with the conditions of violence, a second misconstruction that is important to note relates to the *agents* of violence and more generally to political subjectivity. In this respect, the general tendency of authors is to restore the king's head – namely, to attribute the causes for the phenomenology of violence in 'the camp' to an autonomous power located in the government of the state. In so doing, authors not only decontextualise Agamben's efforts to diagnose the West but they also provide *firmamentum* to sustain their own critique according to which Agamben's subjects 'are rarely agents in their own right'.[44] In this vein, others have claimed that Agamben's exceptionalism 'risks suppressing a political reading of the societal'.[45]

Interpreters have contributed to the perception that Agamben's articulation of 'the camp' exonerates the public by culpabilising the state. In fact, this perception restores the classical theory of sovereignty in which the citizen exists in a pure, neutral capacity. In other words, the over-focus on the responsibility of the state for exceptionalism takes the individual back to the pre-hoplite era. This alleged caesura between 'state' and 'society' (or political subjectivity) in Agamben's work, when scrutinised, will justify an interpretation of 'the sovereign' that takes account of the most fundamental element of democratic political practice, namely, 'the people'. In contrast to assertions by Huysmans,[46] this interpretation is not about correcting Agamben but is in fact about doing justice to his analysis. In the following refocus on 'sovereignty', two points are worth noting: firstly, in *State of Exception*, Agamben calls the state of exception

44 William Walters, 'Acts of Demonstration: Mapping the Territory of (Non)-Citizenship', in *Acts of Citizenship*, ed. Engin Isin and Greg Nielsen (London: Zed Books, 2008), p. 188.

45 Jef Huysmans, 'The Jargon of Exception: On Schmitt, Agamben and the Nascence of Political Society', *International Political Sociology* 2(2) (2008), p. 166.

46 Huysmans, 'The Jargon of Exception'.

a paradigm of *government*, not of sovereignty; and, secondly, in *Homo Sacer*, when Agamben discusses the logic of sovereignty in 'Potentiality and Law', he does not restrict his interpretation of an 'act of sovereignty' to the realm of official politics. He explains: 'an act is sovereign when it realizes itself by simply *taking away* its own potentiality not to be'.[47] In other words, for Agamben, in an act of sovereignty a constituting power (the revolutionary force) is halted and compressed into constituted power (the new order).[48] Acts that arrest potentiality are not the monopoly of government.

There are two reasons for revising the caesura between 'state' and 'society' attributed to Agamben in the *Homo Sacer* series. The first relates to the various ways by which Agamben addresses the deterioration of experience of potentiality, at the very least in his various works including *Infancy and History* (1993), *Stanzas* (1993), *Idea of Prose* (1995), *The Man without Content* (1999), *Potentialities* (1999), *The Open* (2004) *Profanations* (2007) and *The Highest Poverty* (2013) – where that preoccupation is elaborated by looking into a wide range of domains such as poetry, aesthetics, language, tradition, the sacred and the profane, animal life, playing and so on. Particularly in *Infancy and History*[49] and in *The Man without Content*,[50] Agamben uses the Heideggerian idea of destruction to articulate his own preoccupation regarding the Benjaminian concern with the poverty of the current conditions of experience in modernity. I have elsewhere claimed that *Profanations* is nothing less than an activist treatise on political subjectivity.[51] There I analyse Agamben's definition of being

---

47 Agamben, *Homo Sacer*, p. 46 (emphasis added).

48 This is the reason why Agamben prefers to break out of the 'constituting/ constituted, law-founding/law-preserving violence' dialectic: 'For if constituting power is, as the violence that posits law, certainly more noble than the violence that preserves it, constituting power still possesses no tide that might legitimate something other than law-preserving violence and even maintains an ambiguous and ineradicable relation with constituted power' (*Homo Sacer*, p. 40). I would like to thank Jess Whyte (University of Western Sydney) for her comments on these points.

49 Giorgio Agamben, *Infancy and History: The Destruction of Experience*, trans. Liz Heron (London: Verso, 1993).

50 Giorgio Agamben, *The Man without Content*, trans. Georgia Albert (Stanford: Stanford University Press, 1999).

51 Marcelo Svirsky, 'The Mechanics of Profanation: Subjectivity and Zionist Divides', *Cultural Politics* 10(1) (2014), pp. 92–104.

as the double of 'Genius' and 'ego' in terms of 'the complex dialectic between a part that has yet to be individuated and lived and another part that is marked by fate and individual experience', based on his conception of the double structure of potentiality.[52] The book *Profanations* offers a versatile articulation of ways (particularly magic, literature, photography, theology and cinema) through which being reunites with potentiality by escaping the reality principle. In this text, Agamben's concern with the experience of potentiality is not just linked with his aversion of identity. Importantly, as de la Durantaye explains, the tone of these interrogations 'is not that of Dionysian intoxication, and what he is calling for is not merely anarchic'; rather, Agamben 'aims to clear and clarify a field of inquiry'.[53] What does the activity of clarifying 'a field of inquiry' account for if not for a call to re-engage with problems and ideas? In other words, Agamben's explorations of culture and society are explorations of the obstacles that potentiality faces in our times beyond the legal and official domain of government. 'Naked life', then, should not be interpreted as a life stripped bare of the historicity of socio-political life, as something that 'takes precedence over societal categories, like class, socioeconomic exclusions, and pluralism of interests'.[54] Rather, as explained above, from a comprehensive point of view, and not just with reference to the *Homo Sacer* project – the reader finds the ontology that explains the empiricism of 'naked life' in Agamben's interrogations of the experience of potentiality in society, culture and politics.

The second reason for reinterpreting the caesura between the sovereign and the citizenry relates to Agamben's genealogical investigation into the legality of the state of exception, according to which 'the modern state of exception is a creation of the democratic-revolutionary tradition and not the absolutist one'.[55] According to Agamben, democratic and absolutist regimes converge at the point where both appropriate 'bare life' in the functioning of their state mechanisms.[56] But this 'intimate solidarity'[57] or convergence reflects

---

52 Svirsky, 'The Mechanics of Profanation', p. 11.
53 De la Durantaye, *Agamben*, p. 27.
54 Huysmans, 'Jargon of Exception', p. 174.
55 Agamben, *State of Exception*, p. 15.
56 De la Durantaye, *Agamben*, p. 227.
57 Agamben, *Homo Sacer*, p. 10.

the predicament of the first principle of the democratic tradition, namely *popular sovereignty*. There is no need to subscribe to liberal contractualism to agree that it is the quality of popular sovereignty and the potentiality of dissent and rupture that validate it that have given the democratic tradition its genealogy. But, if so, and if we take seriously the differences between the two European traditions – the democratic and the absolutist or totalitarian – then we cannot but critically inquire into the complicity of contemporary democratic virtues and practices with the historical production and maintenance of, and widespread support for, the state of exception and the violence that it brings upon humanity. All those ever substantial resources such as voting, freedom of expression and more generally political participation (or the lack of it) have somehow fuelled, or have allowed, governmental practices that are at odds with the spirit of democracy understood as a spirit of open political spaces. According to Hage, Western societies rationalise this spiral process of engagement with anti-democratic practices by framing it as contingent, temporary – as a matter of exception.[58] That is our predicament. As Brad Evans and Julian Reid have noted, the boundaries between liberalism and fascism have become porous 'to the extent that fascism today is fundamentally a banality of liberal biopolitics, nationally and internationally'.[59]

The end result is the shrinking of democracy as it becomes increasingly evacuated of its traditional and meaningful contents. This is a new global political culture, not just a governmental policy implemented to confront alleged threats to the nation. Therefore, in response to Huysmans, who condemns Agamben for politically neutralising 'the societal as a realm of multi-faceted, historically structured political mediations and mobilizations',[60] it must be said that it is not Agamben who eliminates 'the people' and the societal from view, but it is the people who in Western democracies have finally embodied popular sovereignty – paraphrasing Agamben – by taking away their own potentiality 'not to be'. It is time to revert Deleuze and Guattari's somehow optimistic appraisal, according to

58 Hage, 'Warring Societies'.
59 Brad Evans and Julian Reid (eds), *Deleuze and Fascism: Security, War, Aesthetics* (London: Routledge, 2013).
60 Huysmans, 'Jargon of Exception', p. 166.

which 'at a certain point, [and] under a certain set of conditions, they [the masses] *wanted* fascism'.[61] With a view of Agamben's preoccupation with impotentiality, it is far more exact to claim that, in Western societies, at a certain point, and under a certain set of conditions, people want democracy.

Undoubtedly one of the main corollaries of this process lies with humanity's increasing failure to substantially play with political subjectivity. More and more we latch onto our historical coordinates and normalised vectors from which the engagement with potentially revolutionary and anarchic forces appears to us more and more intimidating to our sense of endurance, as if all that engagement announces is a menace to our existence. Interrogations of character (subjectivity) become threats to existence rather than opportunities to experiment with new 'becomings'. As Hage explains, 'People who engage in reflexivity are traitors because they are wasting their time "thinking about doing" rather than simply "doing"'.[62] Ultimately, playing with potentiality is internalised as unworthy of the effort, though not without persisting with our opulent but empty language of emancipation. It is this weakness – potentiality perceived as excessive – that explains the secular consecration of contemporary political subjectivities, as much as Agamben's insistence on the need for profanations.[63]

Therefore, Agamben's analysis invites scholarship to interrogate political subjectivity, or the social and cultural infrastructure of the law's own suspension – an interrogation he carries out in his numerous works. The question 'how can an anomie be inscribed within the juridical order?'[64] should be supplemented with 'how can despotic rationalities become part of democratic political cultures?' Legal exceptionalism needs to be seen as a sign of political time, not just a juridical term. It is not the tumultuous and dissident character of democratic politics that disappears under the idiom of exception, but it is the currency of that idiom that indicates the infestation of fascist and totalitarian rationalities into the concrete character of liberal and democratic politics.

61 Gilles Deleuze and Felix Guattari, *Anti-Oedipus: Capitalism and Schizophrenia*, trans. Robert Hurley, Mark Seem and Helen R. Lane (Minneapolis: University of Minnesota Press, 1983), p. 29.
62 Hage, 'Warring Societies'
63 Agamben, *Profanations*.
64 Agamben, *State of Exception*, p. 27.

Confronting violence in the world

In the wake of Foucault's analyses of the powers and dangers of 'bio-politics' – the new forms of discipline, control and domination that modernity has brought with it – Agamben identifies what he calls an 'anthropological machine' that threatens to close that which is productively and promisingly open in contemporary politics. The openness in question is the open vocation of humanity, the freedom to refuse to accept the demands of institutionalised forms of power that Agamben sees as seeking to identify, to isolate and to control.[65]

In this context, Agamben's political call for 'inoperativeness' or for disengagement from one's world can hardly be seen as radical.[66] Its urgency lies in the necessity to withdraw from our many identities and vocations in favour of no identity and no vocation, for the sake of an eventually productive return to creative impotentiality by means of de-creation. Agamben calls on the necessity of *Shabbat*, of abstaining from any productive work, as a first step towards *Tikkun Olam* (the repair of the world). Making for us a *Shabbat* in this context ought to address the principle that its current use (namely, popular sovereignty) has turned democracy on its head. 'Not in my name' is one way to caption the sort of profanatory activity that is needed. The deactivation of popular sovereignty necessarily passes through a revision of the act of voting and of our confidence in parliamentary politics. The destruction of representative parliamentary politics appears as one necessary step towards the destruction of the complicity with sovereignty – namely, with the collapse of politics through the severing of potentiality from impotentiality. It suggests that we reflect on new uses of the practice of voting. Regardless of our partisan preferences, by participating in representative elections we inevitably validate the neoliberal political curriculum of which the state of exception is a part. Amal Jamal suggests the principle of 'abstention as participation'[67] to emphasise the act of depletion of consent and legitimacy carried out by the non-voter. This is not a mere act of protest or dissent but an act of 'ungovernability' – as

65 De la Durantaye, *Agamben*, pp. 333–334.
66 Agamben, *Coming Community*.
67 Amal Jamal, 'Beyond "Ethnic Democracy": State Structure, Multi-Cultural Conflict and Differentiated Citizenship in Israel', *New Political Scien*ce (2002), vol. 24, no. 3, pp. 411–431.

Agamben suggests in the *Kingdom and the Glory* (2011) – that opens anew the dialogue with the forces of impotentiality. This constructive dialogue, as Whyte importantly notes, is about 'intervening into our processes of subjectification'.[68] A *Shabbat* of voting denaturalises Western institutions not to eventually resume our engagement with them but in so doing it 'brings the contingent into view'[69] and hence it creates new political territories.

Further reading

Calarco, Matthew and Steven DeCaroli (eds), *Giorgio Agamben: Sovereignty and Life* (Stanford: Stanford University Press, 2007).

Durantaye, Leland de la, *Agamben: A Critical Introduction* (Stanford: Stanford University Press, 2009).

Mills, Catherine, *The Philosophy of Agamben* (Montreal: McGill-Queen's University Press, 2008).

Prozorov, Sergei, *Agamben and Politics: A Critical Introduction* (Edinburgh: Edinburgh University Press, 2014).

Svirsky, Marcelo and Simone Bignall, *Agamben and Colonialism* (Edinburgh: Edinburgh University Press, 2012).

Whyte, Jessica, *Catastrophe and Redemption: The Political Thought of Giorgio Agamben* (Albany: State University of New York Press, 2013).

---

68 Whyte, *Catastrophe and Redemption*, p. 166.
69 De la Durantaye, *Agamben*, p. 23.

12 | SLAVOJ ŽIŽEK

Paul A. Taylor

Biographical details

Slavoj Žižek (1949–) was born in Ljubljana in the People's Republic of Slovenia, Yugoslavia. He gained his PhD from the University of Ljubljana and went on to study psychoanalysis at the University of Paris-VIII with Jacques-Alain Miller and François Regnault. Žižek holds official positions as a senior researcher at the Institute for Sociology and Philosophy, University of Ljubljana, Slovenia, and he is the International Director of the Birkbeck Institute for the Humanities. He has also been appointed as Eminent Scholar at Kyung Hee University, South Korea. His theoretical anchor points are Jacques Lacan's *oeuvre*, Marxist political theory and German Idealist philosophy. Less officially, Žižek is renowned as a prolific author and celebrity academic who sharply divides opinion. The adulation of atypically large crowds for talks on esoteric theory can be clearly seen on numerous YouTube clips, while for others he is a *bête noir* – *à la* Adam Kirsch's characterisation of him as the 'Deadly Jester'.[1]

For a theorist with such seemingly specialised interests, Žižek has made significant contributions to an unusually diverse range of fields including cultural theory, psychoanalysis, theology (Žižek reinterprets the Pentecostal aspect of Christianity in terms of social-ist solidarity – 'whenever two or more are gathered in my name'), politics and film studies. His first international impact came with his break-out book *The Sublime Object of Ideology* (1989),[2] and, in addition to a subsequent disconcertingly large number of theoreti-cal monographs and journalistic articles, Žižek has starred in two feature-length explorations of cinema – *The Pervert's Guide to Cinema*

1 Adam Kirsch, 'The Deadly Jester', *New Republic* (3 December 2008), www.newrepublic.com/article/books/the-deadly-jester.
2 Slavoj Žižek, *The Sublime Object of Ideology* (London: Verso, 1989).

(2006) and *The Pervert's Guide to Ideology* (2012) – both directed by Sophie Fiennes. He has also made a series of appearances on news and cultural affairs programmes including the BBC's *Hard Talk* and *Newsnight*. Žižek's trademark contributions within the media typically involve polemical interpretations of popular culture and world events, for which he uses his eclectic mix of Lacanian psychoanalysis, Hegelian philosophy and Marxist politics. *The International Journal of Žižek Studies*, an open-access on-line journal, was launched in 2007 to reflect the growing level and breadth of intellectual interest in his work.

Both the scale of Žižek's output and the fact he liberally cross-references his own texts, frequently recycling whole paragraphs or even sections,[3] makes identifying key texts somewhat problematic; however, central themes are identifiable. Thus, following *The Sublime Object of Ideology*, Žižek has continued to regularly engage with the ideological aspects of contemporary politics, as illustrated in works such as *The Year of Living Dangerously* (2012),[4] with its reflections upon the political and cultural significance of the Occupy Wall Street movement. His other major focus, albeit with the ultimate aim of illustrating contemporary politics, is popular culture, in particular Hollywood cinema.

Despite the fact that his preferred triad of Lacanian psychoanalysis, Marxist politics and Hegelian philosophy is consistently interwoven throughout Žižek's texts, it is still possible to identify specific works as particularly strong examples of individual elements in the triad, namely:

- Hegelian philosophy: *Tarrying with the Negative* (1993)[5] and *Less than Zero* (2012);[6]
- Marxist political theory: *In Defense of Lost Causes* (2009);[7]

---

3 For some this amounts to a form of self-plagiarism; for others, a careful reading of these apparent repetitions reveals new nuances and fresh contexts that encourage the reader to revisit their previous interpretations.
4 Slavoj Žižek, *The Year of Living Dangerously* (London: Verso, 2012).
5 Slavoj Žižek, *Tarrying with the Negative: Kant, Hegel and the Critique of Ideology* (Durham, NC: Duke University Press, 1993).
6 Slavoj Žižek, *Less than Zero: Hegel and the Shadow of Dialectical Materialism* (London: Verso, 2012).
7 Slavoj Žižek, *In Defense of Lost Causes* (London: Verso, 2009).

- Lacanian psychoanalysis: *Looking Awry: An Introduction to Jacques Lacan through Popular Culture* (1991),[8] *Everything You Always Wanted To Know About Lacan (But Were Afraid To Ask Hitchcock)* (1992),[9] *Enjoy Your Symptom! Jacques Lacan In Hollywood and Out* (2000)[10] and How to Read Lacan (2006).[11]

Theorising violence

Of most relevance to this volume's subject matter is Žižek's appropriately entitled *Violence: Six Sideways Reflections* (2008).[12] The subtitle merits attention: 'sideways reflections' resonates with other titles such as *Looking Awry* and *The Parallax View* (2006)[13] and is typical of the consistent emphasis Žižek has placed throughout his career upon methodological reflexivity. Key to Žižek's analysis of violence is his desire to highlight the need to find a viewing point from which we can clearly observe what we routinely fail to see. To do this, Žižek uses a series of definitional distinctions.

Subjective violence Subjective violence is what we common-sensically understand by the notion of violence and is defined by Žižek as that which is 'performed by a clearly identifiable agent'.[14] In other words, subjective violence does not refer to any notion of an excessively personal interpretation of what constitutes violence; it is violence that can easily be attributed to an individual source. At the time of writing, for example, the disproportionately large number of gun deaths in America (the apparently intractable nature of which many non-Americans struggle to understand) has temporarily been encapsulated in the incident at the Burgers and Bullets gun-range incident in which a nine-year-old girl accidentally shot her shooting instructor. In a similar fashion to the short-term rise in public concern

---

8 Slavoj Žižek, *Looking Awry: An Introduction to Jacques Lacan through Popular Culture* (Cambridge, MA: MIT Press, 1991).

9 Slavoj Žižek, *Everything You Always Wanted to Know about Lacan (But Were Afraid to Ask Hitchcock)* (London: Verso, 1992).

10 Slavoj Žižek, *Enjoy Your Symptom! Jacques Lacan in Hollywood and Out*, 2nd ed. (New York: Routledge, 2000).

11 Slavoj Žižek, *How to Read Lacan* (London: Granta, 2006).

12 Slavoj Žižek, *Violence: Six Sideways Reflections* (London: Profile, 2008).

13 Slavoj Žižek, *The Parallax View* (Cambridge, MA: MIT Press, 2006).

14 Žižek, *Violence* , p. 1.

that accompanies periodic school shooting tragedies, something that normally remains at the level of abstract crime statistics is given fresh import before being subsumed by various normalising processes that Žižek describes using the notion of 'objective violence'.

Objective violence   Objective violence is the pervasive, systemic forms of violence that are not so easily attributed to an easily identifiable source. Žižek subdivides objective violence into two parts.

Firstly, 'symbolic violence' is the basic form of violence 'that pertains to language as such'.[15] The cardinal philosophical point is that all communication has an inescapably violent element; the key political question merely rests in the type of violence a society chooses to privilege. Thus Baudrillard finds in the agonistic, threatening challenges laid down by anthropological forms of symbolic exchange a desirable form of communicational violence. Subtle nuances are contained within traditional rituals of gift-giving that produce a culture full of seductive ambiguities as gift givers and receivers enter into a chain of counter-gifts and 'face'-maintaining protocols. This can be contrasted with the much more pre-ordained, pre-inscribed cultural values transmitted within the commodity culture of mass media society. At one level, the transmission of this technologically mediated commodified order appears to occur in a less symbolically violent form than its more 'primitive' counterparts. This is because much less is demanded from the sender and recipient. On another level, however, it is steeped with systemic violence.

'systemic violence' is 'the often catastrophic consequences of the smooth functioning of our economic and political systems'.[16] This concept refers to the predominantly unrecognised levels of force and repression that form a base level, frequently dispersed, but nevertheless effective and powerful circumscription of social activity. Žižek's concept of objective violence draws attention to those cultural elements that have profound effects but are largely invisible to the ideologically acclimatised eye:

> Objective violence is invisible since it sustains the very zero-level standard against which we perceive something as subjectively

15 Žižek, *Violence*, p. 1.
16 Žižek, *Violence*, p. 1.

violent. Systemic violence is thus something like the notorious 'dark matter' of physics, the counterpart to an all-too visible subjective violence. It may be invisible, but it has to be taken into account if one is to make sense of what otherwise seem to be 'irrational' explosions of subjective violence.[17]

Žižek is fond of pointing out that, although the vast majority of people know that Martin Luther King Jr had a dream, it is much less common for people to be familiar with the unashamedly left-wing political content of that dream. The latter-day media's fabrication of Martin Luther King Jr's highly subjectivised, uncontroversial image as an unquestionably good civil rights leader serves as an example of the ideological consequences of failing to appreciate the objective–subjective violence distinction. Disproportionate emphasis upon Martin Luther King Jr as a charismatic leader displaces attention away from the substantive content of his political struggle and sustained consideration of the pervasive, day-to-day nature of the violent inequality faced by African Americans. In a similar manner across the mediascape, explicit consideration of objective violence tends to be limited to temporary events in which the objective causes of violence are momentarily highlighted before being quickly subsumed again by the symbolic violence of a framework that privileges less politically confrontational, more media-friendly themes. Examples of this process as it relates to the African American experience include the recent uprisings in Ferguson, Missouri, and the Hurricane Katrina disaster. More usual is a situation in which objective violence is unrecognised and in which, *pace* President Dwight D. Eisenhower, it produces a culture that can best be described as the military industrial non-complex.

The cultural violence of the military industrial non-complex

> The thing is, *Schindler's List* is about success, the Holocaust was about failure. (Stanley Kubrick)[18]

---

17 Žižek, *Violence* , p. 2.

18 Terry Gilliam, 'Terry Gilliam Explains the Difference between Kubrick (Great Filmmaker) and Spielberg (Less So)', Open Culture (25 November 2011), www.openculture.com/2011/11/terry_gilliam_on_filmmakers.html.

I don't like the red coat; it gave me a queasy feeling the first time I saw *Schindler's List*. And I know that it was in the profound nature of Hollywood that the concentration camp story could only be told in a big, mainstream picture if someone found a story that had at least a touch of the upbeat. That was Oskar Schindler.[19]

A unique aspect of Žižek's approach to violence is the way that he is able to mine popular culture in order to create both topical and highly practical examples of the way in which our deeper appreciation of its objective nature is blocked as part of the media's standard operating procedure. In particular, Žižek likes to use Hollywood films to further develop the theories of ideology provided by Althusser and others and thereby show how the film industry routinely processes the ideological climate within which violence comes to be recognised as such. Stanley Kubrick's remark about *Schindler's List* succinctly encapsulates the nature of the process whereby the depiction of subjective violence actively displaces consideration of its objective underpinnings. Similarly, Thomson points out how the prioritisation of the individual figure of Oskar Schindler distracts us from the pervasively objective facts of continent-wide genocide. The film's status as an encapsulation of the ideological processing of violence is yet further encapsulated in its most vivid scene – in the midst of the almost incomprehensible horror, a little girl in a bright red coat stands out in an otherwise exclusively monochrome *mis-en-scène*. In Žižekian terms, the red coat is a stain that serves the opposite role to that of the ship at the end of the terraced street in Hitchcock's *Marnie* (1964). Spielberg provides schmaltz even when addressing the industrialised slaughter of a people.

Perhaps Žižek's most significant contribution to understanding this ideological processing of violence is the manner in which his analysis adds a further, more complex, level to this relatively uncontroversial notion that Hollywood typically peddles unrealistic degrees of optimism. In order to show why objective and subjective violence are not more frequently appreciated as distinct entities, Žižek uses the Batman movie franchise in order to explore the role played

19 David Thomson, 'Schindler's Girl in the Red Coat Speaks Out', *New Republic* (7 March 2013), www.newrepublic.com/article/112598/schindlers-girl-red-coat-speaks-out#.

by the predominant social attitude of 'postmodern cynicism' – an ideological climate in which we are shown the truth but continue to act as if we don't know. Žižek frequently summarises this condition with the phrase popularised by the French psychoanalyst Octave Manoni – *je sais bien mais quand même* (I know well, but even so).[20]

The Dark Knight (dir. Nolan, 2008) provides a strong practical demonstration of postmodern cynicism. The character of the Joker explicitly shows how the subjective versus objective violence distinction is socially manifested:

> I just did what I do best. I took your little plan and I turned it on itself. Look what I did to this city with a few drums of gas and a couple of bullets. Hmmm? You know … You know what I've noticed? Nobody panics when things go 'according to plan'. Even if the plan is horrifying! If, tomorrow, I tell the press that, like, a gang banger will get shot, or a truckload of soldiers will be blown up, nobody panics, because it's all 'part of the plan'. But when I say that one little old mayor will die, well then everyone loses their minds![21]

As the most truthful character in the film, the Joker plays a key role in revealing the underlying truth of the social order:

> The film's take-home message is that lying is necessary to sustain public morale: only a lie can redeem us. No wonder the only figure of truth in the film is the Joker, its supreme villain. He makes it clear that his attacks on Gotham City will stop when Batman takes off his mask and reveals his true identity; to prevent this disclosure and protect Batman, Dent tells the press that he is Batman – another lie. In order to entrap the Joker, Gordon fakes his own death – yet another lie. The Joker wants to disclose the truth beneath the mask, convinced that this will destroy the social order. What shall we call him? A terrorist?[22]

20 Octave Manoni, '*Je sais bien, mais quand-même …*': *Clefs pour l'imaginaire ou l'autre scène* (Paris: Editions du Seuil, 1969), pp. 9–33.

21 *The Dark Knight*, dir. Christopher Nolan (2008).

22 Slavoj Žižek, 'Good Manners in the Age of Wikileaks', *London Review of Books* (20 January 2011), www.lrb.co.uk/v33/no2/slavoj-zizek/good-manners-in-the-age-of-wikileaks.

The various films in the Batman franchise do exactly that. The Joker takes his place alongside Ra's Al Ghul and Bane as a clear embodiment of those who, angered by the social injustices of the status quo, refuse to succumb to the mentality of *je sais bien mais quand même* but whom, nevertheless, we are encouraged to view as villains in a latter-day manifestation of Guy Debord's prescient insight into the key ideological role played by the concept of terrorism.

Hollywood's violent projections

> This perfect democracy fabricates its own inconceivable enemy, terrorism. It wants, actually, to be judged by its enemies rather than by its results. The history of terrorism is written by the State and it is thus instructive. The spectating populations must certainly never know everything about terrorism, but they must always know enough to convince them that, compared with terrorism, everything else seems rather acceptable, in any case more rational and democratic.[23]

Žižek's interpretation of violence can be seen as a development of Debord's *The Society of the Spectacle* (1967).[24] In such a society, the low-visibility, background nature of objective violence makes it media unfriendly and therefore less noteworthy. Due to its spectacle-dominated framework, the media *system* proves highly ineffective at highlighting the casual mechanisms of objective violence. For example, attempts by television news to provide historical context for its items tend to be dominated by metronomically metonymic images. Complex cultural histories become inseparable from reductive, excessively familiar pictures – bombed-out Iraqi towns, emaciated African babies, Uzi-toting Israeli soldiers and *keffiyeh*-wearing Palestinian stone throwers. Post-9/11, Debord's earlier observations on the working nature of contemporary democracies have proved particularly accurate. Žižek's texts in general, and *Violence* more specifically, enable us to understand more precisely the various elements of the government-sponsored construction of democratic reason.

23 Guy Debord, *Comments on the Society of Spectacle*, trans. Malcom Imrie (London: Verso, 1990), sect. 9.
24 Guy Debord, *The Society of the Spectacle* (Detroit: Black and Red, 1977 [1967]).

The Žižekian interpretation in which Batman-type films represent explicit ideological expressions of the postmodern cynicism that underlies democratic reason is validated by Christopher Nolan, the director of the most recent trilogy:

> Ra's Al Ghul is a fascinating character, because he's not a boilerplate nefarious villain who wants to dominate the world, he's an ideological villain. He seems to have been ripped from today's headlines, especially with his rhetoric about the decadence of the capitalist West. With my co-writers David Goyer and my brother [Jonathan Nolan], we decided early on that the greatest villains in movies, the people who most get under our skin, are the people who speak the truth.[25]

Nolan openly recognises a key ideological aspect of postmodern cynicism. His 'villains' are undoubtedly guilty of violence, but, as Nolan freely admits, it is a violence carried out in the service of truth. Hollywood representations of villainous violence, therefore, serve to highlight the under-acknowledged nature of the objective violence that liberal democracies depend upon for their normal functioning. Film-goers are presented with an institutionalised form of disingenuous contradiction. Obvious parallels between the League of Shadows and the Occupy Wall Street movement are designed to undermine the notion of political activism while we are simultaneously predisposed to accept and then promptly overlook dramatic images of establishment duplicity. In *The Dark Knight*, for example, with one side of his face burnt to bone and sinew, the pillar of the establishment, District Attorney Harvey Dent, is reduced to a grossly disfigured character – he is literally two-faced.

A crucial feature of postmodern cynicism is thus its tendency to hide the truth of society's fundamental structural flaws in plain sight. Beyond the fictional world of Gotham City, the same processes are evident in films that address topical world events. For Žižek, Kathryn Bigelow's film *Zero Dark Thirty* (2012) typifies the sort of film used to propagate the *je sais bien mais quand même* mind-set.

25 Christopher Nolan, quoted in Scott Foundas, 'Cinematic Faith', *Film Comment* (2013), http://filmcomment.com/article/cinematic-faith-christopher-nolan-scott-foundas.

When criticised for the film's graphic depiction of state-condoned torture, Bigelow responded that 'Those of us who work in the arts know that depiction is not endorsement',[26] but for Žižek this is an unconvincing justification:

> Really? One doesn't need to be a moralist, or naive about the urgencies of fighting terrorist attacks, to think that torturing a human being is in itself something so profoundly shattering that to depict it neutrally – i.e. to neutralise this shattering dimension – is already a kind of endorsement.

> Imagine a documentary that depicted the Holocaust in a cool, disinterested way as a big industrial-logistic operation, focusing on the technical problems involved (transport, disposal of the bodies, preventing panic among the prisoners to be gassed). Such a film would either embody a deeply immoral fascination with its topic, or it would count on the obscene neutrality of its style to engender dismay and horror in spectators. Where is Bigelow here?[27]

Žižek's argument raises some complex questions about the contrasting roles of art and theory in examining the ideological status of violence. For Žižek, the neutral depiction of violence is a form of symbolic violence that cultivates and facilitates the cultural normalisation of immoral fascination. This is a fascination that shares qualities similar to the pervasive rise of celebrity culture as a now generalised social mentality. When attempting to analyse this obscenity, however, theorists encounter a paradoxical difficulty – they themselves can be subjected to the knee-jerk accusation that they are endorsing the very immorality they are opening to critique.

Acheronta movebo: The violent reactions to Zizek's psychoanalytical theory

> This obscene underground, the unconscious terrain of habits, is what is really difficult to change. This is why the motto of every

26 Slavoj Žižek, 'Zero Dark Thirty: Hollywood's Gift to American Power', *The Guardian* (13 January 2013), www.theguardian.com/commentisfree/2013/jan/25/zero-dark-thirty-normalises-torture-unjustifiable.

27 Žižek, 'Zero Dark Thirty'.

radical revolution is the same as the quote from Virgil that Freud chose as the epigraph for his *Interpretation of Dreams*: *acheronta movebo* – I will move the infernal regions. Dare to disturb the underground of the unspoken underpinnings of our everyday lives![28]

Žižek's claim that it is difficult to change the unconscious terrain of habits has been borne out by the hostile reception that his heavily theoretical and, perhaps even worse than that for some, psychoanalytically influenced approach has evoked. As Žižek points out in the quote above, this stems not from the inaccuracy of the analysis but from the entrenched emotional and psychological investments, the unspoken underpinnings, threatened by it. *Ad hominem*, subjective critique is used to displace the substance of the conceptual points being made about objective processes. Resistance to shedding a light on our infernal regions occurs across the political spectrum. Thus, one of Žižek's most violently dismissive critics in recent times has been Noam Chomsky, who elaborated as follows on his dislike of Theory with a capital 'T':

> When I said I'm not interested in Theory, what I meant is, I'm not interested in posturing – using fancy terms like polysyllables and pretending you have a theory when you have no theory whatsoever. So there's no theory in any of this stuff, not in the sense of theory that anyone is familiar with in the sciences or any other serious field. Try to find in all of the work you mentioned some principles from which you can deduce conclusions, empirically testable propositions where it all goes beyond the level of something you can explain in five minutes to a twelve-year-old. See if you can find that when the fancy words are decoded. I can't. So I'm not interested in that kind of posturing. Žižek is an extreme example of it. I don't see anything to what he's saying.[29]

Other equally biting examples of critical reaction include statements such as 'this work does not even approach the standards of academic

28 Žižek, *Violence*.
29 Noam Chomsky, 'Virtual Town Hall', interview with Noam Chomsky (December 2012), www.goodreads.com/quotes/838704-what-you-re-referring-to-is-what-s-called-theory-and-when.

rigour that would normally be expected of an undergraduate essay'[30] and John Gray's play on the title of Žižek's Hegelian magnum opus *Less than Zero*:[31] 'Achieving a deceptive substance by endlessly reiterating an essentially empty vision, Žižek's work – nicely illustrating the principles of paraconsistent logic – amounts in the end to less than nothing.'[32]

The fact that Chomsky and others reject out of hand any substantive content to Žižek's work when it involves close readings of such major figures of Western thought as G. W. F. Hegel, Karl Marx and Lacan, to name but three, serves to clearly outline the demarcation dispute that exists for some between serious and non-serious thinking. For Chomsky, seriousness is synonymous with the scientific mode of enquiry, but to go from this position of empirical fundamentalism to not seeing *anything* in Žižek's work (beyond what could be explained in five minutes to a twelve-year-old) clearly goes beyond an all-excluding love of scientific punctiliousness alone. The reaction of Chomsky *et al.* inadvertently demonstrates the sort of deep libidinal investments that are made in order not to consider essential features of contemporary society – its infernal regions, which are underpinned by unacknowledged levels of objective violence.

One of the most infamous examples of this tension between subjective and objective elements of violence is contained within the controversy that has surrounded Martin Heidegger's reprehensible links with the Nazi party. At the most basic subjective level, his initial membership of the Nazi party and subsequent preternaturally stubborn post-war refusal to apologise for his actions means that some people are unable to look beyond his disreputable character to find any value in his whole philosophical *oeuvre*. At a deeper level, however, an interesting aspect of how commentators struggle to disassociate subjective and objective considerations arises when one considers that part of the evidence (in particular his rare direct reference to the Holocaust) used to condemn Heidegger the person actually shed light upon the same issue of obscene neutrality that

30 Jeremy Gilbert, 'All the Right Questions, All the Wrong Answers', in *The Truth of Žižek*, ed. Paul Bowman and Richard Stamp (London: Continuum, 2007), pp. 61–81.
31 Žižek, *Less than Zero*.
32 John Gray, 'The Violent Visions of Slavoj Žižek', *New York Times* (12 July 2012), www.nybooks.com/articles/2012/07/12/violent-visions-slavoj-zizek.

interests Žižek. Rather than demonstrating Heidegger's Nazi sympathies, his reference to the Holocaust instead goes straight to the essence of objective violence.

The essence of the problem with violence

> Agriculture is now a mechanized food industry, in essence the same as the production of corpses in the gas chambers and extermination camps, the same thing as the blockading and starving of countries, the same thing as the production of hydrogen bombs.[33]

The above, repeatedly asserted, equivalence Heidegger made between processes of apparently contrasting degrees of technological sophistication using the phrase 'the same thing' led to such representative criticisms as Davidson's observation that:

> When one encounters Heidegger's 1949 pronouncement, one cannot but be staggered by his inability – call it metaphysical inability – to acknowledge the everyday fate of bodies and souls, as if the bureaucratized burning of selected human beings were not all that different from the threat to humanity posed in the organization of the food industry by the forces of technology.[34]

Using the phrase, 'were not all that different', Davidson fundamentally misses Heidegger's central philosophical point. By concentrating solely on Heidegger's expression 'the same thing as' to the exclusion of the crucial qualification contained in the immediately preceding 'in essence', Davidson and others miss how, with his use of this specific phrase, Heidegger draws attention to the fact that it is possible for activities that are vastly different in both their substantive content and the overt intentions that lie behind them to share, nevertheless, a common underlying quality of violence. Heidegger's egregious personal past means that his philosophical desire to highlight an essential equivalence that has profound implications for our

---

33 Martin Heidegger, in *Bremen and Freiburg Lectures: Insight into That Which Is and Basic Principles of Thinking*, trans. A. J. Mitchell (Bloomington: Indiana University Press, 2012 [1949]), p. 27.

34 Arnold I. Davidson, 'Questions concerning Heidegger: Opening the Debate', *Critical Inquiry* 15(2) (1989), p. 424.

understanding of violence and its place within society is also susceptible to the previous accusation Žižek made against Bigelow – for many, it suffers from a fatal flaw of the 'obscene neutrality of its style'.[35] Žižek attempts to avoid the obscene neutrality of dispassionate discussion. He tries to obtain a suitably parallax view of violence by looking awry (to use two of his book titles), as conveyed in the subtitle of *Violence: Six Sideways Reflections*.

In his highly influential essay 'The Question concerning Technology' (1962), Heidegger points out that there are many different forms of technological artefact, but, common across such diverse forms, there is an overarching quality that transcends any particular manifestation: 'The essence of technology is by no means anything technological'.[36] Any individual piece of technology embodies a more general aspect – it is the specific instrumental facilitation of a more general objectifying attitude towards human experience. Similarly, for Žižek, individual instances of violence belie their role within a wider ideological schema. The fact that Heidegger's reprehensible past makes him vulnerable to charges of heraldic insensitivity does not, on its own, explain away the persistence elsewhere among other prominent Jewish thinkers – such as Zygmunt Bauman and Richard Bernstein – of sentiments that, like Heidegger's, insist upon the wider and more generalisable significance of the industrial nature of the Holocaust.

Thus, in terms reminiscent of imagery present in Heidegger's work, Bauman argues:

> Like everything else in our modern society, the Holocaust was an accomplishment in every respect superior if measured by the standards that this society has preached and institutionalized. It towers high above the past genocidal episodes in the same way as the modern industrial plant towers above the craftsman's cottage workshop, or the modern industrial farm with its tractors, combines and pesticides, towers above the peasant farmstead with its horse, hoe and hand-weeding.[37]

35 Žižek, '*Zero Dark Thirty*'.
36 Martin Heidegger, 'The Question concerning Technology', in *The Question Concerning Technology and Other Essays*, trans. William Lovitt (New York: Harper, 1977 [1962]), p. 20.
37 Zygmunt Bauman, *Modernity and the Holocaust* (Cambridge: Polity, 1989), p. 89.

It is understandable that, in such horrific instances as the Holocaust, subjective factors cannot always be dispassionately removed from discussions of objective processes and that there is a natural human tendency to seek to embody and anchor objective causes of violence in human subjects. This explains the perennial resonance of Hannah Arendt's characterisation of Adolf Eichmann as the embodiment of the banality of evil. However, this approach still leaves important questions regarding the relationship between subjective and objective violence unaddressed, and these Žižek's psychoanalytically influenced theory is uniquely suited to help answer.

The violence of the symbolic order

> The trouble with Eichmann was precisely that so many were like him, and that the many were neither perverted nor sadistic, that they were, and still are, terribly and terrifyingly normal. From the viewpoint of our legal institutions and of our moral standards of judgment, this normality was much more terrifying than all the atrocities put together.[38]

It has become an almost standard and predictable trope after the eventual discovery of a serial killer or other serial criminal that, when interviewed by the media, the criminal's neighbours comment upon how normal and unassuming the killer appeared to be. From Peter Sutcliffe ('the Yorkshire Ripper') to Josef Fritzl, evil acts are frequently carried out by perfectly normal people.

On the much greater scale of the Holocaust, Arendt's *Eichmann in Jerusalem* is devoted to exploring the obvious difficulty in reconciling almost unimaginable levels of killing and the superficially mundane demeanour of the perpetrators. Such was Eichmann's unassuming appearance that Arendt describes how: 'Half a dozen psychiatrists had certified him as "normal" – "More normal, at any rate, than I am after having examined him", one of them was said to have exclaimed.'[39] That Eichmann still grips the collective imagination so strongly – not, as Arendt points out in the quotation above, because

---

38 Hannah Arendt, *Between Past and Future: Eight Exercises in Political Thought* (London: Penguin, 1993 [1954]), p. 276.
39 Arendt, *Between Past and Future*, p. 25.

of his sadism, but precisely because his normality – hints at what we have previously seen Žižek describe as the infernal region, the dark underpinnings of conventional society.

The disquiet that met Heidegger's claim of similarity 'in essence' between the death camps and modern technology relates to this difficulty of squaring the normal/evil circle so that:

> We may find it almost impossible to image how someone could 'think' (or rather, not think) in this manner, whereby manufacturing food, bombs, or corpses are 'in essence the same' and where this can become 'normal', 'ordinary' behavior. This is the mentality that Arendt believed she was facing in Eichmann.[40]

A full understanding of Nazi violence therefore requires not just recognition of the degree of barbarity involved but also acknowledgement of the necessary tension and juxtaposition of the barbaric and the civilised that is required for truly horrific violence – that is, the relationship between violence and the symbolic order within which it is defined and understood. For Žižek, the problematic aspect of Arendt's thesis resides in its failure to account adequately for the libidinal investment involved in otherwise seemingly normal bureaucratic processes.

The falsity of *Schindler's List* is thus the same as the falsity of those who seek the clue to the horrors of Nazism in the 'psychological profiles' of Hitler and other Nazi figures. Here Arendt was right in her otherwise problematic thesis on the 'banality of evil': if we take Eichmann as a psychological entity, a person, we discover nothing monstrous about him – he was just an average bureaucrat, and his 'psychological profile' gives us no clue to the horrors he executed.[41]

It is the conventional failure to appreciate the frequently close relationship between the evil and the everyday that, on the one hand, makes people surprised when faced with the banality of Eichmann-like figures and, on the other hand, allows for the uncritical fetishisation of extreme violence as some sort of unthinkable,

40 Richard Bernstein, 'Evil, Thinking, and Judging', in *Hannah Arendt and the Jewish Question* (Cambridge: MIT Press, 1996), p. 170.
41 Slavoj Žižek, 'Laugh Yourself to Death: The New Wave of Holocaust Comedies!' (15 December 1999), www.lacan.com/zizekholocaust.htm.

inconceivable aberration. The commonly portrayed status of the Holocaust's exceptionality occurs, however, alongside its continued use as an ideological stick with which to beat down a more nuanced understanding of violence. Žižek argues that:

> this very depoliticization of the holocaust, its elevation into the properly sublime Evil, can also be a political act of utter cynical manipulation, a political intervention aiming at legitimizing a certain kind of hierarchical political relations. First, it is part of the postmodern strategy of depoliticization and/or victimization: is holocaust not the supreme proof that to be human today means to be a victim, not an active political agent? Second, it disqualifies forms of the Third World violations of human rights for which Western states are (co)responsible as minor in comparison with the Absolute Evil of the holocaust. Third, it serves to cast a shadow on every radical political project, i.e. to reinforce the Denkverbot (prohibition to think) against the radical political imagination: 'Are you aware that what you propose ultimately leads to the holocaust?' In short: notwithstanding the unquestionable sincerity of some of its proponents, the 'objective' ideologico-political content of the depoliticization of the holocaust, of its elevation into the abyssal absolute Evil, is the political pact of the aggressive Zionists and the Western Rightist anti-Semites at the expense of TODAY's radical political potentials.[42]

Thus, rather than be puzzled that German officers were able to perform atrocities and then go home and be ideal family men, listen to Mozart and so on, we should instead recognise 'the way ideology and power function at the level of their "microphysics"'.[43] Viewing evil only as banal fails to see 'the obscene, publicly unacknowledged surplus-enjoyment provided by executing orders'.[44] From Žižek's perspective, therefore, it is a mistake to think of the horrors of Nazi violence as either the product of commonplace banality or a complete

42 Žižek, 'Laugh Yourself To Death'.
43 Slavoj Žižek, *The Plague of Fantasies (Wo Es War)* (London: Verso, 1997), p. 55.
44 Žižek, *Plague of Fantasies*, p. 56.

historical aberration. Instead, to understand the underlying truth of violence, we need to appreciate how our easy familiarity with the excuse 'I was just following orders' hides the profound import lying behind such a glib phrase. The broader social order, from which myriad individual orders spring, is maintained by powerful libidinal forces, whether in Nazi Germany or contemporary democracies.

The essential gap in Zizek's repugnant hermeneutics of violence

Žižek is a fashionable Slovenian 'cultural theorist' and author of books on Lacan, Lenin and David Lynch ... but he is perhaps most famous for his judgement on 9/11: 'In a way, America got what it fantasised about'. That 'in a way' is pure Žižek: moral relativism masked by rhetorical evasion.[45]

'America got what it fantasised about' – which Žižek insinuates, echoing Baudrillard, is merely another way of saying that America got what it had coming ... Amid the fog of postmodern relativism disseminated by Baudrillard, Žižek, and others, something essential is missing.[46]

In the context of much higher death tolls from other tragedies elsewhere in the world, the 9/11 attack on New York's 'twin towers' was notable for the unparalleled traumatic effect it created around the globe, to the extent that even the usually less than sympathetic French attitude to America was summed up in the *Le Monde* heading of 12 September: 'We are All Americans'. In *Welcome to the Desert of the Real* (2002)[47] and *Iraq: The Borrowed Kettle* (2004),[48] Žižek explores the politics of this violent event from a range of perspectives, but, interestingly, it was his linking of the event to the American collective fantasy that produced the most ire from his critics. For example, in the quotes above, Bearn and Wolin encapsulated a particular type of

45 Mark Bearn, 'On the Rampage: Generation Kill', *New Statesman* (2 August 2004), www.newstatesman.com/node/160291.
46 Richard Wolin, *The Seduction of Unreason: The Intellectual Romance with Fascism from Nietzsche to Postmodernism* (Princeton: Princeton University Press, 2004), p. 307.
47 Slavoj Žižek, *Welcome to the Desert of the Real* (New York: Verso, 2002).
48 Slavoj Žižek, *Iraq: The Borrowed Kettle* (New York: Verso, 2004).

reaction that objected in principle to the understanding of violence through the prism of psychoanalytical thought. The symbolically violent resistance to psychoanalytical insight begins with difficulty in even recognising the *a priori* legitimacy of theorising about cultural fantasies. This is indicated by Bearn putting 'cultural theorist' in apparently ironic quotation marks, and by Wolin's insistence that 'something essential is missing'. Like Wolin's criticisms, John Gray's condemnatory review of Zizek in the *New York Times*, entitled 'The Violent Visions of Slavoj Žižek', also focused upon his 'essentially empty vision'.

We have seen from the reaction caused by Heidegger's analysis of technology's essence that attempts to discuss the objective causes behind subjective manifestations can lead to reactions of defensive incomprehension; however, in the above responses there is a particular irony in how Gray and Wolin focus upon the idea that something essential is missing when it is this very 'something essential' missing from conventional understandings of violence that Žižek wishes to highlight. In the sort of psychological terms Žižek's critics are predisposed to reject, this qualifies as an instance of projection. Part of Gray's critique cites Žižek's description of how, in Stalinist Russia, paranoid denunciation became institutionalised so that

> The art of identifying a kulak was thus no longer a matter of objective social analysis; it became a kind of complex 'hermeneutics of suspicion', of identifying an individual's 'true political attitudes' hidden beneath his or her deceptive public proclamations.[49]

Gray then proceeds to argue, 'Describing mass murder in this way as an exercise in hermeneutics is repugnant and grotesque; it is also characteristic of Žižek's work.'[50] In other words, for Gray, Zizek's analysis of how the essence of violence may be found in the symbolic order from which ideological categories are generated makes him guilty of condoning actual acts of violence.

The crucial distinction to be made here is between Žižek's explanation of the cultural and psychological processes that enable

49 Žižek, quoted in Gray, 'Violent Visions'.
50 Žižek, quoted in Gray, 'Violent Visions'.

mass murder and a repugnant and grotesque justification of mass murder itself. Ironically, the fact that a professional philosopher is willing to deliberately conflate (the alternative conclusion that he is unable to make the distinction is even more unflattering) a justification and an explanation serves to illustrate how the institutionalisation of paranoid denunciation works in a contemporary, non-Stalinist context. Gray's denunciation of Žižek's analysis of Stalin's violence represents an active refusal to recognise the links between the frequently arbitrary, irrational and intangible features of the overarching abstract ideology of a social order and the no less horrendous actual lived consequences of such abstract systems. Similarly, in the case of 9/11, to refuse to acknowledge the role played in our experience of violence by the psychological superstructure of fantasy can lead to an inability to recognise the truly fantastical scenario of the world's most powerful military force declaring war on an abstract noun – the *über*-Debordian notion of the global war on terror.

Confronting violence in the world

> There is an old story about a worker suspected of stealing: every evening, as he leaves the factory, the wheelbarrow he rolls in front of him is carefully inspected. The guards can find nothing. It is always empty. Finally the penny drops: what the worker is stealing are the wheelbarrows themselves.[51]

Contemporary democratic reason is dominated by a Manichean world view summarised by President George W. Bush in his address to a joint session of Congress: 'either you are with us, or you are with the terrorists'. An important aspect of Žižek's analysis of violence is the way in which he explores its innate quality within rather than outside democratic structures. The anecdote of the stolen wheelbarrows is one that Žižek frequently uses to illustrate the important political paradox that essential ideological elements can be hidden in plain sight. The day-to-day functioning of democratic governments requires a baseline level of (objective) violence that ceases to be recognised as such. The (subjective) violence that *is*

51 Žižek, *Violence*, p. 1.

recognised by the media systems that form the ideological backbone of the body politic, as the Joker points out, comes from what occurs outside state-recognised plans. Žižek conveys the strength of the resultant ideological consensus that dominates our understanding of violence by pointing out that, while the media finds itself able to discuss the potential end of human life on earth due to ecological disaster, it is structurally unable to imagine any political alternative to capitalism. The ideological construction of violence represents an important aspect of this political blind spot. It means that democratically sponsored violence occurs largely unrecognised, apart from occasional flash points such as Ferguson, Missouri or when presented by Western governments as unequivocally self-justified, yet nevertheless inchoate, bellicose rhetoric.

The fact that war can be declared on an abstract noun demonstrates the degree to which Debord's observations on the deeply ideological conceptualisation of terrorism have become an organic part of democratic reason. Like the commodity form whose 'theological niceties and metaphysical subtleties'[52] are supplanted by the uncritical society-wide fetishisation explored so influentially by Marx, Žižek shows how violence is subjected to a ubiquitous de-politicisation. The current media treatment of ISIS as an absolute form of evil, for example, partakes of the same essentially ideological series of manipulations that have previously been seen in the portrayal of the Holocaust as a historically unique form of evil. This is the ultimate significance of the Joker's claim that 'Nobody panics when things go "according to plan" ... But when I say that one little old mayor will die, well then everyone loses their minds!' R'as Al Ghul, Bane, the Joker – the villainous status of all these characters resides not in their telling of lies but rather in the fact that they tell the truth in a way that directly threatens the powerful investments we have made in society's various noble lies. Žižek's work demonstrates how Hollywood villains act as easily identifiable poster-boys for subjective violence. This is a violence processed in a fantasy realm that democratic governments keep corralled in the cultural reservation of Hollywood. Meanwhile, objective violence

52 Karl Marx, 'The Fetishism of Commodities and the Secret Thereof', in *Capital*, vol. 1 (1867), http://web.stanford.edu/~davies/Symbsys100-Spring0708/Marx-Commodity-Fetishism.pdf.

remains stubbornly immune to either fictional representation or political accountability.

Further reading

Taylor, Paul A., *Žižek and the Media* (Cambridge: Polity, 2010).

Žižek, Slavoj, *Iraq: The Borrowed Kettle* (New York: Verso, 2004).

Žižek, Slavoj, *The Sublime Object of Ideology* (London: Verso, 1989).

Žižek, Slavoj, *Violence: Six Sideways Reflections* (London: Profile, 2008).

Žižek, Slavoj, *The Year of Living Dangerously* (London: Verso, 2012).

13 | CYNTHIA ENLOE

Terrell Carver

Biographical details

Cynthia Enloe (1938–) was born on Long Island near New York City and grew up in a suburban setting. She graduated from Connecticut College in 1960 and earned an MA (1963) and PhD (1967) in political science at the University of California, Berkeley. At graduate level, Enloe trained in comparative politics, specialising in Southeast Asia and completing a dissertation on the ethnic politics of education in Malaysia. After a short stay at Miami University, Ohio, she taught for many years at Clark University in Worcester, Massachusetts, and continues teaching in a post-retirement capacity. Her first academic books did not, as she says, have the '"W" word' (for 'woman') in them at all, because she thought then that ethnic politics (or any politics of significance) was 'comprised merely of the ideas and actions of ungendered … men'.[1]

Enloe's subsequent involvement in the women's movement of the early 1970s and onwards influenced first her teaching and then her academic work. This trajectory resulted in the publication of her first feminist book, *Does Khaki Become You?*, a study in 'the militarization of women's lives' (its subtitle) in 1983.[2] Enloe is known for her international involvement in feminist activisms and for her pioneering work in international relations, notably for writing the now classic *Bananas, Beaches and Bases* (1989, 2nd ed. 2014). This book is continually cited as a 'discipline-changing' work, though opinions differ on whether or how much the discipline has changed. Enloe was the first to undertake a thorough feminist revisioning of international politics, and did so by asking an apparently simple question: 'Where are the women?'[3]

1 Cynthia Enloe, *The Curious Feminist: Searching for Women in a New Age of Empire* (Berkeley: University of California Press, 2004), pp. 155–166.
2 Enloe, *Curious Feminist*, pp. 166–168.
3 Cynthia Enloe, *Bananas, Beaches and Bases: Making Feminist Sense of International Politics*, 2nd ed. (Berkeley: University of California Press, 2014 [1989]), p. 1.

Theorising violence

The answer to Enloe's question 'Where are the women?' is also a good answer to the question 'Where is the violence?' But it is not the usual answer to this question, nor is the question the usual one, nor is the violence the usual thing we look for. Why should we have to ask 'Where is the violence?' when 'everyone already knows' where to look and what to look for? Overwhelmingly, the obvious presents an answer and thus obviates the need to ask the questions.

Violence for most readers and thinkers is obviously located in two quite different places: 'at home' and 'abroad'. When it is 'at home' it is criminality. Or rather criminality as we conceive it draws a line – or tries to – between violence and mere fisticuffs, high jinks, accidents, misadventure, corporal punishment, self-defence, legitimate restraint, drunken 'fun', contact sports, push-and-shove, consensual role-play and any number of other familiar and sometimes bruising phenomena and experiences.[4] When it is 'abroad' it is war. Or rather war as we conceive it draws a line – or tries to – between legitimate, proportionate and 'civilised' responses to unwarranted attacks, incursions, threats and subversion.[5] However, owing to the lack of sovereign institutions that rule on 'international' events, such that they are unambiguously known to be legitimate and justified, or illegitimate and unjustified, we experience a 'fog' of war-like ideas, rather than clarity. These ideas include conflict, civil war, 'troubles', terrorism, guerrilla action, Realpolitik, black ops, collateral damage, rebellion, partisan warfare, regime change, aerial bombing, improvised explosive devices, banditry, piracy, mass killing, genocide and any number of other versions of what's going on 'abroad'. Unlike most criminality 'at home', though, these phenomena hog the headlines and befog the citizenry.

When you find yourself off the plane and in a 'warzone', you experience a conflation of these two supposedly separate realms: criminality (where archetypically violence lurks in the shadows) and war (where archetypically violence rains down from the skies). When

4 See Adrian Howe, *Sex, Violence and Crime: Foucault and the Man Question* (Milton Park: Routledge-Cavendish, 2008).
5 See Helen Kinsella, *The Image before the Weapon: A Critical History of the Distinction between Combatant and Civilian* (Ithaca: Cornell University Press, 2011).

you find yourself in an office or on a subway train and 'under attack' (whether from small-arms fire or human-size explosives), much the same conflation applies. But overall 'war' trumps criminality, so 'the international' trumps the domestic, and what goes up the scale in that way seldom comes down again to 'mere' criminality. Or, rather, attempts to bring what are construed as instances of 'international' violence down to criminal jurisdictions, even 'international ones', do not get very far, or get as far as they have got only with difficulty. This is because criminality has its origins in individualised guilt and *mens rea*, and, in general, nation-states have more resources to deploy in order to keep themselves and their 'spokesmen' out of the dock than do individuals. Indeed individuals in the dock – even when addressed as epigones of a 'criminal' state – will always look like apparatchiks who have wandered into the 'banality of evil', as Hannah Arendt so famously summed up the situation.[6]

Enloe looked around the back of all these issues, all this language and all these presumptions, all this familiarity and obviousness, to the everyday lives of individuals, in particular women – women, *rather than* just 'individuals'. 'Individuals' as such appear ungendered, either men or women indifferently. In actuality this is a 'male-shaped' category; the 'individual' isn't really a woman, and womanly things are not first on the list – or even on the list at all – when filling in this abstraction with specifics. 'Woman' appears *in opposition* to this abstraction, as feminists have shown.[7]

Enloe grasped this intuitively and then made two revolutionary moves in one. The first was to begin the study of politics away from the 'high politics' of nation-states, international agencies and war/peace rhetorics, and move instead to the everyday, domestic, non-international and even non-public 'hearth and home' of the household and neighbourhood: 'Wars are never "over there"'.[8] The second was to enquire into the most basic building-block of the 'woman question'. Exactly whose question was this, and why was it a question? And who should 'obviously' be in charge of the solution? Enloe's feminist friends and colleagues were crucial to what became

---

6 Hannah Arendt, *Eichmann in Jerusalem: A Report on the Banality of Evil* (London: Faber, 1963).
7 Terrell Carver, 'Public Man and the Critique of Masculinities', *Political Theory* 24(4) (1996), pp. 673–686.
8 Enloe, *Curious Feminist*, p. 97.

the obvious conclusion: authoritative answers and non-obvious solutions would come from women.[9]

Once Enloe had liberated the study of politics from the international–domestic divide and thus from the sometimes conflationary character of the war–criminality divide, then the 'obvious' hierarchies of importance through which academia and the media characteristically operate had been levelled out. Moreover, on this newly levelled playing field, women could be anywhere and do anything, at least potentially. And potentially they were as interesting doing 'domestic' things as 'international' things, since the distinction had vanished and the hierarchy had been inverted. Whew. The world looks different after this, and so does the violence within it.

Curiouser and curiouser   Enloe deconstructed the categories through which the world of violence is normally parsed, and, more to the point, she created a non-hierarchy of significance. That is, she redefined what is potentially of interest and where to find information about it. This sets the stage for her 'curious feminist' to get to work in order to 'make the link' (as she put it in the subtitle to her book *Globalization and Militarism*, 2007).[10]

There is a methodological turnover here as well. Readers will struggle to find any 'major philosophers', political or international theorists, or 'great thinkers' cited in her work. This was not her training, which was in empirical and comparative studies in political science, though how closely related such 'empirics' were to anyone's actual experiences in politics was an early worry of hers. These worries led her to think 'Seriously!' (another of Enloe's book titles, published in 2013) about who anyone actually is – and, more pertinently, who anyone 'obviously' isn't. In Enloe's hands, who is 'obviously' a causal agent and who 'supposedly' couldn't be one is a major 'theoretical argument about causality'.[11] Her insight here is of specific reference to how feminism is often conceived, sometimes by feminists themselves (though Enloe carefully doesn't say so):

9 See, e.g., Cynthia Enloe, *Does Khaki Become You? The Militarization of Women's Lives* (London: Pandora, 1983), pp. xvii–xviii, though almost any page of her writings would do.
10 Cynthia Enloe, *Globalization and Militarism: Feminists Make the Link* (Boulder: Rowman & Littlefield, 2007), pp. 1–18.
11 Enloe, *Curious Feminist*, p. 169.

It's a mistake, I think, to portray feminist analyses as merely about impacts – for example, revealing the effects of war on women or of international debt on women ... *Bananas* [, *Beaches and Bases*] tries to show why the colonial project occurred the way it did ... [and] why states are so needful of ideas about masculinity and femininity.[12]

Enloe's curiosity was not so much about what *else* is going on outside the (formerly) 'obvious' hierarchies of significance but rather about how *all* of what is going on is there so that *any* of it can go on. Studies of ambassadorial wives, military 'camp followers' and nimble-fingered banana-packers could of course be of more (or 'obviously' less) interest in putting together the global picture of international 'high politics', armed servicemen's 'issues' and the political economy of client-state trade. Enloe's first book, *Bananas, Beaches and Bases* (1989), made some sense for many readers in those terms, because they were assuming that Enloe was highlighting women's 'bit-parts' in the larger scheme of things.

But that is not what really happens in this book. Enloe was able to show – through careful marshalling of anecdotal evidence and insistently persuasive common-sensical knowledge – that all was not what it was made out to be in the 'normal' frames of knowledge accumulation. And how it was made out to be was that women as such and women's activities in general were always and already an 'auxiliary', an 'add-on', something for 'them' to be interested in and 'us' (men) not to be curious about, since – by definition and by education – what's interesting is elsewhere, and 'obviously' comprises the 'real' world (as men have set it up to be seen and as it 'makes sense'). Enloe decided that 'making sense' (a phrase in the subtitle to her first book) should start all over again.[13]

Enloe did this in two ways. She argued that trivialisation and marginalisation were important forces in getting readers and viewers to foregone conclusions, and that foremost among these was the 'obvious' conclusion that women's activities were and are trivial and marginal. As she says, 'No individual or social group finds itself on the "margins" ... without some other individual or group having

12 Enloe, *Curious Feminist*, p. 169.
13 Enloe, *Bananas*, pp. 1–36.

accumulated enough power to create the "center" somewhere else.'[14] By demonstrating the functional centrality, causal importance and sheer economic necessity of women and what they do in the 'larger' scheme of things, Enloe made a very big claim. What makes the claim stick is a further Enloe-ism: a lot of *work* goes into making readers and viewers, students and 'the general public' *incurious* – that is, already invested in normalities, already in possession of what anyone needs to know, and knowing already who it is who *really* knows what's going on.[15]

Wising up and winning out   The 'who' in all these normalities, foregone conclusions and 'wise heads' is – men. Enloe was hardly the only person noticing this – most men took it as not just obvious but also unproblematic, and still do. Moreover she was hardly the first woman to find malestream knowledge and patriarchal institutions problematic and to take issue not just with 'obvious' appearances but also with 'deeper' claims that this was all as it should be, or indeed could ever be. These self-serving claims are generally rooted in supposed 'biological realities', reproductive morphologies, physical or hormonal difference, gender difference, God's will or any number of other explanations, 'incontrovertible facts' or commandments.

But the ground on which Enloe took issue with this was unusual (or perhaps unusual only outside some feminist circles of curiosity and debate). She made the link by demonstrating that men had bothered with women for various gender-centric reasons but had then disavowed this work by abjecting women as incapable of reason, or at least not nearly so good at it as the 'superior' sex, or anyway hardly any were as good, so that proved the rule.[16]

A corollary to that was the trivialisation, even invisibilisation, of 'women's activities' as (paradoxically) inessential, clearly a contradiction of the initial premise. Or, in other words, Enloe – with her curiosity, observation and reportage – did not create knowledge that men had somehow overlooked, given that it was obvious to them how and why they had overlooked these things, so perhaps they

---

14 Enloe, *Curious Feminist*, pp. 19–20.
15 Cynthia Enloe, *Seriously! Investigating Crashes and Crises as if Women Mattered* (Berkeley: University of California Press, 2013), pp. 10–12.
16 Enloe, *Bananas*, pp. 1–36.

should (possibly) change their minds. Instead she overturned how knowledge was conceived at all and in what knowledge consists, and argued – in books accessibly written for 'trade' rather than academia – that 'feminist sense' could make sense to anyone. As Enloe explains, 'a "text edition" ... is a book that most bookshops cannot afford to carry' because the wholesale discount to them is less than it is for a 'trade' book. 'Caring about a combined academic and non-academic readership has become part of my politics', she writes.[17]

This communication strategy also reconceives academic knowledge as a 'for whom' question; Enloe makes set-piece appeals to (and on behalf of) women who know what's going on (but are afraid to say). Or, in some cases, as documented by Enloe, not afraid to say:

> Some mothers began to collect the stories, to add up the
> suicides, to challenge officials' sanguine explanations ...
> some of the women whose sons had been officially listed as
> missing in action began to form groups ... The first objective
> of these groups was to extract more information ... It was
> the unresponsiveness and even contempt with which officials
> greeted these requests that sparked more radical thinking ...
> These women were redefining motherhood. Being a good Soviet
> mother and being a Soviet patriot no longer seemed mutually
> reinforcing.[18]

Rather than appealing to know-all philosophers and known-to-death texts, Enloe's opening salvo – in a typical example – is to cite Pocahontas, the seventeenth-century 'Indian' Princess, and Carmen Miranda, the 1930s movie star. After that, in the same passage, we get 'a foreign male soldier' and 'an impoverished, local woman'. Why should we be curious about any of these? What exactly is the link that will hold our interest? Why does Enloe start from here? And what does this (start to) tell us about violence? Enloe proceeds through storytelling, apparently oblivious to – or at least very uninterested in – the usual boundaries between historical mythologies, biographical 'brief lives' and anonymised tales of everyday folk. Rubbing it in, we

17 Enloe, *Curious Feminist*, pp. 167–168.
18 Cynthia Enloe, *The Morning After: Sexual Politics at the End of the Cold War* (Berkeley: University of California Press, 1993), pp. 12–13.

get a list – in no particular order, and thus disrupting any particular hierarchy:

> The woman tourist and the chambermaid; the schoolteacher and her students; the film star, her studio owners, the banana company executives, the American housewife, and contemporary YouTube enthusiasts; the male soldier, the brothel owner and the woman working as a prostitute.[19]

But where are the guns, the victims, the perpetrators, the violence – the 'real' action? They may all be out of sight, but they are not 'somewhere else' at all. The link that Enloe makes concerns gender relations, specifically between males and females, between masculinities and femininities, between the unfraternal 'opposites' of heterosexuality, since heterosexuality is the default presumption through which anyone 'becomes' – as Simone de Beauvoir famously put it – a 'woman'.[20] But, rather than labour the point, Enloe puts it to work.

Firstly, Enloe denies the distinction between 'scandal' (where violence is suddenly and 'inexplicably' made visible) and 'normality' (where it doesn't exist! until someone reveals it). Secondly, rather than reveal more scandal, the feminist 'link' shows how 'normality' stokes up the potential for violence, rather like the way that electrostatic charges accumulate – invisibly – and then flash forth violently for all to see. People have no doubt been curious about lighting flashes as long as there have been people, but only the empirical and theoretical work of curious amateurs (over the years) got us to the point of understanding the more general phenomenon of electrical *potential*. Enloe's picture of the human potential for violence turned the 'normality' of peaceful 'individual' relations and domestic relationships inside out. Sexual violence by men on women in the military, or located in a combat or 'R&R' zone, for instance, isn't different when 'abroad' from sexual violence perpetrated on women in or out of the military 'at home', media assertions about geography, legality and necessity or normality notwithstanding. The

---

19 Enloe, *Bananas*, pp. 7–8.
20 Simone de Beauvoir, *The Second Sex*, trans. and ed. H. M. Parshley, new ed. (London: Vintage, 1997 [1949]), bk 2, pt 4, ch. 1.

link is a general one, but Enloe puts it as a question rather than an answer:

> How exactly do diverse men inside the military absorb the
> masculinized idea that women are property to be used by
> men in ways that allegedly confirm their own manhood and
> simultaneously preserve the masculinized atmosphere in certain
> institutional spaces?[21]

This question is of course very general, but also refreshingly specific. And it is applicable to masculinised institutions generally. For Enloe the sordid tale of violence at the Sofitel in New York City, and subsequent allegations, court hearings and media coverage, was not an act when Dominique Strauss-Kahn was 'off duty' from his job as head of the International Monetary Fund. In classic style, she attacked the internal/external, domestic/international, high politics/low crime, government/business, masculine-aggression/female-passivity distinctions through which the 'incident' was reported and evaluated. Most importantly, she inverted the hierarchy of significance through which 'mere' workplace and other day-to-day cultures (where women mostly are) were invisibilised so that 'important' political summits were *visibilised* through the media as out-of-the-ordinary headline events. Giving due credit to feminists who already had their eye on such workplaces (both 'international' hotels and 'international' offices), Enloe asserted a *causal* link between organisational *cultures* that tolerate – indeed inculcate – misogyny and organisational *decisions* that tolerate – indeed create – the enormous 'gender gap' between men's and women's income, wealth, power and prospects over which the International Monetary Fund presides.[22]

What has happened here is interesting. Enloe was not the first to notice 'structural violence' – that is, conditions that (as with atmospheric electrical charges) prepare the way for (inevitable yet unpredictable) lightning strikes. Rather, what she did with an assertion of causation, but with a conclusion consisting of questions, was to subvert *both* a 'gendered' *reduction* of violence to individual specifics and subsequent court cases and lawsuits, *and* a 'gendered'

21 Enloe, *Bananas*, p. 156.
22 Enloe, *Seriously!*, pp. 49–56.

expansion of violence to cultural norms and patterns, zones of tolerance and resistance. Enloe vaporises the notions that seeing is believing and that well-founded belief can only rest on a retrospective causal chain of events. Instead, via her questions she poses a *prospective* view that privileges the future and challenges her readers – a rather hopeful 'us' in my sentence here – to wonder 'Seriously!' whether a sexist and misogynist organisational culture 'locally' can possibly *not* be linked to sexist and misogynist policy decisions 'internationally'.[23] Rhetorically, the question invites her readership to action and to summon the will to grapple with uncertainty. This is not a characteristic philosophically 'reflective' stance, nor does it look much like the certainty through which 'empirical' claims are usually made.

Rather than finding violence in the human potential 'to do evil', Enloe locates what could appear to be violence between individuals in a recognisable contemporary setting of modern-day militaries and other 'liberal' areas of public and private concern. Yet masculinisation has a long history and bad track record, and – in Enloe's brief but potent sketch – her power-vision is clearly applicable and visible in relation to all the institutions of modern-day societies, not just the military. This is quite a triumph of the everyday, but the terms are changed and the ground has shifted. Suddenly men are the problem, and we're no longer in 'a man's world' but in a world of worries about the 'man question'. Sexual violence – by men on women – isn't incidental to the violence of war or conflict or Realpolitik or 'defence' or 'security' or any of these other national or international frames of reference and discrete policy-spheres. Rather, sexual violence is a dynamic of international politics, not because it is nasty but because it is an easy place to normalise violence and brutality. The gender–sex hierarchy has already set this up: men do the slapping and pinching, punching and raping, and women (or perforce femininised men) get 'the business'. As Enloe details, military men (and others in similarly masculinised institutions) get 'into practice' in these 'small ways' – that is, by learning to do and to enjoy (or at least to accept) an active role in doing violence to other human beings, particularly women. Conveniently, women are generally defined as, and said by nature to be, smaller, weaker, more caring and nurturing, and, in

23 Enloe, *Seriously!*, p. 52.

those and other ways, a lesser order of humanity than their opposites and superiors.

Of course this hierarchy can be projected onto any number of other targets through race, class, religion, speciesism or any other way of organising beings into hierarchies of worth. Enloe goes for sexual difference here, inverts the romanticising narratives of 'two hearts beat as one' through a spectacular ideology-critique, and comes up with a genuinely universal proposition. As she says, in a homely touch, 'the politics of masculinity has been swept under the militarized rug'.[24] And, detailing this in a list, she says:

> Taking women seriously always has the effect of enabling us to see men as men. That is, when only men are treated as if they matter, those men appear to be generals, authorities, activists, police, farmers, soldiers, managers, investors, economists, writers, and insurgents. That serves to hide their masculinities. It makes us incurious about how male revolutionaries, male budget directors, male soldiers, male bankers imagine their own manliness, worry about expressing their manliness, and make choices based on their efforts to prove their manliness to their male rivals and male superiors.[25]

This is not a popular research programme. The chapter 'When Soldiers Rape' in *Maneuvers* (2000) makes harrowing reading. The evidence – finding truth conditions in the rhetoric of storytelling – comes from Bosnia, Kosovo, Okinawa, the Philippines, Rwanda – any number of places.[26] It could be responsible, fact-finding journalism, something a *Guardian* or BBC or *New Yorker* or New York or London *Review of Books* writer would come up with. But it isn't. Enloe has been to some of these places, and not others, and certainly not there as an eye-witness to most of what she recounts. Like academic writers, college professors like herself, she has research assistants, though paradoxically she denies this: 'No. I don't have research assistants.'[27] Unlike other college professors and academic

24 Enloe, *Bananas*, p. 156.
25 Enloe, *Seriously!*, p. 17.
26 Cynthia Enloe, *Maneuvers: The International Politics of Militarizing Women's Lives* (Berkeley: University of California Press, 2000), pp. 108–152.
27 Enloe, *Curious Feminist*, p. 165.

writers, though, Enloe's work is crowd-sourced, drawn from a wide network of international contacts, tried and trusted by herself. As she says, 'I have found that it is only by lots of us piecing together all sorts of information that we can make full sense of how militaries rely both on women and on presumptions about femininity.'[28] These are overwhelmingly feminist activists, curious and smart (a pair of Enloe-isms), *using* their reportage in protest, campaigning, lobbying for what they see as feminist causes and women's 'take' on issues. In their hands, and in Enloe's, these issues are not 'merely' local but – with effort – 'global'. Enloe is doubtless 'on side' for any or all of these, and doubtless also a respectful critic (if asked). But her books and writings are not issue-specific in that way.

Enloe's work has footnotes, references and formatting that tell us it's academic, since she is an academic (Research Professor of Women's Studies). But the methodology, as other academics might say, isn't a familiar one, nor is the writing style, even among feminist scholars, where there are others daring enough to experiment and push the boundaries. Sometimes her writing, she says, began as talks. But, in recounting these circumstances, Enloe tells us what she heard from the audience, and her talk hardly ever appears as such. She emerges from the text, and methodologically, as a listener. 'More and more', she says, 'listeners became contributors. Each taught me to pay fresh attention to puzzles, connections and implications, I earlier had missed.'[29]

In *Nimo's War, Emma's War* (2010), Enloe 'profiles', as she says, eight women – four Iraqi and four American – in order to make 'feminist sense of the Iraq War' (identified as such to reach the anglophone audience).[30] These are 'brief lives' in the classic tradition, assembled to give us an accessible way in to an era, an age, a culture, a window on hard human experience. Unlike John Aubrey, though, Enloe had never met the 'originals' and didn't intend to; and, unlike Aubrey, she wasn't interested in gossip and getting a 'personal' angle on the famous, titled, rich – and their wannabes.[31] Enloe constructed these extended narratives entirely from published

28 Enloe, *Maneuvers*, pp. ix–x.
29 Cynthia Enloe, *Nimo's War, Emma's War: Making Feminist Sense of the Iraq War* (Berkeley: University of California Press, 2010), p. xiii.
30 Enloe, *Nimo's War, Emma's War*, p. 1 and passim.
31 See John Aubrey, *Aubrey's Brief Lives* (Harmondsworth: Penguin, 1972)

sources. This makes two epistemological points: firstly, that anyone could have had access to this information and so could have generated knowledge from it for activist purposes, and, secondly, that activism does not require academic experts to generate or validate information as 'knowledge'.[32]

Phenomenologically, Enloe's method here makes a substantial point: people are a summation of their experiences, violent ones included, perhaps especially these. Such experiences are in some visceral and emotional sense the person, not 'things' that happen and go away, but with which 'the person' deals, more or less successfully. The stuff that happens is already around the person; they are already in it, and the process rolls on, leaving testimonial traces and reportage on which Enloe draws. But there is a project here, not just human interest. The project is an ontological and epistemological one: 'I was just trying', Enloe says, 'to find a way to make the complex wartime lives of Iraqi women as *real* as those of American women'.[33] Enloe is interestingly indifferent to nationality (her own and others') as a supposedly obvious epistemological boundary line – a limit to one's own knowledge or even curiosity and a get-out that others know-what-they-know 'over there'. In fact she says explicitly:

> I think it's very dangerous intellectually to be an American writer
> because it's too easy to mentally stand in the United States
> and see the world from New York or Boston or Chicago. The
> American brand of parochialism (and arrogance) is so seductive
> and so risky.[34]

The art of this (rather than the methodology) is making a link and testing it again and again, gathering information from all over the world, going places to find a different perspective, finding a vital clue in a whirl of diversity, and not letting go of it. One thing that really disappears in Enloe's text, though, is the courage it took in 2003 and for some time after to go out into the United States, even to college campuses, and 'talk about the war', as if there were really something to talk about, rather than simply to watch and celebrate on the (Fox) news.

32 Enloe, *Nimo's War, Emma's War*, p. 11.
33 Enloe, *Nimo's War, Emma's War*, p. xii (emphasis added).
34 Enloe, *Curious Feminist*, p. 169.

There is an Enloe-esque art of surprise and an interestingly 'material' turn in her work. Sometimes feminists are visibly a bit less than comfortable as Enloe – the famous feminist – talks entirely about men and masculinities for twenty minutes and – until she takes a deep breath – then mentions 'women'. Everyone is surprised, though, when the subject of an academic talk is billed as a can of soup[35] or a seminar opens with a polite request for a volunteer to remove a sports shoe and put it in the middle of the table for all to view.[36] Cans of soup are more dangerous than they look, and sports shoes far more puzzling than anyone realises. Enloe has effectively queered both in quite a deep way, way beyond what Andy Warhol did with his 32 *Campbell's Soup Cans* (1962) or what an economic geographer or labour economist might make of a handy metonymy before getting on with the data-sets.

Both these exemplars are genuinely quite sinister, 'creeping out' the audience. Enloe's point is not just that militarism and – a concept she virtually owns – militarisation are everywhere but that children and youth are both specific targets here ('get 'em young') and that gendering is how this process works. In the latter case Enloe makes the link between (un)naturally 'cheap' female labour, 'local' industries, revenue-chasing governments and 'a masculinized state development strategy'.[37] This is an exact picture of the storm-charges mentioned above; at some point material violence – bodies, machines, objects – will blow up, because people have set the devices, pulled the triggers, given the orders, cheated on the inspections. In the former case – probably the creepier – Enloe imagines the kind of thinking at the Heinz corporation headquarters that made substituting Star Wars[38] pasta shapes for alphabetical ones a good idea. That kind of thinking presumes the normality of mothers who find it normal that children can be enticed with weaponry, even when everyone around is normal (i.e., not in the military).

The military does not find it normal to have mothers and children on board and 'out there' in the field (or rather some militaries are coming to terms with this in one way or another, but all very

35 Enloe, *Maneuvers*, pp. 1–34.
36 Enloe, *Globalization and Militarism*, pp. 19–38.
37 Enloe, *Globalization and Militarism*, p. 38.
38 The 'outer-space' weaponry proposed by the Reagan administration, not the epic movie franchise.

quietly). Rather Enloe can show convincingly that 'food companies, toy companies, clothing companies, film studios, stock brokerages, and advertising agencies' are militarised in so far as they and their employees 'imagine that promoting military ends serves the general welfare'.[39] So political gendering in Enloe's work is not a strategy of difference, even though that is how the concept is supposed to work – surely it divides the world into men and women, men's things and women's things. Rather, Enloe reveals gendering to be a strategy of ontological and epistemological differentiation working towards a 'home *and* away' common goal, which – given the pervasiveness and relentlessness of militarisation as a global dynamic – is decidedly not 'world peace'.

Back to the philosophers of the future   Suppose we put Enloe into conversation with philosophers on the subject of violence, say the philosophers and thinkers of this volume. No doubt she would express appropriate appreciation of their work and disclaimers from doing philosophy or being a philosopher. As detailed above there are obvious differences in the framing, diction, points of reference and academic packaging (at the time or subsequently) between the philosophers – or anyway those thinkers who have been framed as such – and Enloe, the 'curious feminist' (another of Enloe's book titles, published in 2004). Rather than pursue such an apparent stand-off, or render in detail an episode of people talking past one another, I am going to suggest a philosophical proxy for Enloe, possibly a kind of fraternal (*sic*) twin. My candidate for this role is Ludwig Wittgenstein, or at least the philosopher in his later incarnation, edited up by others in a number of 'books', notably the *Philosophical Investigations* (1953).

At first sight this seems a worse pairing than would occur with almost any of the other writers in this collection; possibly the better candidates would be Arendt and Fanon, both personally involved in struggles famously reflected in their writings and movingly presented in their prose. Both moved many contemporaries and many more later readers; both interpreted the world in ways meant to change it in quite specific ways, aiming at very large problems, notably those of violence, cruelty, brutality, colonialism, war crimes and the like. But reading them doesn't make one think of Enloe, nor does reading

---

39 Enloe, *Maneuvers*, p. 2.

Enloe lead one at all directly to their works, which are not cited substantively in her corpus.[40] In fact, reading through the indices to Enloe's books, one fails to find even one philosopher of violence or even of anything else. Why pursue this trope?

The later Wittgenstein – at least in some readings – is overtly an anti-philosopher, remarking ironically that 'philosophy leaves everything as it is',[41] hardly an Enloe-esque ambition. But intentions to change the world or not are not really the point here. Rather the alignment that I am suggesting is one of curiosity and of thinking through the everyday. Wittgenstein's cast of characters isn't as wide or as colourful as Enloe's, but it's actually wider than one might think after a casual reading. The *Investigations* has 'parts' for children, various animals, ordinary workers (evidently male) and the like (though not 'a woman'), even if the situations are somewhat abstracted. But one senses the urge on Wittgenstein's part to break out of a philosophical and therefore an academic frame, so as to reason things through from commonplace situations. Enloe could have written this:

> When I talk about language (words, sentences, etc.) I must speak the language of every day. Is this language somehow too coarse and material for what we want to say?[42]

Of course Wittgenstein's curiosity was actually directed towards philosophy and philosophers, making them curiouser and curiouser and concluding that they are like flies in fly bottles.[43] He thus used ordinary life to puncture their hermeticism and – as is gently hinted – silliness. What unites him with Enloe – in my view – is not even the curiosity but the will 'to look and see' and thus test out what is always and already, normally and 'rightly', philosophically and academically, said to 'be the case' or 'natural' or 'normal'.[44]

---

40 Arendt is mentioned by Enloe in a historical list of women intellectuals accorded some *gravitas* by men and as possibly the only woman social science author Enloe had heard of around 1970; Enloe, *Seriously!*, pp. 4, 20, 22.
41 Ludwig Wittgenstein, *Philosophical Investigations*, trans. G. E. M. Anscombe, 2nd ed. (Oxford: Blackwell, 1958), §124.
42 Wittgenstein, *Investigations*, §120.
43 Wittgenstein, *Investigations*, §309.
44 Enloe says much the same thing in *Curious Feminist*, pp. 3–4.

Confronting violence in the world

Enloe's feminism and her famous question 'Where are the women?' are not a summation of what to do and how to do it. Rather they are a way of 'troubling' the hierarchies and normalities of a masculinised view of the world to which (some few) women might – with suitable condescension – be allowed (by 'them') to contribute. Wittgenstein was rather too self-absorbed to pick up such an idea, and it took many women of his time – and earlier and later – much effort to get this kind of activism going. Enloe's contribution to the study of violence was not to reinscribe woman as victim but to point to women as an essential – if often brutalised and unwitting – part of the mechanisms through which violence accumulates wherever, whenever, whoever.

Further reading

Enloe, Cynthia, *Bananas, Beaches and Bases: Making Feminist Sense of International Politics* (Berkeley: University of California Press, 2014 [1989]).

Enloe, Cynthia, *The Curious Feminist: Searching for Women in a New Age of Empire* (Berkeley: University of California Press, 2004).

Enloe, Cynthia, *Globalization and Militarism: Feminists Make the Link* (Boulder: Rowman & Littlefield, 2007).

Enloe, Cynthia, *Nimo's War, Emma's War: Making Feminist Sense of the Iraq War* (Berkeley: University of California Press, 2010).

Enloe, Cynthia, *Seriously! Investigating Crashes and Crises as if Women Mattered* (Berkeley: University of California Press, 2013).

INDEX